Shellfish

AUSTRALIAN COOKERY SERIES

Shellfish

Christian
COUPE

With all my love

Christian

Hodder & Stoughton
SYDNEY AUCKLAND LONDON TORONTO

First published in 1991
by Hodder & Stoughton (Australia) Pty Limited
ACN 000 884855
10–16 South Street, Rydalmere, NSW, 2116.

Line drawings by Sophie Tourrier.

National Library of Australia Cataloguing-in-Publication entry

Coupe, Christian.
  Shellfish.

  Includes index.
  ISBN 0 340 54961 0.

  1. Cookery (Shellfish). I. Title.

641.694

Typeset by G.T. Setters Pty Limited, Kenthurst
Printed in Hong Kong by Colorcraft Ltd.

Contents

Introduction

Shellfish have been part of the food chain of humanity from the earliest times. The middens of ancient waterside communities give testimony to the eating of the oysters and abalone, mussels and clams found along the shores of lakes and seas all over the world. Palaeolithic tribes in North America wiped out whole colonies of abalone after the last Ice Age in their enthusiasm (fishing methods don't seem to have changed much), and convict builders in 19th-century Australia found a ready source of lime supply in the great oyster middens of the local Aborigines.

Crabs, lobsters and prawns have been cooked in the ashes of a fire, enclosed in their own packaging, ever since fire was first employed to heat food. Cockles and mussels and scallops could be opened in the embers too; winkles and abalone and limpets prised off the rock-face and eaten raw; sea-urchins split apart and the roe scooped out; oyster and clam shells opened and the contents tipped straight down a waiting throat.

Nowadays the majority of people live in towns or large cities and we no longer have to catch the food we eat. For most of us, these creatures are to be found on the ice beds or in the fish tanks of fish markets or shops. They are expensive, luxurious items which need careful treatment, special sauces, delicate accompaniments. Many of them are considered special occasion foods rather than everyday ones. But this needn't be so: buying shellfish fresh from the fish markets is far cheaper than eating them in a restaurant, and while some species may take a while to prepare, cooking them is usually very quick and easy. And not all shellfish are expensive—cuttlefish, octopus and squid are cheap, as are clams and cockles, and prawns in season make one of the simplest and cheapest feasts imaginable.

So, this book is about the creatures themselves and how to deal with them—how to buy them, prepare them, and cook them. And most of all, how to enjoy them.

BUYING SHELLFISH

Buying shellfish of any description has one basic rule—whatever the species it must be fresh. If it is stale or old it is not only unpalatable, it can be dangerous, as seafood goes off very quickly. Oysters should look juicy and plump in their shells, not deflated and dry around the edges. Scallops, clams, mussels and cockles should close when the shells are tapped; prawns should be bright and shiny, with glowing colours and tight shells, and live crabs and rock lobsters active and aggressive. Shells should be checked to make sure they are undamaged and never broken or pierced.

Remember that locally caught and sold shellfish is always freshest, and that anything from a distance will have been transported in cold storage or deep frozen. Some creatures from fishing grounds far from their main markets are frozen immediately they are caught and sold still frozen or defrosted on ice. If the latter, they should be cooked as soon as possible and never refrozen. Scampi, from the warm waters of north-west Australia, are a case in point: these are deep-frozen as soon as they are caught, packed into trays, and exported throughout South-East Asia and Australia.

On the subject of frozen seafood, bear in mind that some species freeze much better than others. The cephalopods don't seem to come to too much harm in a freezer and neither do abalone (often the only ways to buy abalone are frozen or in tins). Lobster and crayfish tails, even yabby and bug tails, seem to remain reasonably intact and can be substituted for fresh ones if they are not available, or if the idea of wrestling with a lively cray doesn't appeal at all. But prawns don't seem to freeze well and it is always much better to buy the local ones in season. Frozen prawns lose all their taste and much of their texture.

Oysters, mussels and clams will survive for a few days if kept damp and cool in a dark place (*not* the fridge, which is far too cold) packed in hessian bags or seaweed. Contained in this way they have been transported great distances since before Roman times.

If the shellfish are to be eaten cold they can be bought ready-cooked, but always buy green specimens if they are to be served hot—the delicate flesh of a rock lobster can easily become a piece of indigestible rubber if overcooked. It's really much better to cook them oneself, even the prawns for a picnic lunch, because they always seem to taste so much better.

Most crustaceans are in season in summer, and while lobsters, crabs, and some varieties of prawns are available all year round, on the average they are heavier and meatier in the warmer months. For some species there are laws governing the sale of females with eggs, and for others closed fishing seasons. Large octopus are in short supply in winter, but squid and cuttlefish appear all year round. So do oysters—although they are at their best just before spawning, which takes place in the summer months—and scallops. Pipis and cockles appear and disappear from the markets and freshwater crayfish of any description are frequently very difficult to find. Because of this variability of supply, it's much better to shop first and decide on a particular dish second, rather than set your heart on something that is unavailable.

KITCHEN UTENSILS

There is no special tool required in the kitchen to deal with shellfish and indeed the most used implements are the fingers, as so much of the preparation involves scrubbing and cleaning shells, twisting off claws from crabs, and peeling prawns. But there are two things that are really useful. The first is a Chinese meat cleaver, ideal for splitting crayfish and lobsters down the middle. The second is a crab cracker, by far the best tool for cracking recalcitrant crab claws although a heavy nutcracker will do, or even a hammer (but don't smash them completely). A steamer is useful: the bamboo ones (sold in Asian emporiums and markets) that come in various sizes to fit over ordinary saucepans are very efficient. If you are going to go into the business of opening your own oysters then an oyster knife is a must, but this is a dangerous occupation to my way of thinking, and far better left to the experts, or at any rate 'Other People'.

INGREDIENTS

Again, there are no special ingredients for shellfish, no special herbs and spices or cunning flavourings. But there are certain items which are used all the time and these are listed here.

Butter

Always use unsalted butter in cooking, especially with seafood, as the salt content of the butter could easily unbalance the rest of the flavours in the dish. If you have to use margarine, again the unsalted type is best. Clarified butter, or export-quality, pure butter-fat ghee (bought in smart green-and-gold tins from Asian stores although it comes from Australia or New Zealand) is always best for cooking over high heat as it doesn't burn so easily.

Coconut milk

This is made by pouring hot or boiling water over the grated flesh of the nut. While I'm sure that using fresh coconut is best, sadly coconuts and I just don't mix. The nut ends up looking as if shredded by shrapnel, the kitchen like a war zone, and I'm nursing a mangled hand. Essential for so many Thai, Indian and other South-East Asian dishes, coconut milk can be bought fully constituted in tins or sachets, in powdered form (just add water), or it can be made by pouring hot or boiling water over shredded desiccated coconut. *Coconut cream* comes as a solid bar to be cut or shaved as required, adding a deeper, richer flavour and texture to the milk itself.

Oil

Light, tasteless oils with high burning temperatures are the ones to use for deep-frying or cooking over high heat. Oil for frying should always be completely clean and preferably not have been already used: no matter how careful one is, used oil always smells of the food that was cooked in it before. Olive oil is best for Mediterranean flavours but save the virgin oil for salads and cold dishes—it's for flavour not for cooking.

Rice

Brown white long round fluffy sticky wild American Italian Indian Pakistani Thai . . . rice is indispensable in any kitchen and although not all of the hundreds of different kinds are necessary, it's worthwhile having at least a few of them in the cupboard:

Thai rice or Jasmine rice is meant to be sticky, unlike the long-grain Indian type. It is faintly perfumed and is best cooked by the absoprtion method (usually printed on the packet).

Brown rice is unpolished so that some of the outer covering remains. It takes longer to cook than polished rice, about 20 minutes, and has a chewier texture and a stronger, grainier flavour. It is best with smooth, rich, creamy dishes, balancing the unctuousness with its roughness.

Long-grain rice Basmati is the best quality white long-grain rice, with slightly curved grains and a subtle but distinctive perfume and taste. When properly cooked the grains remain separate and dry, not at all sticky. I find the Iranian method the best way to cook it. Soak the rice for at least two hours, drain, dry it for an hour then cook for no more than one or two minutes in boiling, lightly salted water until still firm but no longer hard in the centre. Drain. Melt some butter in the saucepan (which should be a heavy-based one) and put back the rice. Fold a cloth over the top of the pan, fit the lid on top, turn up the edges of the cloth over the lid so they don't burn and steam over a low heat for 15-20 minutes. The rice comes out fluffy and dry, and on the bottom of the pan a lovely layer of crispy, crusty, buttery grains has formed, adding their different taste and texture to the rest of the dish.

Round-grain or short-grain rice is the sort used for puddings, Italian risottos and Spanish paella. It will go mushy if not cooked carefully. The best type is oval rather than round in shape. Good quality varieties take a long time to cook: they lend themselves perfectly to being fried in butter or oil, then cooked gently in stock for 20-30 minutes (add other ingredients as it simmers—shellfish last) and served directly from the pan.

Wild rice is wonderful, but not rice. It is a grass which grows wild in America and some parts of China and Japan. It should be washed, drained, cooked in boiling water for 10 minutes or so, then steamed in the same way as Basmati. Wild rice goes particularly well with mussels, cockles and oysters.

Nuts
Almonds, hazelnuts, pine nuts and walnuts are the most useful nuts, with pistachios and peanuts close behind. They should be bought unsalted, whole, and in fairly small packs unless you consistently use large quantities, and stored in airtight containers in the fridge. To blanch nuts, pour boiling water over them and rub off their skin with the fingers.

Almonds make lovely sauces, and are good thickeners for soups and casseroles. A potent mixture of ground almonds and dried chillies, soaked in water, boiled and blended—about 20 almonds to 5 hot dried chillies, and 100 ml water—can be kept in a stoppered bottle in the fridge for some time, to be doled out in small drops to spice up sauces and such. Don't try to taste it—it raises blisters on the lips with astounding speed.

Pine nuts, apart from being essential in pesto sauce, impart a wild, earthy flavour to dishes. They go rancid fairly quickly so it's best to buy them from Middle-Eastern shops with a good turnover of stock.

Hazelnuts make one of the most delicious of tarators, the wonderful nut-based sauces of the Eastern Mediterranean. The skins of hazelnuts cling tightly and are hard to remove so it is easiest to grind the nuts whole in a blender and then shake them through a fairly coarse sieve, which will hold back most of the skin.

Walnuts are easy to blanch by pouring boiling water over them and peeling away the skin. They are especially good with salads of lobster and crab.

Dried beans

There seem to be endless varieties of dried beans on the market, although many of them appear to be the same ones under different names. As beans become harder the older they are, they are best used in the season they are picked (which makes life difficult as that information is not given on the packets). The older they are the longer they take to cook, and the time stretches from 30 minutes to two and a half hours—or never, in the case of really ancient ones. Varieties such as cannelloni, haricot and small lima beans are useful in salads with prawns and green mussels. The black beans used in Chinese cooking are fermented soy beans, but there is also a variety native to Mexico with a strong, spicy flavour.

Cooking liquids

Apart from water and fish stock, the most useful cooking liquid must be alcohol, regardless of whether it comes from rice, grain or grape. Wine, sherry, rice wine from either Japan (mirin) or China (mai-tai), and flavoured vermouths, liqueurs, port and brandy, gin and whisky are all used in cooking, and some of them are indispensable to the basic methods of preparation. In both Chinese and Japanese cooking rice wine, like soy sauce, is an element in almost every dish.

Wine is also used enormously in Western cookery. For cooking shellfish it is mainly dry white wine that is required, or a dry vermouth, which adds a particularly subtle flavour. Sherry (which marries brilliantly with crab and lobster) should be dry and smooth. Port, like marsala, should be used with discretion as its heavy sweetness can overpower a delicately flavoured dish. The same applies to flavoured liqueurs such as Cointreau, although a little adds an extra dimension to an orange sauce. Brandy is often used, Pernod and whisky are wonderful with scallops, and gin adds a smoky, faintly bitter-sweet taste to crayfish dishes.

Vinegar

The list of vinegars can be very long, but really all that's needed is a good white wine vinegar and a good red wine one. Make your own if you have some good quality wine left over and don't feel like drinking it. Good vinegar is made from good wine, so it's not worth making it from cask or flagon wines. Simply pour it into a container with a small amount of ordinary wine vinegar, red or white, and let it sit in the kitchen to sour slowly, with a lid on to stop it becoming contaminated. The vinegar produced is smooth and soft, not at all harsh, and is magnificent for salads. Cider vinegar is also useful, but avoid malt vinegar as it's too strong for delicate dishes. Rice vinegar is smoother and sweeter than European types and is used in both Japanese and Chinese cooking.

Dashi

Dashi is the basic stock used in Japanese cooking, and is made from dried bonito, shaved from a block into water to produce a taste unlike any other. It isn't necessary to hunt for dried bonito as all Japanese stores and many Chinese ones stock a bewildering variety of dashi powders. All one has to do is shake in the quantity required, or dip in the tea-bag, or measure in the spoonful, depending on the instructions. Some of them seem to be extremely high in monosodium glutamate, so check the ingredients carefully.

The strength of the powder varies with the brand as well, so it's a question of trial and error to get the right blend. The best way is to start with a small amount and keep adding and tasting until the required strength is achieved.

Sauces

Soy sauce, both light and heavy, and Teriyaki are important and so are other bottled sauces like Worcestershire and Tabasco. I also have a volcanic mixture called Hot Chilli Relish, bought at the local flea market from a home-made-pickle stall, which I add in judicious quantities to dishes with a South American or Caribbean slant.

Fish stock

Fish stock, like chicken or veal stock, should be a staple item in the freezer, either in containers large enough to hold at least a half litre, or frozen into ice cubes for adding to sauces as required. Either way, the container should be clearly labelled: fish-stock ice-cubes in the Campari would be a shock to the system from which it would take a long time to recover! To make a basic fish stock, use:

head and bones of a firm,
  white-fleshed 'fish
1 cup dry white wine
1–4 cups water
1 small onion

1 small stick celery
1 sprig each parsley, thyme,
  and oregano or tarragon
1 bay leaf
5–6 black peppercorns

Place all the ingredients in a large saucepan and bring to the boil, skimming off the scum as it rises. Simmer gently with the lid on for 1 hour, then strain through a muslin-lined sieve into a clean saucepan and allow to cool. Separate an egg, crush the shell and beat the white a little, and add them to the stock. Whisking with a wire whisk, bring the stock back to the boil, allow the foam to rise to the edge of the pan, then remove from the heat and let it die down before returning to the boil again. Do this one more time, then turn off the heat, put the lid on the pan and let it sit for 5 minutes before straining through muslin and a fine sieve into a clean container. If necessary, reduce the stock a little to concentrate the flavours before cooling and freezing for future use.

The liquid in which prawns, mussels and pipis are cooked is always full of flavour (with pipis it's full of sand and grit as well!) and can be used to add extra strength to stocks and soups, but remember that prawns have a fairly powerful taste and prawn stock could swamp a more delicate flavour. Octopus is very salty and the skin turns pink when it is cooked, so the liquid in which it is poached becomes a cloudy, old-rose pink, tasting of sea and salt and seaweed.

Dairy products

Light (35 per cent milk fat) and heavy (45 per cent) cream, crème fraîche if you can get it, sour cream and yoghurt are all used extensively in shellfish recipes. One of the simplest of all sauces is dry white wine and cream reduced to a smooth, thick consistency and poured over lobster, crab, scallops or prawns.

Crème fraîche is lighter, thicker and sharper than ordinary cream, and is very useful for finishing sauces. If it can't be found it is very easy to make and keeps for a week or so in the fridge. Pour 1 ½ cups light cream into a saucepan, add a good tablespoonful of buttermilk and heat until it feels tepid to the finger. Take it off the heat, cover the pan with a cloth, and leave it in a warm place for 24 hours. The cream will thicken, and become solid when refrigerated.

Sour cream for cooking should always be full fat rather than the light variety, which will curdle if subjected to heat. The same applies to *yoghurt* if it isn't stabilised. This is done by adding one egg white to 2 cups of yoghurt in a saucepan and bringing it slowly to the boil, stirring all the time. As soon as it boils lower the heat and simmer very gently for about 10 minutes, or until it is thick and glossy. Cool and refrigerate and use in the same way as cream and sour cream.

Spices
Black, green and pink peppercorns, ground pepper chilli and paprika are all important. Frequently in Morocco a small amount of each is added to a dish, all of them together giving a subtle intangible savour. Other spices in constant use include mustard seed, turmeric, saffron, fenugreek, cinnamon in sticks, coriander and cardamon and cumin seeds, cloves, fennel seeds and juniper berries, whole nutmeg, garam masala, five-spice powder, star anise and, if you can get it, filé powder from New Orleans. Buy spices whole and in small amounts rather than ready ground, as they lose their pungency quite quickly. Grind them as they are needed.

Curry powder and paste, hot mango pickle in oil, capers and dried tomatoes in glass jars (use the tomatoes in hors d'oeuvres and casseroles and the oil they are stored in for cooking with); tahina and the dried peel of both oranges and mandarins (pare the skin thinly, dry in the sun in a bright, sheltered spot until it will snap in two if you try to bend it, then store in a jar for use in sauces and stews); French mustard; black olives, kalamata and those shrivelled sun-dried ones that always taste of salt and summer; red capsicum, seeded and skinned, cut into strips and stored in olive oil; and anchovies, in tins or jars, or bought from round tins of salted fish at a delicatessen and rinsed, filleted and packed in oil at home.

Herbs
Fresh herbs are much nicer than dried ones, which always seem to taste and smell suspiciously the same. During the winter there is no alternative to dried tarragon, but even then there are other herbs.

Rosemary and sorrel, marjoram, chives and parsley will grow in cold weather; thyme never seems to stop growing; and dill, coriander and fennel can be bought from fruit shops. In summer fresh basil, tarragon, chervil and savoury are available and dried bay leaves are available all the time.

Vegetables

Capsicums Red, green, yellow or black, fat and bulging or long and tapering, capsicums (or sweet peppers) are used in a variety of ways. Peel red capsicums by grilling them until the skin blisters and blackens and comes away from the flesh beneath; discard the seeds, stem and white pulpy pith along the inside ribs; cut into strips and store covered with good olive 'oil in jars in the fridge. The strips can be used as required in salads and hors d'oeuvres, or blended with the oil to make a simple and delicious sauce for octopus and mussels.

Daikon Daikon is the large white Japanese or Chinese radish, and is an essential ingredient in Japanese cooking. It is milder and sweeter than the red kind.

Lettuce There are four main types of lettuce available: soft-leaved varieties such as butterhead and mignonette; crisp, firm-hearted ones like iceberg; curly headed types; and the long-leaved Romaine or cos. The choice depends on the season and taste. The soft-leaved types are easier to use in salads.

Onions The allium group includes onions, spring onions, leeks, garlic and shallots, all of which have been indispensable to cooking for thousands of years. Onions and leeks formed a major part of the diet of the Ancient Egyptians and later the Greeks and Romans, and the Chinese have been using onions and garlic for as long as they have been cooking.

Garlic Strong-smelling and pungent but tamed by long cooking, garlic is the most powerful allium member. Garlic is good for you. 'Its use against intestinal worms', says *Fruits of the Earth* rather dauntingly, 'has been known since very early times. . . [and it] is said to promote hypertensive and cardiovascular activity'. So garlic is medicinal as well as flavoursome. Eating it could cure consumption, snake bites, lethargy and the plague; you could get rid of a cold by rubbing it on the soles of the feet; and hanging it outside the door will stop witches, warlocks and vampires from entering. The only problem is that the smell is as powerful as its medicinal and protective qualities, so you could easily end up super-healthy but socially unacceptable. But it is one of the most important ingredients in the kitchen and very easy to deal with. If it is to be added to stocks or long-cooked sauces, just hit the clove with the flat side of a wide knife, squashing it slightly and splitting the skin so that it comes away from the bulb. It can then be easily peeled, or dropped into the liquid still with the skin on to be retrieved later. For frying, peel and chop finely and add after long-cooking ingredients like onion and carrot have softened, as garlic becomes bitter if allowed to burn.

Leeks Leeks are milder, sweeter and softer than ordinary onions, bulbless like spring onions but thicker and longer. The tough outer leaves and fibrous dark green tops should be discarded, and the cut end notched with a knife so that the tightly-furled leaves can be splayed back and rinsed under running water to release any mud and grit trapped inside. Their mildness enhances the taste of all shellfish, especially scallops. They can also be used as a substitute for Japanese long onions.

Onions There are countless varieties of cultivated onions, ranging from the relatively mild species high in water and sugar to the drier, harder, stronger ones. As a rough rule, purple or red-and-white onions are mild and yellow ones stronger, but the only way to find out is to try each type and decide which one suits you best.

Shallots Shallots look like brown-skinned garlic cloves, and the bulbs grow singly or in twos or threes, held together at the roots. They have a distinctive taste, at once penetrating and refined, and are used mainly as a seasoning for sauces.

Spring onions Spring onions are also called scallions, green onions and—incorrectly—shallots. They form no bulb or only a small one when mature, and the green and white parts are both edible. Eaten raw in salads or added at the last minute to hot dishes, spring onions are also used extensively in Chinese cooking, and are useful substitutes for Japanese green onions.

Silver beet or Swiss Chard is often called spinach but has long, thick, ribbed stems which are the nicest part of the vegetable, and curly, glossy green leaves. These are coarser in taste and texture than spinach but can be used in the same way. A few leaves of sorrel added to the dish will give a cleaner, sharper taste.

Spinach Spinach is sometimes called English Spinach but in fact it probably originated in Persia. The slender stalks which form ribs in the middle of the leaves should be removed before cooking. Spinach harbours an enormous amount of grit and sand and should be washed in various changes of water before cooking. If the leaves are to be used as a wrapping for stuffings (prawns, say, or scallops) peel away the centre stem very carefully so that it doesn't tear the leaf. Bring a shallow, wide pan of water to the boil and drop in each leaf separately, taking it out with a slotted spoon or fish slice as soon as it wilts (about two seconds). Drain the leaves on kitchen paper before wrapping around the stuffing and place the little bundles join-side down in the dish in which they are to be cooked. Spinach clings like plastic wrap, so they don't need to be tied with string.

Tomatoes The best tomatoes are home-grown and picked when they are fully ripe, but when they have to be bought from shops and markets choose deep-red, ripe ones with a sweet, fresh smell. Rather than use canned tomatoes for casseroles and stocks, buy tomatoes during the glut periods and make tomato puree to freeze for future use. Just place the washed tomatoes in a saucepan, put on the lid, set the heat at the lowest setting and cook for 30 minutes or so, or until they have separated into clear liquid and red flesh. Cool and tip them into a blender, whizz for a few seconds, and strain through a sieve, pressing down on the pulp so that everything goes through except the skin and the seeds. Put into containers and freeze until needed for sauces, soups and casseroles.

Other important vegetables are cucumbers, carrots and mushrooms, both dried and fresh; chicory and endive, radicchio and watercress; avocados (delicious with crab and prawns); aubergines and zucchini; potatoes, and sweep potatoes to make a soup with scallops; artichokes and asparagus for salads with prawns and mussels; fennel; and celery and celeriac, the former as a major seasoning component in stocks and stews as well as a crisp addition to salads, and the latter for soups and purees, and mixing with mayonnaise to eat with scampi.

Fruit

The citrus group is the one usually associated with fish and shellfish, and lemon the most common accompaniment. But limes are delicious with seafood, oranges make very good sauces, and mandarins imbue any dish they are in with a sweet, tangy taste. Grapefruit, if not too sour, go well with crab, as do lychee nuts; apples and pears make lovely salads with lobster; melon goes with prawns; and grapes with almost anything.

Abalone

'Origin uncertain' says my dictionary about the word 'abalone'. It sounds quintessentially Spanish but in Spain as in France and Italy the colloquial name describes the flattened, whorled shape of the shell itself — 'oreja de mar', the sea-ear. So perhaps the word derives from the area where the species is most prolific and diverse — the Pacific coasts of the Americas, especially Chile and California. Here pink, red, green, black, white and even pinto varieties are found among the rocks and crevices of the coastal shallows and intertidal waters. In protected pools, they can be so prolific as to cover every part of the rock shelf, touching and even overlapping each other as they graze on the weed and algae in the water.

Abalone are gastropods, members of the family Haliotidae and related to snails and limpets, but the shells are neither humped nor pointed. They curve instead in a shallow oval dome pierced by a line of small holes, with a barnacle-encrusted top and a lustrous mother-of-pearl lining. Their habitats range from the Channel Isles between France and England, through the tropics and as far south as New Zealand, where a particularly beautiful species, the paua, is found. The shell of the paua, with its spectacular opalescent lining of blues and greens, is carved by the Maoris into intricate designs and patterns for jewellery and decoration, and was once used as money.

Single-shelled, able to attach themselves firmly to rock and to crawl (albeit slowly) over the floor and sides of a pool, abalone are vulnerable to few predators other than human beings who discovered them to be delicious. In California after the last Ice Age Palaeolithic hunters gathered so many that they became extinct in some areas. Indeed people consumed abalone with such enthusiasm that they turned to oysters and mussels only after the once-vast abalone beds were turned into huge middens. Australian Aborigines have been eating the creatures for thousands of years, as have the Chinese and Japanese. In Japan women traditionally dived for abalone, carrying a stone to help drop down to the required depth. As all the specimens at the higher levels were removed they had to dive deeper and deeper to collect them, a fact which probably saved the species from total extinction before the days of scuba gear. Nowadays most countries have fairly restrictive fishing laws on the collection of abalone, with quota systems or closed seasons.

Abalone can be eaten raw as well as cooked. If the foot or muscle is taken from the shell as soon as it is prised off the rock the flesh is fairly tender, but the muscles contract when torn away from the stone and remain contracted, so abalone must be tenderised by beating if it is to be eaten later. The Chinese use it enormously, though more as a flavouring agent or for the introduction of a different texture than as the main component of a dish. It is considered a delicacy in the Channel Islands; and in California it is fried, grilled, minced and added to chowders and casseroles.

Abalone can be bought live (held by the fishmonger in tanks where the creatures cling to the glass like thick, pale, oval suction pads) but is more often available only frozen, with or without the shells, or in tins. If abalone is live or frozen, the muscle should be taken from the shell, the dark mantle discarded and the frilly edge of the foot scrubbed thoroughly to get rid of all the sand and grit the ridges can hold. Cut the foot into thin slices and beat gently with a smooth-faced mallet until the texture becomes soft and velvety, using a stroking motion so that the surfaces of the slices are evenly tenderised. They are then ready to be used in various ways.

Buying tins of abalone gives the added bonus of the liquid in which they are packed, especially for Chinese dises, and the already tenderised slices need no preparation. As with all shellfish, abalone needs very little cooking and will toughen quickly if overdone. If added to other ingredients, stir it in at the last minute so that the flavour and perfume are released but the flesh itself doesn't toughen.

ABALONE AND ASPARAGUS

2 abalone
lemon juice
black pepper, freshly ground
200 g (6–8 spears) fresh
* asparagus*

100 ml (½ cup) chicken stock
1 tablespoon soy sauce
oil for frying

Clean the abalone thoroughly, slice into thin strips and pound them to a smooth, velvety texture. Sprinkle with some lemon juice and freshly ground black pepper and set aside.

Clean the asparagus, snapping off the tough bases and scraping away the outer layer of skin from the stems. Cut the spears into short lengths and drop them into the boiling chicken stock to simmer for no more than 1 minute. Take them out of the pan and set aside. Add the soy sauce to the stock and reduce to about 3 tablespoons.

Heat some oil in a wok or frying pan and cook the abalone for no more than a few seconds on either side, then add the rest of the ingredients. Stir very gently, so as not to break up the asparagus tips, for a few seconds longer and arrange on a heated serving dish.

Serve with boiled rice or, much better, Chinese noodles that have also been cooked in the chicken stock before it has been reduced with the soy sauce. If serving with noodles add a little more soy to the stock as they can be very bland otherwise. The textures of the soft noodles, the asparagus still crisp and crunchy, and the smooth chewiness of the abalone are disparate yet complementary to each other, adding an extra dimension to a very simple dish. *Serves 2.*

ABALONE BALLS

2 abalone	*pepper*
2 spring onions	*1 egg white*
1 large sprig fresh mint	*oil for frying*

Scrub, slice and beat the abalone and place in a food processor or blender with the spring onions, mint and pepper. Whizz for a few seconds until minced and blended, then add the egg white and process for a few seconds more to blend well together. Form the mixture into little balls and chill them for at least 1 hour in the refrigerator.

Heat some oil for deep-frying in a deep pan (use a light tasteless vegetable oil for preference) until a piece of bread will brown in 1 minute. Cook the little balls a few at a time, taking them out of the oil as soon as they turn puffy and golden. Drain on kitchen paper and serve at once, with a dipping sauce of soy sauce mixed with a little grated ginger. *Serves 2.*

ABALONE IN BREADCRUMBS

2 abalone	black pepper
lemon juice	dried breadcrumbs
1 egg	clarified butter for frying

Scrub, slice and beat the abalone, sprinkle the slices with lemon juice and set aside for 1 hour.

Beat the egg, season with some black pepper and dip the abalone slices first into the beaten egg and then into breadcrumbs. Chill them in the fridge for 30 minutes or so before cooking so that the coating is firmly attached and dried. Fry the slices in clarified butter over a high heat for no more than a few seconds each side. Serve at once. *Serves 2.*

ABALONE AND CHINESE CABBAGE

2 abalone	1 tablespoon soy sauce
1 small Chinese cabbage	1 tablespoon rice wine
1 leek	1 tablespoon water
1 small piece fresh ginger	2 spring onions, finely
2 tablespoons sesame oil	chopped

Clean the abalone and slice thinly across the grain. Beat the slices lightly with a meat mallet and set aside. Discard the outer leaves of the cabbage and slice the rest into thin shreds. Clean the leek and slice thinly. Grate the ginger.

Heat the oil in a frying pan or wok, stir the leek rings for a few seconds, then add the cabbage and stir-fry until all the shreds are coated and glistening. Pour in the soy sauce, rice wine and water and continue to cook over a high heat, stirring all the time, for another 1–2 minutes.

Transfer the cabbage and leek to a pre-heated serving dish. Turn the abalone quickly in the liquid in the pan for no more than 1 minute and arrange it over the cabbage. Scatter the finely chopped spring onions on top, pour over the liquid and serve at once with plenty of rice. *Serves 2.*

ABALONE CROQUETTES

2 abalone   1 handful parsley leaves
1 leek   pepper to taste
unsalted butter   1 egg white
1 slice white bread without   vegetable oil for frying
  crusts

Clean the abalone, slice across the grain and beat with a meat tenderiser until soft. Peel and clean the leek, chop into thin slices and cook gently for 5 minutes or so in a little butter to soften.

Place all the ingredients except the egg white in a food processor or blender and whizz until finely chopped and blended. Whip the egg white until standing in stiff peaks, fold it into the abalone mixture and refrigerate for at least 20 minutes.

Heat some tasteless vegetable oil in a deep saucepan until a piece of bread turns golden brown in 1 minute. Form the abalone mixture into little balls and fry them, a few at a time, until swollen and crisp and golden. Serve at once, with salad and plenty of lemon slices, and perhaps a sauce tartare. *Serves 2.*

ABALONE IN COCONUT MILK

2 abalone   clarified butter
lemon juice   150 ml (¾ cup) coconut milk
chilli powder   small piece coconut cream
1 onion   1 egg yolk
½ green capsicum

Clean, slice and beat the abalone. Sprinkle the slices with lemon juice and chilli powder and set aside for at least 1 hour.

Peel the onion, seed the capsicum and chop them both finely. Melt some clarified butter in a saucepan and cook them with a pinch more chilli powder until the onion is soft. Add the coconut milk, bring to the boil, lower the heat and continue to cook for a few minutes before adding the coconut cream and stirring for a minute more while the sauce thickens. Put in the abalone slices and go on stirring for another minute, then withdraw from the heat.

Beat the egg yolk, pour in a little of the sauce, mix together and return to the sauce, stirring over a very low heat until smooth and rich. Pour into a heated bowl and serve at once with rice and a few strips of fresh green capsicum to give crispness and sharpness to the dish. *Serves 2.*

ABALONE PIE

2 abalone	clarified butter
lemon juice	1 large handful fresh
black pepper	coriander leaves
1 large onion	200 g (7 oz) shortcrust pastry

Scrub, slice and beat the abalone and cut into thin shreds. Sprinkle with lemon juice and pepper and set aside.

Peel the onions, slice thinly and cook in clarified butter until soft. Mix the abalone strips, onion and finely chopped coriander together, grind over some black pepper and set aside.

Roll out the pastry into an oblong and cut it in half. Lay one half on a buttered baking sheet and spread the abalone mixture on top leaving a wide rim free all round, then fold over the second half. Dampen the edges and press them together so that they stick and seal. Prick the top with a fork, brush with some melted butter and cook in a hot oven for 30 minutes or until the pastry is crisp and golden. *Serves 2.*

ABALONE SALAD

2 abalone	1 tomato
vinaigrette dressing spiced	1 avocado
with chilli powder	fresh coriander, chopped
1 soft-leaved lettuce	1 spring onion, chopped

Clean, slice and beat the abalone. Place the slices in a small saucepan with just enough water to cover and bring to the boil, stirring so that the pieces don't stick together. As soon as the water boils remove from the heat and rinse the slices quickly under cold water to stop them from cooking further. Dry them on kitchen paper, chop into small pieces and put into a bowl with the chilli-spiced vinaigrette to marinate for at least 1 hour.

Arrange the lettuce on two salad plates. Slice the tomato into thin rounds and lay in a circle on top, add the avocado flesh chopped into chunks, then pile the abalone pieces in the middle. Sprinkle with chopped coriander and spring onion and pour over the vinaigrette.

This salad should be served at room temperature, and the flavours should be spicy and peppery, smooth and sharp at the same time. *Serves 2.*

ABALONE AS SASHIMI

1 abalone	*¼ small cucumber*
lemon juice	*1 spring onion*
¼ small daikon	*1 slice fresh ginger*
1 small carrot	*wasabi*

Clean, slice and beat the abalone and pour boiling water over the slices, dropping them instantly into cold water so that they are merely cleansed, not cooked. Dry the slices thoroughly, sprinkle with lemon juice and set aside.

Grate the daikon, drain off the liquid and arrange the shreds in a pile on one side of a plate. Lay the abalone slices against it in a falling pattern, spreading them across the dish. Slice the carrot, cucumber and spring onion into long, fine shreds and drop them into iced water for a minute or so, to make them curl. Drain and dry, and arrange in little piles beside or around the abalone. Grate the ginger and pile it in a little mound. Do the same with the wasabi. Serve with a dipping sauce of soy. *Serves 2.*

ABALONE SOUP

1 abalone	*300 ml (1½ cups) water*
1 small carrot	*1 sachet dashi powder*
150 g (½ small) buck choy	*1 handful fresh coriander*

Clean, slice and beat the abalone, and slice once more into thin shreds. Peel the carrot, discard the inner core, and shred the rest into thin strips. Remove any coarse leaves from the buck choy and chop it into small pieces.

Bring the water and dashi powder to the boil, add the vegetables and abalone and simmer for 2–3 minutes. Pour into bowls and serve, sprinkled with finely shredded coriander leaves. *Serves 2.*

ABALONE STEW

2 abalone
lemon juice
1 onion
1 ear sweet corn
1 green capsicum

1 tomato
1 clove garlic
oil for frying
100 ml (½ cup) coconut milk

Clean and scrub the abalone thoroughly. Slice and beat the slices until soft and smooth, sprinkle with a little lemon juice and set aside. Peel the onion and slice thinly. Strip the husks from the sweet corn, chop into thick slices and boil for 10 minutes. Slice and seed the capsicum, skin and seed the tomato, chopping it roughly into chunks.

Heat some oil in a frying pan and add the onions and crushed garlic, cooking until the onion softens. Add the drained sweet corn and the rest of the vegetables, stir in the oil for 1 minute, then pour in the coconut milk and bring to the boil. Cover and simmer for 10 minutes. Remove the vegetables to a heated casserole and turn up the heat to reduce the liquid and thicken the sauce slightly. Add the abalone and continue to cook over a low flame for another minute or so, then add to the bowl. Serve at once, with sweet potato and mint, or just with bread and a side salad. *Serves 2.*

Clams or Pipis

The problem with clams is their habitat. They live along the shoreline in the sand, gathering their food as the waves wash microscopic particles through the open shells. To them, therefore sand is no difficulty—part of the digestive system, almost—but to any creature who likes its seafood sandless it poses a problem: how to get the grit out.

Treatises could be written (and probably have been) on how to de-grit clams, although cookbooks are often coy on the subject. The Portuguese and Spanish don't seem to worry too much, and their clams always taste terrific. The Americans rarley mention the problem when describing the archetypal clam bake ('dig a pit 20 metres square and 2 metres deep, cover the bottom with large, white-hot stones, lay on top 30 kilos of clams, 30 kilos of oysters, 300 crabs, and 150 lobsters, cover with half a tonne of seaweed, put back the earth and leave for 5 hours. . .'), although they have been known to admit to soaking them in sea water and oatmeal for several hours before the event.

The Japanese soak them in clean salt water for at least 6 hours, the Chinese get round the problem by using dried ones, and the French (like the New Zealanders and the British) farm them, putting thcm in seawater tanks under ultraviolet lights before marketing to rid them of all sand. But for those of us who buy them at local fish shops, or catch them live, the best method seems to be long soaking in sea water that has been liberally dosed with oatmeal. This method doesn't get rid of the sand entirely (only the ultraviolet light method seems to do that), but it does reduce the amount considerably, adding a smooth, rich creamy flavour as well. And, of course, if the shells aren't needed, one can always cheat and buy a can, in which case they only need to be heated through, and the juice comes as an added bonus.

When buying clams, it's always worthwhile getting more than you need in case some are dead. Any that are gaping wide, or which don't open during soaking, should be discarded.

Clams have a good ratio of flesh to shell (about 45–50 per cent) and have a delicious flavour, but they toughen with amazing speed, so be careful not to leave them in the steamer for too long or they can become inedible. Because of this, and also because of the grit problem, most of the recipes here are for minced clams.

CLAMS WITH GARLIC BUTTER

12 clams
oatmeal
rock salt
60 g (3 tablespoons) unsalted
  butter

2 cloves garlic, crushed
1 handful parsley, chopped
lemon juice
black pepper, freshly ground

Scrub the clams and soak them for at least 6 hours in sea water, or salted fresh water with a generous handful of oatmeal, changing the water occasionally. Drain them, rinse thoroughly, and open the shells fully by inserting a knife between the two sides, holding the point against the hinge, and twisting. The top shell will come away easily. Place the clams on the half shell on a grid, or on a fireproof plate pressed into a good depth of rock salt to hold them steady. Mix together the softened butter, crushed garlic, finely chopped parsley and a little lemon juice. Sprinkle with freshly ground pepper and place spoonfuls of the garlic butter on each clam, spreading it so that they are completely covered. Place the rack or plate under a hot grill for 2 minutes, or until the butter is melted and sizzling. Take out and serve at once, with the butter still bubbling. *Serves 2.*

CLAM PASTA

300 g (10 oz) clams
oatmeal
1 tablespoon brandy
1 tomato
1 tablespon fresh tomato puree
pepper
1 sprig each basil, oregano,
  parsley

1 clove garlic
oil
300 g (10 oz) sheet pasta
semolina
salt
unsalted butter
extra parsley for garnish

Scrub the clams, then soak them in clean sea water or salted fresh water with a large handful of oatmeal for at least 6 hours, changing the water occasionally.

Heat the brandy in a pan and add the clams, taking each one out as soon as the shells open and tipping the liquid inside into the pan. Discard the shells and mince the flesh in a food processor or blender, then push it through a fine sieve so that all the sand and grit is left behind. Strain the brandy and clam stock through a muslin-lined sieve into a clean saucepan. Skin the tomato, seed it over a sieve so that the juice can be collected, and add it with the tomato puree to the saucepan. Season with pepper, cover and cook over a low heat for 15 minutes.

Finely chop the herbs, peel and crush the garlic, and cook in the oil for a few seconds, then mix with the clams and cool.

Roll out the pasta and place tiny spoonfuls of the clam mixture in rows on one half, leaving a wide margin between each spoonful. Dampen the spaces with water and fold over the other half of pasta, pressing down between each mound to seal the two layers together. Cut along the rows or press out the mounds with a cutter, dust with semolina, and leave to dry for 5 minutes.

Bring a pan of water to the boil, put in a spoonful of oil and some salt, and cook the pasta for 3 minutes. Drain in a sieve, put into a pre-warmed dish and toss with a little butter.

Heat the sauce and pour over the pasta, sprinkle with some parsley and serve at once. *Serves 2.*

CLAM STUFFED MUSHROOMS

400 g (14 oz) clams	*unsalted butter*
oatmeal	*6 large mushrooms*
2 tablespoons white	*1 handful parsley leaves*
* breadcrumbs*	*1 small egg*
1 small leek	*pepper*

Soak the scrubbed clams for at least 6 hours in sea water, or salted fresh water, and oatmeal, changing the water occasionally. Put them in a wide, shallow pan, cover with the lid, and turn on the heat. Remove the clams as soon as the shells open (they make a loud clicking noise) and tip the liquid into the pan. Mince the flesh, force it through a fine sieve to get rid of any grit and sand, and mix with the breadcrumbs.

Peel the leek, chop finely and cook in butter until soft. Detach the stems from the mushrooms, chop them finely with the parsley and add to the leek to continue cooking for another minute, then cool and mix with the clams and breadcrumbs. Beat in the egg, season with pepper.

Wipe the caps of the mushrooms with butter and place them, undersides upwards, in a shallow, fireproof, buttered dish. Pile the stuffing on top, pour over the reserved clam liquid, and cook in a medium oven for 20 minutes, or until the stuffing is slightly risen and puffy. Serve at once. *Serves 2.*

CLAMS STUFFED WITH PINE NUTS

12 clams
ghee or unsalted butter
1 tablespoon uncooked
   long-grain rice
1 tablespoon pine nuts

1 tablespoon currants
black pepper
lemon juice
1 sprig mint, finely chopped

Prepare, steam and mince the clams as in the previous recipe. Discard the top shells and wipe the others inside and out with a little melted butter. Boil the rice until cooked, drain thoroughly and mix together with the ground pine nuts, the currants (which should be soaked in water to cover for a few minutes before they are used), some black pepper, lemon juice and plenty of finely chopped mint. Pile the mixture into the shells, drizzle a little melted ghee or butter over them, and place under a hot grill for 2–3 minutes, until the stuffing is sizzling and hot. Serve at once. *Serves 2.*

STUFFED CLAMS

400 g (14 oz) clams
oatmeal
2 tablespoons dry white wine
1 leek
1 thick slice white bread,
   crumbed

1 tablespoon parsley
1 teaspoon oregano
olive oil
2 tablespoons grated parmesan
   cheese

Soak the clams for at least 6 hours in sea water, or salted fresh water, and oatmeal, changing the water occasionally.

Heat the wine and steam the clams open over it, removing them as soon as the shells click open and tipping the juices into the wine. Twist off the top shells and discard. Mince the flesh in a blender or food processor and push it through a fine, muslin-lined sieve to get rid of the grit.

Peel the leek and process in the blender with half the breadcrumbs, some parsley and the oregano until finely chopped. Heat the oil and cook the leek mixture until softened, then add the minced clam flesh and the wine.

Wipe the shells with oil and pile in the stuffing. Cover with the other half of the breadcrumbs mixed with the parmesan, drizzle with a little oil, and place under a hot griller for 3–5 minutes, or until the tops are golden brown and sizzling. *Serves 2.*

Cockles

Cockles are burrowers living in the sand and mud of seashores and estuaries. Their thick, deeply domed, heavily ridged shells are found scattered profusely on beaches all over the world. There are various species, belonging in the main to the Arcidae, Cardiidae and Veneridae families, and all of them are edible. Living as they do in intertidal reaches cockles are easy to find and collect. Indeed, cockles have been found, collected and eaten by humans ever since someone first prised open the shells and tasted the fat, fleshy creature inside. Some varieties are disconcertingly bright red as they have haemoglobin in the blood, but they are just as readily eaten as all the others. One species of 'blood cockle' is the largest of them all: a tropical West African type that can grow up to 14 cm in diameter. Most species, however, range between 3 and 5 centimetres.

Cockles have been commemorated in rhymes and songs for centuries. Their shells were part of the garden that Mary, Mary quite contrary grew, and Molly Malone carried them in a basket on her head along with mussels as she called her wares through the streets of 18th-century Dublin. They were also part of the diet of the London poor, along with winkles and whelks and mussels and oysters and jellied eels.

Meaty and solid, with a seaweedy, iodine flavour, they can be eaten raw with just black pepper and lemon juice, but I think the strong taste really should be tempered by cooking with other ingredients. Because they are mud-dwellers they need to be soaked in frequent changes of salty water before being used so that they have a chance of sluicing away at least some of the sand and grit inside. The exterior of the shells should be well scrubbed to get rid of any attached weed before they are soaked. They can be left for 12 hours or overnight, as long as they have plenty of room and the water has enough oxygen.

Any that don't close but remain gaping open when moved about are suspect, but cockles don't react to outside pressure anywhere near as quickly as mussels and scallops. To open, insert a knife blade between the shells and twist it against the hinge, or steam them over a pan of boiling water until the shells part, then remove the flesh and tip the liquid through a muslin-lined sieve into the water to make the basis of a sauce or soup. The cockles are then ready to use.

COCKLES AND AUBERGINE

300 g (10 oz) cockles
1 medium aubergine
salt
1 handful each fresh basil and parsley

black pepper, freshly ground
lemon juice
100 ml (½ cup) olive oil
2 tablespoons fresh white breadcrumbs

Long, slender aubergines are better for these sorts of dishes as they cook more quickly. Cut the aubergine in half lengthwise, and score the face deeply in a diamond pattern, leaving a rim of at least 1 cm around the edges. Rub with salt and turn cut side down in a colander to drain off the bitter juices for 1 hour.

Scrub and soak the cockles. Twist a knife against the hinges and remove the flesh from the shells. Chop it roughly and the parsley and basily finely and mix them all together. Season with freshly ground black pepper and some lemon juice and set aside.

Rinse off the salt from the aubergine, drain and dry. Bring a large pan of water to the boil and blanch the two halves for 1–2 minutes (aubergines in boiling water have an unnerving capacity to collapse without warning, so watch them carefully: they should be soft while still retaining their shape). Drain them, and as soon as they are cool enough to handle scoop out the cubes of flesh. Mix these with the cockles and herbs, wipe the skins inside and out with a little olive oil, and pile the aubergine-and-cockle mixture into them. Cover with the rest of the olive oil, sprinkle with the breadcrumbs, and cook under a low to medium-hot griller for 10 minutes, turning up the heat at the last minute to brown and crisp the breadcrumbs. *Serves 2.*

COCKLES AND CAPSICUMS

300 g (10 oz) cockles
½ each red and green
  capsicums
1 clove garlic
4 tablespoons olive oil

1 tablespoon white wine
  vinegar
½ teaspoon French mustard
black pepper

Scrub and soak and cockles. Steam them open, remove the flesh and discard the shells. Seed the capsicums, slice them thinly, and mix with the cockles. Blend together the garlic, oil, vinegar, mustard and pepper and pour over the cockles and capsicum slices. Place the bowl in the refrigerator, covered, for 2 hours so that all the flavours can meld, then take it out of the fridge at least 1 hour before eating (if it's too cold the tastes will be deadened).

Covered with plenty of chopped parsley, this is a delicious salad on its own, but is even better served with thin slices of avocado, added at the last minute and brushed with the vinaigrette. *Serves 2.*

COCKLE AND CAULIFLOWER SALAD

300 g (10 oz) cockles
200 g (7 oz) clams
juice ½ lemon
pinch chilli powder
black pepper, freshly ground
1 medium onion
1 carrot
1 stick celery

200 g (¼ small) cauliflower
½ red capsicum
1 tomato
1 clove garlic
3 tablespoons olive oil
½ teaspoon each ground
  coriander and cumin seeds

Scrub the cockles thoroughly, using a wire brush to remove the weed, and soak them with the clams for at least 6 hours in plenty of changes of sea or salted water. Steam them open, removing them from the steamer as soon as the shells open so that they don't overcook. Rinse the clams under cold water to get rid of as much sand and grit as possible, then marinate the molluscs with the lemon juice, chilli powder and black pepper while the rest of the ingredients are being prepared.

Peel and thinly slice the onion and carrot; string and slice the celery; separate the cauliflower into florets; skin, seed and chop the capsicum and tomato; and chop the garlic finely. Heat the oil in a shallow pan and cook the onion in it until soft. Add the coriander and cumin seeds, garlic, carrot, cauliflower and celery and cook for 1 minute more. Add the tomato and capsicum, put on the lid, lower the heat and continue to cook for another 3 minutes (the vegetables should still retain their crispness).

Add the molluscs and their marinade to the pan, stir into the vegetables and serve the salad warm. *Serves 4.*

COCKLES AND CHORIZO

300 g (10 oz) cockles
1 onion
1 chorizo sausage
1 clove garlic
½ each red and green
* capsicums*

1 tomato
olive oil for frying
100 ml (½ cup) dry white
* wine*
pinch chilli powder

Scrub and soak the cockles. Peel the onion and cut it into thin rounds with the chorizo sausage and the garlic. Seed and slice the capsicums; and peel, seed and roughly chop the tomato.

Heat some oil in a shallow pan and cook the onion, garlic and sausage with a pinch of chilli until the onion is soft. Pour in the wine, add the tomatoes and their liquid and bring to the boil. Cover the pan, lower the heat and simmer for 2 minutes, then put in the cockles and steam them open. Lift them out of the pan with a slotted spoon and place them in heated soup plates. Ladle the rest of the ingredients over and around them and serve at once, with plenty of bread to mop up the sauce. *Serves 2.*

GINGER COCKLES

300 g (10 oz) cockles
2 tablespoons dry vermouth
200 ml (1 cup) chicken stock
1 onion
1 stick celery
1 rasher bacon
1 tomato
1 slice fresh ginger
4–6 black olives

1 tablespoon oil
1 clove garlic
175 g (½ cup) uncooked
* long-grain rice*
1 sprig each tarragon and
* thyme*
juice ½ lemon
sliced almonds for garnish

Scrub and soak the cockles and steam them open over the vermouth and chicken stock. Strain the juices through muslin into the simmering stock, discard the shells and set the meat aside.

Peel the onion, string the celery, rind the bacon, skin and seed the tomato, and chop them all finely. Grate the ginger, and stone and halve the olives. Cook the bacon in a pan with the tablespoon of oil until brown and crisp. Remove it from the pan and drain on absorbent paper. In the same pan, cook the onions until soft. Add the celery and garlic and continue to cook for 1 minute, drain, and set on one side with the cockles and bacon.

Tip the rice into the oil in the pan and stir until all the grains are coated and starting to pop in the heat, then add the stock and bring to the boil. Lower the heat, stir in the ginger and herbs, cover the pan and cook for 10 minutes, checking the liquid occasionally so that it doesn't dry out and burn. Add the tomato, lemon juice, onions and celery and continue to cook over a low heat for 20–30 minutes or until the rice is cooked through. Stir in the olives, bacon and cockles and turn onto a warmed serving dish.

Toss the almonds in a little butter until crisp and golden. Sprinkle them over the top and serve. *Serves 2.*

COCKLE PIE

For the filling:
300 g (10 oz) cockles
¼ teaspoon chilli powder
1 onion
1 potato
1 stick celery
1 chorizo sausage

For the pastry:
200 g (½ cup) plain flour
3 tablespoons butter
1 small egg
70 ml (3 tablespoons) chilled
*   water*

First make the pastry by sifting the flour into a bowl, adding the chilled, cubed butter and cutting it quickly with 2 knives until the mixture looks like coarse breadcrumbs. Mix the egg and chilled water together and stir into the flour, mixing until the dough forms a ball. Cut into 2 pieces, one slightly larger than the other, cover them with plastic wrap and chill for at least 1 hour or preferably overnight.

Scrub and soak the cockles and steam them open over about ½ cup of water. Tip the juices from the shells into the water through a muslin-lined sieve, discard the shells and chop the cockle meat roughly. Sprinkle with the chilli powder and set aside.

Peel the onion and potato, string the celery and dice them all finely. Cut the sausage into the same size pieces as the cockles. Simmer them all in the cockle stock until the onion and potato are soft, then remove the chorizo with half the vegetables and puree the rest with the stock in a blender to a smooth sauce.

Roll out the bigger of the 2 pieces of dough into a circle large enough to fit a buttered baking plate or flan tin, with a wide margin overhanging all round. Mix together the cockles, vegetables, chorizo and sauce and pile it into the pastry case, then place the second piece of dough, rolled out to fit, on top. Bring up the overhanging ends and press the edges together to seal. Brush the top with melted butter or milk, prick with a fork and cook in a hot oven (200°C or 400°F) for 30–35 minutes, or until the top is golden brown and crisp.

While this is very good served straight away hot from the oven, it is also good warm, like a quiche. It needs no accompaniment either way except perhaps a salad. But fruit afterwards is better. *Serves 2.*

COCKLE SOUP (1)

250 g (8 oz) cockles
1 onion
1 small potato
½ each small red and green capsicums

unsalted butter
100 ml (½ cup) dry white wine or vermouth
100 ml (½ cup) water

Peel the onion and potato, seed the capsicum and chop them all finely. Cook the onion in a little butter until soft, stir in the capsicum and potato and add the wine and water. Bring to the boil, cover and simmer for 10 minutes then place a muslin-lined steamer over the pan and steam open the scrubbed and soaked cockles, tipping the liquid from the shells into the soup below as soon as they open. Discard the shells, chop the flesh roughly and set aside until the vegetables are cooked.

Cool the stock, then puree it with the vegetables and half of the cockles until smooth and thick. Strain it through a fine sieve into a clean saucepan, bring back to the boil, add the rest of the cockles and serve at once.

Clams or mussels can also be used as the basis for this very simple and very good soup. Mussels are treated in just the same way as cockles, but clams need to be very finely sieved to make sure there is no grit in the soup. *Serves 2.*

COCKLE SOUP (2)

250 g (8 oz) cockles
2 tablespoons olive oil
2 small onions
sprig each of parsley,
  rosemary, mint, thyme
1 bay leaf
1 clove garlic
1 tablespoon dry vermouth
200 ml (1 cup) fresh tomato
  puree

1 piece preserved red capsicum
1 piece dried tomato
1 teaspoon hot chilli sauce
  or
½ teaspoon chilli powder
black pepper, freshly ground
1 large, ripe, red tomato

Scrub the cockles and soak them for at least 6 hours in frequent changes of salted water.

Heat the olive oil (the flavour is immensely improved by using the oil in which the dried tomato and preserved grilled capsicum are stored) in a frying pan and cook the finely chopped onions until soft. Add the herbs, garlic and dry vermouth and bring to the boil. Bubble for a minute or two then add the tomato puree, chopped capsicum, dried tomato and the chilli sauce or powder. Grind in some black pepper, lower the heat, put on the cover and cook, barely bubbling, for 20 minutes.

Peel and seed the tomato, add the juice to the soup and dice the flesh. Place the cockles in a muslin-lined steamer over the soup and as soon as they open tip the liquid from the shells into the stock and take them out. Discard the shells, chop the cockles roughly and stir them into the soup with the diced tomato. Pour into bowls and serve at once with lots of crusty bread to dip into it.

This is perhaps more of a casserole than a soup, but is one of the best ways to eat cockles regardless of what it's called. *Serves 2.*

CURRIED COCKLE SOUP

250 g (8 oz) cockles
1 dried chilli
1 teaspoon coriander seed
½ teaspoon each cumin,
  fennel seed, fenugreek,
  garam masala, cardamon
2 cloves
8 black peppercorns

2 tablespons uncooked rice
1 tablespoon ghee
1 onion
1 clove garlic
1 slice ginger root
250 ml (1 cup) water
1 tablespoon white wine
  vinegar

Grind the spices (including the chilli) and the rice very finely and put in a small saucepan over a low heat to release the aromatics. Add the ghee and continue to cook for 2–3 minutes.

Peel and thinly slice the onion and garlic, shred the ginger and cook them with the spices until the onion is soft, adding the garlic last so that it doesn't brown and become bitter. Pour in the water with the vinegar and bring to the boil. Cover, lower the heat and simmer for 10–15 minutes or until the ground rice has thickened the stock.

Steam open the scrubbed, soaked cockles over the stock, tip their liquid into the pan below, shell them and add the flesh to the soup. Stir for 30 seconds to heat and amalgamate the juices with the spicy liquid. Pour into heated soup plates and serve at once. *Serves 2.*

STUFFED COCKLES

12 cockles	*1 rasher bacon*
2 tablespons dry sherry	*½ each small red and green*
oil	*capsicums*
1 onion	*unsalted butter*
1 thick slice white bread	*pinch chilli pepper*

Scrub and soak the cockles, steam them open over the sherry and strain the juices from the shells into the pan below. Chop the flesh roughly, dry the shells and wipe them inside and out with oil.

Peel the onion, remove the crusts from the bread, rind the bacon, seed the capsicums and mince them all finely in a food processor or mincer. Melt some butter in a saucepan and cook the mixture until the onion softens. Add the cockle juice and sherry and continue to cook for another minute. Remove the pan from the heat, stir in the chopped cockles with a little chilli pepper and pile the mixture into the shells. Dab each one with butter and bake in a medium oven for 15 minutes or until the tops are brown and bubbling.

The most difficult part of this operation is keeping these deeply-dished, inherently unstable shells the right way up. A good method (or one that seems to work anyway) is to crumple some foil loosely and place the stuffed shells into the folds so that they are held in place. Put the crumpled foil into a baking plate that will hold it firmly, and bed the cockles into it. Another method is to fix them into a bed of rock salt like oysters. *Serves 2.*

Crabs

Crabs are found almost everywhere—under ledges on rocky shores, scuttling across the sand and mud of tidal flats, in mangrove swamps and estuaries, in ocean depths and freshwater rivers. One species has even adapted to tree climbing and claws its way up palm trees to get to the coconuts on top.

They range in size from tiny, transparent creatures no larger than a grain of sand to the monster deep-sea spider crabs of the Pacific. They belong to the family Decapoda and instead of having round bodies they have flattened ones with legs at the sides and large claws in the front. Some species have only one claw, many have one much larger than the other, but all are armed with nippers of some sort and even small ones can give a sharp bite to the unwary.

Crab shells have been found in excavations of settlements beside the ancient riverbeds and waterways between the Tigris and the Euphrates. Freshwater crabs have always been a favourite food in China, where some restaurants specialise in cooking them, usually steamed and served with various dipping sauces. In America and Italy soft-shelled ones are a delicacy (soft-shelled because they are moulting and therefore without a shell, which seems to me a rather unsporting time to catch them). Apicius describes crab sausages and Shakespeare talks of roast crabs hissing in the bowl, but in general crabs do not seem to be mentioned all that much in literature, perhaps because everyone was too busy eating them.

While there are hundreds of different species, most of them edible, the really useful ones, so far as home cooking is concerned, are the species that are readily available commercially, and those which weigh between 200 g (7 oz) and 2 kg (4 lb). Anything above or below that weight is either too fiddly to deal with or so big it's better left to restaurants. The three described here illustrate methods of dealing with crabs small (blue swimmer), crabs medium (spanner) and crabs large (mud).

BLUE SWIMMER CRABS

Blue swimmer crabs are sand crabs. Found in shallow waters and estuaries, they have mottled dark blue shells and the claws are a stunning purple-indigo, almost iridescent in its vividness. They are available throughout the year in reasonable quantities both raw and cooked, and the average weight is around 350 to 400 g (12–14 oz), although they can be bigger than that. Because of their long, rather spindly legs and claws they do not have a high ratio of flesh to shell (there is little meat in the legs for instance). A medium-sized crab will give just under one-third its weight in meat, but a little crab meat goes a long way and the taste and texture of one crab will permeate a dish for two people if stretched with other ingredients. Blue swimmers are fragile and therefore easy to extract the flesh from, unlike some of the larger, more heavily shelled varieties. They are also delicious with a sweet, nutty flavour and soft, delicate texture.

To clean uncooked swimmer crabs, lift the tail or flap on the underside and the top shell will come away easily. Remove the stomach, intestines and the grey-white, gritty, papery gills and break open the inner structure to remove the meat inside, carefully separating it from the stiff, transparent cartilage surrounding it. Twist off the claws, hit them lightly with a mallet or nutcracker and peel away the shell from the flesh, loosening it carefully so it doesn't break up. It is then ready to be cooked, either by poaching in a little white wine or stock, or by turning in butter until the flesh stiffens and becomes white with pink-tinged edges.

To cook a swimmer crab whole, twist off the claws beforehand and steam or simmer the body for 8 to 10 minutes depending on size, adding the claws halfway through (if they are given the same amount of time as the main shell, the flesh inside will over-cook, becoming mushy). The shell will turn from mottled blue to bright red when the flesh is cooked. Take the crab out of the steamer or pan and as soon as it is cool enough to handle, clean it the same way you would if it were raw. If the crab meat is not to be used immediately, it is a good idea to plunge the whole thing into cold water to stop the cooking process as soon as it's ready, otherwise it will overcook.

CRAB AND ALMOND SALAD

1 blue swimmer crab
4–6 leaves soft lettuce
50 g (2 tablespoons) unsalted
  butter

50 g (2 tablespoons) blanched
  almonds
black pepper, freshly ground

Arrange the washed, dried lettuce leaves on salad plates. Clean the crab and remove all the flesh from the body and claws. Melt the butter in a frying pan, add the crab meat and stir gently until it turns white, then remove from the pan and arrange on the lettuce.

Turn up the heat under the butter and put in the almonds, tossing and stirring them until they become crisp and golden. Sprinkle over the crab meat, pour on the sizzling butter, give a couple of generous turns with the pepper grinder and serve immediately. *Serves 2.*

CRAB AND AVOCADO

Crab and avocado are a wonderful combination, each seeming to add an extra dimension to the other, but there are problems in dealing with avocados as they don't take kindly to being cooked. The trick is to just heat them gently to warm and never let them get to the stage where the flesh and oil separate, as then the taste changes to one reminiscent of brass.

CRAB AND AVOCADO MOUSSE

1 medium blue swimmer crab
½ teaspoon gelatine
1 tablespoon hot water
50 ml (2 tablespoons) cream

1 egg white
½ ripe avocado
1 tablespoon dry vermouth
cayenne pepper

Steam the crab and remove the flesh from body and claws. Sprinkle the gelatine on the hot water to dissolve it. Whip the cream, beat the egg white until stiff and standing in peaks, and mash the avocado.

Mix together the vermouth, avocado, crab meat, gelatine and cream, sprinkle with a little cayenne pepper and fold in the egg white. Pour into a lightly oiled terrine or mould and chill for at least 2 hours before serving. *Serves 2.*

CRAB AND AVOCADO PANCAKES

For the filling:
1 blue swimmer crab
1 tablespoon dry vermouth
½ ripe avocado, mashed
2 tablespoons light cream
1 tablespoon heavy cream
pepper

For the pancakes:
1 egg yolk
100 ml (½ cup) milk
100 ml (½ cup) water
50 g (½ cup) plain flour
salt and pepper
butter for frying

The batter for the pancakes should be made at least 2 hours before. Mix together the egg yolk, milk and water. Sift the flour with a little salt and pepper into a bowl. Pour in the egg, milk and water, stirring constantly and adding a little at a time, making sure the first lot is absorbed and smoothly incorporated before adding the next. Beat together so that the batter is smooth and leave for 2 hours.

Melt a little butter in a frying pan. Bring to a high heat (using clarified butter makes it much easier) and pour in a ladleful of the batter, swirling it quickly round the pan to coat the bottom and pouring back any left over—the pancakes should be thin and crisp, not thick and heavy—into the bowl. Cook until the top surface has dried out and the edges are crisp, then turn and cook the other side for a few moments longer. Place on a heated plate and keep warm in the oven. Continue until all the batter is used up, and cover the plate with foil to stop the pancakes from drying out in the oven.

Remove the flesh from the crab. Cook gently in butter and vermouth until the flesh loses its translucence, then add the mashed avocado. Heat the cream in a separate saucepan and beat in the crab and avocado mixture. Place spoonfuls in each pancake, roll up and arrange on a warm serving dish. Pour the rest of the mixture over as a sauce.

The crab and avocado filling can also be used as a sauce poured over pasta, scallops poached in vermouth, or crab cakes. *Serves 2.*

CRAB AND AVOCADO PIES

1 blue swimmer crab
unsalted butter
1 tablespoon dry vermouth

½ ripe avocado, mashed
black pepper, freshly ground
250 g (9 oz) shortcrust pastry

Take the flesh from the body and claws of the crab and cook very gently in butter until the translucency changes to white. Pour in the vermouth, allow to bubble briefly, then remove from the heat and stir in the mashed avocado and some black pepper.

Roll out the pastry as thinly as possible and on one half spoon little mounds of the mixture, leaving a wide margin between each and keeping them in straight lines. Dampen the spaces around each mound with water, fold over the other half of the pastry and press down around each spoonful to seal the two halves together. Cut out the little pies with a circular biscuit or pastry cutter and chill for 10 minutes before placing on a baking sheet brushed with butter.

Brush the tops of the pies with more melted butter and put in a hot oven for 15 minutes. Allow to cool a little before eating. *Makes 6–8 pies.*

CRAB AND AVOCADO SALAD

1 blue swimmer crab
1 soft-leaved lettuce
1 ripe avocado

2 tablespoons mayonnaise
juice of 1 mandarin
black pepper, freshly ground

Steam, cool and remove the flesh from the crab. Rinse, dry and arrange the lettuce on plates. Halve and peel the avocado and cut across each half diagonally into thin slices. Arrange these on each plate on top of the lettuce and add the crab meat. Mix together the mayonnaise and mandarin juice and pour over the crab and avocado. Grind a little black pepper over the top and serve. *Serves 2.*

CAULIFLOWER WITH CRAB SAUCE

1 blue swimmer crab
1 small white tight cauliflower
unsalted butter
pepper
lemon juice

100 ml (½ cup) dry vermouth
1 onion
40 g (2 tablespoons) fresh
    cream cheese
parsley for garnish

Trim the cauliflower stem and cut a notch in the bottom. Cook for 10–15 minutes in lightly salted, boiling water, until the white flower (which should steam above the water rather than be immersed in it) is still firm but no longer friable. Drain the cauliflower throughly, retaining the liquid, and set in a deep buttered dish, into which it just fits. Sprinkle with pepper, wipe the top with lemon juice and melted butter, cover with foil or a lid and keep warm in the oven.

Poach the crab in the cauliflower liquid until the shell turns bright red (about 5–8 minutes, depending on the size) then take it out and remove the crab meat, discarding the inner organs. Take the flesh from the claws and set aside. Crush the shells and return them to the liquid with the dry vermouth, the onion and some pepper. Turn up the heat and boil for another 5–10 minutes, then cool and whizz in the blender to break down the shells. Sieve into a clean saucepan, pressing down on the residue in the sieve to push through all the juices. Rinse out the blender and return the stock to it with the cream cheese. Blend until thick and smooth, then pour back into the pan and bring back to the boil. Stir in the crab meat and pour over the cauliflower. Serve at once, sprinkled with finely chopped parsley. *Serves 2.*

CRAB WITH CORIANDER BUTTER

1 blue swimmer crab	*60 g (3 tablespoons) unsalted*
70 ml (3 tablespoons) dry	*butter, chilled*
white wine	*salt*
1 large handful fresh	*black pepper, freshly ground*
coriander leaves	*lemon juice*

Scrub the crab and remove all the flesh from the body and claws. Bring the white wine to the boil, lower the heat, and poach the crab meat for 2–3 minutes or until it turns white. Transfer it to a heated serving dish and keep warm.

Turn up the heat and boil the wine briskly until reduced to 2 tablespoons. Chop the coriander leaves finely and add to the wine. Cut the chilled butter into little cubes and whisk into the mixture a few at a time until the sauce amalgamates into a glossy, green-flecked smoothness. Add a little salt and freshly ground black pepper, squeeze in some lemon juice to spark the buttery richness and pour round the crab.

Serve with rice or tiny boiled potatoes, or just fresh bread to mop up the juices. *Serves 2.*

FETTUCINE WITH CRAB SAUCE

1 blue swimmer crab
olive oil
½ small green capsicum
2 ripe red tomatoes
1 clove garlic
1 dried chilli

1 sprig oregano
1 tablespoon parsley leaves
black pepper, freshly ground
300 g (10 oz) fettucine
basil for garnish

Remove all the flesh from the crab and stir gently in heated oil until it turns white. Take out and set aside. Peel and seed the capsicum and tomatoes, retaining as much tomato juice as possible, and add to the pan with the finely chopped garlic, chilli, oregano and parsley. Season with pepper and continue to cook for 5–10 minutes.

Bring a large pan of water to the boil, put in a pinch of salt and a teaspoonful of oil and cook the fettucine until soft but still slightly firm to the teeth. Drain in a colander and toss with a little olive oil until all the moisture is driven off, then pile into a pre-heated bowl.

Return the crab meat to the sauce to reheat and pour it over the pasta. Finely chop the basil, sprinkle over the top and serve at once. *Serves 2.*

CRAB AND LEEK SOUP

2 blue swimmer crabs
70 ml (3 tablespoons) dry
   white wine
100 ml (½ cup) water

1 bay leaf
1 leek
unsalted butter
salt and pepper to taste

Put the water, the wine and the bay leaf into a large saucepan, bring to the boil and cook the crabs for 8 minutes or so until the shells are bright red. Shell them, discard the guts and intestines, and return the shells to the liquid. Set the crab meat aside.

Clean the leek, cut off the tough tops and discard the outer leaves. Add the inner pale-yellow part of the green section to the liquid. Cut the white part into slender rounds. Melt some butter in a pan and cook the leek rounds until soft.

Simmer the stock for 20 minutes then cool and strain. Pour it into a blender with the leek and the flesh of one of the crabs and blend until smooth. Return to the pan and bring it back to the boil. Season with salt and pepper, pour into pre-heated bowls and garnish with the meat from the second crab. *Serves 2.*

CRAB OMELETTE

1 blue swimmer crab	*salt*
unsalted butter	*pepper*
3 large eggs	*1 tablespoon cream*

Carefully remove the flesh from the body and claws of the crab, heat some butter in an omelette pan and put in the crab meat. Cook for no more than 1–2 minutes over a low flame until the flesh is no longer translucent. Set aside and keep warm.

Beat the eggs with a little salt and pepper. Turn up the heat beneath the pan until the butter starts to brown lightly. Pour in the beaten eggs, shaking the pan so that the base is evenly covered. As the edges start to set spread the crab meat on top, pour over the tablespoon of warmed cream, flip over one side of the omelette and slide onto a warm plate. Cut in half and serve at once. (Alternatively, make two separate omelettes. This is probably more aesthetically attractive but omelettes don't wait for anyone and should be eaten the instant they hit the plate. This could cause problems if you like eating together.) *Serves 2.*

CRAB AND RED CAPSICUM SOUP

1 blue swimmer crab	*1 sprig mint*
200 ml (1 cup) water	*black pepper, freshly ground*
1 sweet red capsicum	

Bring the water to the boil in a deep pan, add the crab and simmer for 6–8 minutes. Take it out and remove the flesh. Set the crab meat aside. Return the shells to the water and simmer for 20 minutes to extract all the flavour. Strain the stock into a clean pan and cool.

Grill the capsicum, peel off the skin, discard the seeds and white ribs of pith. Slice off 6 long, slender strips and set them aside. Put the rest in a blender with the crab meat, mint, pepper and stock and blend until smooth and brilliant red. Pour the soup back into the pan, heat to just on boiling point, and serve at once in pre-heated bowls. Garnish with the slender capsicum strips.

This soup is open to variation. A hot red chilli added to the stock will enliven it no end; or you could blend all the capsicum with the stock and garnish instead with plenty of mint. In either case the soup is a brilliant, beautiful colour, and can be served hot or cold. While the addition of hot chilli is very good, the smooth sweetness of the soup without it is surprising and delicious. *Serves 2.*

CRAB IN SHERRY CREAM

2 blue swimmer crabs
60 g (3 tablespoons) unsalted
   butter
2 tablespoons dry sherry

50 ml (2 tablespoons) cream
black pepper, freshly ground
2–3 sprigs chervil

Shell the crabs, discarding everything except the meat. Melt the butter in a frying pan. Cook the crab gently until the flesh becomes opaque then transfer to a serving dish and keep it warm in the oven.

Add the sherry to the juices in the pan. Bring to the boil, pour in the cream, grind in some pepper and simmer until reduced to a rich sauce. Chop the chervil finely, stir into the sherry cream, and pour over the crab. Serve at once with rice, or in vol-au-vent cases with snow peas. *Serves 2.*

STUFFED CRAB

2 small blue swimmer crabs
1 small onion
¼ red capsicum
1 small carrot
unsalted butter

2 tablespoons fresh
   breadcrumbs
1 sprig each fresh mint and
   coriander
1 medium tomato
black pepper, freshly ground

The wide, pointed top shells make good holders for grilled or baked crab dishes, but they must be trimmed first to remove the pale, brittle undershell (it breaks away along the edge quite easily) to leave a shallow, gently curved bowl. Scrub and boil each thoroughly and brush with a little melted butter before filling.

Twist off the claws and place the crabs on a steamer rack over boiling water. Cook for 5 minutes. Add the claws and cook for 2–3 minutes longer. Cool by plunging into cold water and then remove the flesh.

Peel and finely chop the onion, capsicum and carrot and cook over a low heat in some butter until the onion is soft. Stir in half the breadcrumbs and continue to cook until they are lightly browned and have absorbed some of the moisture. Add the coriander and mint, both finely chopped.

While the onion is cooking peel and seed the tomato and drain off the juice by turning the cut side down on kitchen paper. Chop into small pieces and mix into the onion and breadcrumbs.

Fold the crab carefully into the vegetables, grind in some black pepper, butter the two crab shells, pile in the crab mixture, sprinkle with the rest of the breadcrumbs and dot with butter. Place under a hot grill for 3 minutes or until the breadcrumbs are golden-brown and the stuffing sizzling. Serve at once as a first course. *Serves 2.*

CRAB WITH TAWNY PORT

2 blue swimmer crabs　　　　　*juice of ½ lemon*
unsalted butter　　　　　　　　*1 sprig parsley*
1 onion　　　　　　　　　　　　*3 tablespoons fresh white*
50 ml (2 tablespoons) tawny　　　*breadcrumbs*
*　port*

Remove the crab meat from the shells, discarding the guts and gills and all shell except the top ones. Boil these until they turn bright red then drain and rub them, inside and out, with a little melted butter and set aside.

Peel and finely chop the onion and cook in a little butter until soft. Add the crab meat and stir gently. When the flesh turns white take it out. Pour the port into the pan, raise the heat, add the lemon juice and boil fiercely until the mixture has reduced to no more than 2 tablespoons. Allow to cool for a minute or so, then fold in the crab meat and pile it into the shells.

Chop the parsley finely, mix it together with the breadcrumbs and cover the crab meat, patting the crumbs down lightly so they don't fall off. Melt some butter and pour it over the top. Place the shells under a hot grill for 2–3 minutes until the top is crisp and bubbling. *Serves 2.*

SPANNER CRABS

Spanner crabs *(Ranina ranina)* are square, shield-shaped creatures with flattened claws and brown-fringed, red-brown carapaces. They are sand and mud dwellers, living in the shallows throughout the warmer waters of the Indo-Pacific region, including Hawaii and Japan and the warmer coastal areas of Australia.

They have solid, no-nonsense shapes, sensible rather than frightening or beautiful. They lack the brilliantly-coloured fragility of the blue swimmer on the one hand and the awesome claws and massive carapace of the mud crab on the other. But they are very good to eat, with firmer, denser flesh than the swimmers. The claws are flattened and much of the meat is in the body. The ratio of flesh to gross weight is quite good—roughly a third for a medium-sized one, including that from the legs and claws.

The carapaces are thick and hard and a mallet or hammer is a necessary piece of equipment for breaking them. The 'tail', clamped tight to the red-and-white underside, is shorter than that of a blue swimmer crab and the top shell fits much more tightly—it needs to be prised away by lifting the tail and inserting a broad-bladed knife, using it as a lever to pull it away from the body. Inside the shell is a viscous, fawn, scarlet-veined liquid which is called 'brown meat' in England and 'crab butter' in America but doesn't seem to rate a mention in Australia. This is a pity, because it makes a wonderful sauce or addition to sauces. Mixed with breadcrumbs for stiffening, it can be added to the white crab meat in certain dishes. In spanner crabs, it turns brick-red when cooked and is delicious, used either as a sauce or, added to fresh breadcrumbs, as a component of a crab salad.

The body shell is also hard, but once cracked open, after the guts and grey, gritty gills have been discarded, it is an easy matter to separate the flesh from the thin, transparent inner walls. The legs are surprisingly meaty and repay either cracking to eat at the table, or removing the flesh beforehand, depending on the dish. The claws need to be bashed with care. Though hard they are thin, and too hearty a bang will send crab shards scattering, leaving no crab meat to eat.

If the crabs are to be cooked in the shell, they should be steamed or simmered for 10 to 12 minutes, depending on size, then plunged into cold water to stop the process so that the shells can be removed and the crab cleaned. If the flesh is extracted before cooking it takes no more than 2 to 3 minutes to poach or cook gently in butter.

CRAB CAKES WITH MUSTARD

1 medium spanner crab
1 thick slice white bread
1 teaspoon French mustard
1 sprig parsley

1 tablespoon cream
black pepper, freshly ground
40 g (2 tablespoons) unsalted
  butter

Steam the crab for 10–12 minutes depending on size, then plunge it at once into cold water to arrest the cooking process. As soon as it's cool enough to handle remove all the flesh from the body and claws, discarding everything else.

Cut off the crusts and whizz the bread in a blender or food processor to fine crumbs. Take out about ⅓ of these and set aside. To the remainder add the crab meat, mustard, parsley and just enough cream to hold the mixture together and process until smooth. Season with black pepper, turn onto a plate, cover with plastic film and chill for at least 30 minutes.

Shape the mixture into small balls then flatten them into cakes. Melt the butter and dip them into it, roll them in the rest of the breadcrumbs, and chill again until needed.

Cook them, brushed with melted butter, on a sheet of foil under a griller or in a hot oven for 5–8 minutes, or fried in clarified butter. Serve the crab cakes with mustard-flavoured mayonnaise and a salad. *Serves 2.*

CRAB CLAWS WITH SHERRY MAYONNAISE

legs and claws of 1 cooked
  medium spanner crab
1 tablespoon dry sherry

4 tablespoons mayonnaise
salt
black pepper, freshly ground

Twist the claws and legs away from the body carefully, pulling slowly but firmly, and much of the body meat will come out at the same time. Crack the claws and legs with a hammer or crab cracker and carefully pick off the loose shards so that the flesh is exposed but the ends remain to be used as handles.

Beat the sherry and mayonnaise together, adding a little salt to taste and some freshly ground black pepper. Pour into a bowl and place it in the centre of a large dish, surrounded by the crab.

This is delicious but messy food, wonderful as a first course or as tapas with drinks (large table napkins and finger bowls are highly desirable extras), but even better as part of a lavish picnic. *Serves 2.*

CRAB AND CORN SALAD

*1 cooked medium spanner
 crab
1 ear sweet corn
1 teaspoon sugar
black pepper, freshly ground
salt
4 tablespoons olive oil*

*1 bunch watercress
1 small radicchio
1 tablespoon white wine
 vinegar
1 handful chervil leaves
1 tablespoon cream*

Cook the sweet corn in plenty of boiling water with a teaspoonful of sugar for 20 minutes. Drain, cool and scrape off the kernels into a bowl with a sharp knife. Sprinkle them with pepper, salt and a little oil and set aside.

Spread the washed, dried watercress on four salad plates. Shred the radicchio and spread on top, then scatter over the corn kernels. Remove the flesh from the body, claws and legs of the crab and pile in the centre of the plates.

Put the oil, vinegar, chervil and cream with a pinch of salt and some freshly ground black pepper in a blender or food processor. Blend to a smooth, creamy-green dressing and drizzle it in wavy lines over the crab meat. Drape a few shreds of radicchio and some cress leaves over the top and serve.

This salad is vividly pretty and the sharp, deep colours of the vegetables contrast with the pale richness of the crab and its dressing in the same way the flavours do, echoing the bite of the radicchio and the smoothness of the crab. *Serves 2.*

DEVILLED CRAB

*1 cooked medium spanner
 crab
1 small onion
½ green capsicum
½ stick celery
unsalted butter
1 tablespoon heavy cream*

*¼ teaspoon Worcestershire
 sauce
dash Tabasco sauce
black pepper, freshly ground
1 sprig parsley
3 tablespoons fresh white
 breadcrumbs*

Peel the onion, seed the capsicum and string the celery. Chop them all very finely and cook in a little butter until soft but not browned.

Remove all the flesh from the body, claws and legs of the crab, carefully picking out the cartilage. Mix together with the onion, celery, capsicum, cream, Worcestershire and Tabasco sauces and pepper and pile into four buttered ramekins (or small crab or scallop shells). Finely chop the parsley, stir it into the breadcrumbs, and sprinkle over the crab mixture. Dot with butter and place beneath a medium-hot grill for 2–5 minutes, until the surface is golden-brown and the mixture beneath is sizzling. *Serves 4.*

CRAB WITH LEEKS

1 green medium spanner crab
1 leek
60 g (3 tablespoons) unsalted
* butter & extra for frying*
1 egg yolk
black pepper, freshly ground
salt
lemon juice

This dish is very good as a stuffing or garnish for artichokes or any other vegetable that can be hollowed out and used as a case. It also can be used for vol-au-vents or feuilletes.

Take the crab flesh from the shells, claws and legs and pour the fawn, scarlet-flecked liquid from the top shell into a saucepan. Over a low heat, stir until the liquid thickens and turns brick-red. Remove the pan from the heat and set aside.

Peel the leek, clean it and slice thinly. Melt some butter in a pan and cook the slices gently until they are soft. Add the crab meat and continue to cook, stirring carefully so that the flesh doesn't break up, until it turns white. Pile the crab and leek mixture onto pre-heated plates and keep warm in the oven.

Break the egg yolk into the crab sauce and cook for a few moments until the sauce thickens, then start adding the butter in small, chilled cubes, a little at a time, stirring until the sauce becomes thick, glossy and glowing red. Season with pepper, lemon juice, and a little salt. Pour around the crab and leek mixture and serve.

An alternative sauce can be made by adding cooked leeks and celery and blending or processing until smooth.

MARINATED CRAB

1 green medium spanner crab	*black pepper, freshly ground*
1 clove garlic	*½ cucumber*
1 stalk and leaves parsley	*salt*
2 tablespoons olive oil	*4–6 leaves butter or other*
1 tablespoon red wine vinegar	*soft-leaved lettuce*

Steam the crab for 10–12 minutes depending on size, then plunge into cold water. As soon as it's cool enough to handle, remove all the flesh from the body. Then crack the legs and claws, opening the shell so that the marinade can be poured onto the meat inside. Put body meat, legs and claws into a deep bowl.

Crush the garlic, chop the parsley, and blend them together with the oil, red wine vinegar and pepper. Pour the marinade over the crab and leave for at least 2 hours for all the flavours to develop.

Peel, seed and slice thinly the cucumber, sprinkle with salt, place in a colander and leave to drain for at least 1 hour, then rinse under cold water and dry. Wash and dry the lettuce, place the leaves on a large dish, arrange the crab meat on top, surrounded by the legs and claws and decorated with the cucumber slices. Grind black pepper over the top, pour on any remaining marinade and serve. *Serves 2.*

CRAB PILAFF

1 green medium spanner crab	*1 large sprig fresh mint*
2 tablespoons olive oil	*100 ml (½ cup) water*
1 onion	*100 g (5 tablespoons) long-*
1 clove garlic	*grain rice*
2 large ripe tomatoes	*juice 1 lemon*

Twist off the claws and legs from the crab, pull away the top shell from the body, and discard the guts and gills. Carefully separate the flesh from the cartilage and set it aside. Pour the fawn-coloured liquid from the top shell into a basin and set it aside as well.

Heat the olive oil and add the crab shell, claws and legs, stirring for about 5 minutes until the colour changes to bright red. Remove, discard the shell and put the claws and legs aside.

Peel the onion and slice it thinly with the garlic. Skin and seed the tomatoes, retaining their juice, and chop the flesh. Chop the mint. Cook the onion in the olive oil until soft, add the garlic and stir for a moment or two. Add the tomatoes and their juice, the water, and the crab liquid and bring to the boil. Stir in the rice, lower the heat and cook, covered, for 20–30 minutes until the rice is cooked and most of the liquid absorbed.

Stir the crab meat and the mint into the rice, carefully so that the grains don't break, and cook for a minute or so longer. Check the seasoning, squeeze in half the lemon juice, taste again to see if more is needed, then pile into a pre-heated bowl. Decorate with more chopped mint and serve. *Serves 2.*

WARM CRAB SALAD

*1 cooked medium spanner
    crab
60 g (3 tablespoons) unsalted
    butter, plus extra for frying
2 tablespoons dry sherry*

*1 tablespoon sour cream
few drops Tabasco sauce
1 handful parsley leaves
black pepper, freshly ground*

Take all the flesh from the body of the crab and crack the legs and claws, peeling away as much of the shell as possible without it falling apart. Melt a little butter in a pan and heat the crab in it gently, grind over some black pepper, then transfer to a pre-heated dish, cover with foil or a lid and place in a warm oven.

Boil the sherry, reducing it to about 1 teaspoon. Add the sour cream and Tabasco, return to the boil and simmer for a minute or so. Lower the heat and beat in the butter, chilled and cubed, a little at a time until all the cubes are incorporated and the sauce is thick and smooth. Taste for seasoning, adding some more Tabasco if necessary, then pour over the crab and sprinkle the chopped parsley leaves on top.

Serve piled on lettuce leaves and surrounded by a warm salad— shredded zucchini and carrots; thinly cut leeks and skinny slices of grilled, seeded red capsicum; or asparagus and mushrooms. *Serves 2.*

MUD CRABS

The World's Best Mud Crab was eaten in a restaurant on a wharf in Southern Thailand. Out front, packed on ice-laden trays, fish and shellfish were displayed in shining piles, with fruit and vegetables arranged to one side. Attended by a suitably serious restaurateur, we walked slowly past the trays of seafood, trying to choose between briliantly-coloured parrot fish and coral trout, scampi and huge prawns, squid and rock lobster, and a grim, dark, glowering mud crab doing its best to unwind the string that bound its great claws and escape its inevitable fate.

Some time later, sitting at a table with the shallow water of the bay lapping and plopping under the planks beneath our feet, we ate that crab. It had been simply cleaned, cracked, and steamed with ginger and soy sauce, and was utterly delicious.

Scylla serrata, the mud or mangrove crab, is found throughout the Indo-Pacific region in the shallows and estuaries and mangrove swamps of the tropical and semi-tropical waters. It has a dull, green-grey shell and enormous claws in which lie much of the flesh, unlike the blue swimmer and spanner crab. In fish markets and shops mud crabs, their claws tied with string, are kept in plastic tubs or water tanks, where they stumble and fall over each other as they move about. Occasionally someone with more bravado than sense undoes the string and the great nippers flail and wave, sending the crowd involuntarily backwards. Getting a hand or finger caught between those claws would undoubtedly cause anguish, and more than likely a broken bone or two.

The wide top shell has a serrated edge, and the body, like the claws, is thick and heavy. The shell is much stronger than that of swimmer or spanner crabs, and commensurately harder to crack—a large, heavy hammer and a great deal of willpower are required to get at the crab meat in the fat claws.Mud crabs are sold either live or ready cooked, and a pre-cooked one is fine for serving cold with a salad. If it is to be served hot however, it should be bought not only still alive but still lively. Choose the one struggling gamely over all the others, not the one lying tamely underneath. As soon as you get it home, put it in the freezer for 30 minutes to an hour (but remember you came to cook Caesar not to freeze him), and once the creature is dead, cook it as soon as possible.

To clean a mud crab, lift the attenuated tail tucked beneath the body and pull away the top shell. Inside is the brown, semi-fluid 'brown meat' or 'crab butter'. It should not be thrown away as it makes lovely sauces and, mixed with breadcrumbs, adds considerably to the quantity of meat from what is always a very expensive creature. Remove the grey, gritty finger-like gills, stomach and intestines, rinse the body quickly under cold water to get rid of any grit, and drain. If the crab is to be eaten whole it is simpler to steam or simmer it first and clean it afterwards. When cooked, the crab butter changes colour and texture, becoming thick and pale yellow.

Being served with a large crab, whole but cracked, in a restaurant is one thing. There, surrounded by table napkins and hot towels, finger bowls and special utensils with which to crack the claws and poke out the flesh from the body, one can feel pampered and deliciously grubby at the same time. At home, however, it's usually somewhat more difficult. A hammer doesn't have quite the same cachet as crab crackers, and there is never enough room on the table for the finger bowls, so really the easiest method is to remove all the flesh beforehand. When fresh and uncooked, the meat clings tightly to the shell, so that it tears and breaks instead of coming away in one piece. To overcome this you can cheat by partly cooking it then removing the shell and continuing the cooking afterwards.

Simply place the crab in a large pan of cold water and bring slowly to the boil with the lid on. As soon as the water starts to bubble remove the crab and plunge into cold water to stop the cooking process. Take off the top shell, discard the gills, stomach and intestines, and rinse. Crack the claws, either opening the shell wide enough to pour in a marinade or removing the flesh entirely (it's a good idea to leave on one of the nippers for a handle), and break open the body to remove all the flesh inside. Twist the legs away from the body, break the joints and take out all the flesh. Partly cooked, it will come away easily. The crab meat is then ready for finishing by whatever method you wish.

A mud crab gives from 25 to 28 per cent of flesh to gross weight, but a little goes a long way, and a large mud crab will feed four easily, especially if stretched with other ingredients. The first recipe in this section gives the basic method of simmering a crab.

MUD CRAB WITH ARTICHOKES

1 large live mud crab
4 artichokes
1 slice lemon
1 tablespoon dry vermouth
1 tablespoon lemon juice

1 large egg yolk
70 g (3 tablespoons) unsalted
  butter
pepper (optional)

Place the crab in the freezer until it stops moving, then put it in a deep saucepan and cover with cold water. Bring to the boil, lower the heat and simmer for 8–10 minutes. Plunge it at once into cold water to stop the cooking process. As soon as it's cool enough to handle take off the top shell by lifting the tail and pulling it away from the body; the shell will come away quite easily. Scrape out the soft, butter-yellow material clinging to the shell and set it aside. Discard the gills, stomach and guts, rinse the body quickly under running water and dry it. Break open the carapace and twist off the claws and legs. Pick out all the flesh from the body, carefully discarding any shards of shell or cartilage, and crack the legs and claws with a hammer or crab cracker to remove the meat inside.

Remove the outer leaves of the artichokes, cut off the tops, trim the stems and rub the cut edges with lemon. Cook them, uncovered, in boiling water for 15–20 minutes until the stems can be pierced with a fork, then drain. As soon as they are cool enough to handle remove the centre leaves and the chokes. Place on a buttered, heat-proof dish, pile the crab meat into and around them, cover with foil and put the dish in a warm oven while the sauce is prepared.

Heat the vermouth and lemon juice in a saucepan, and boil rapidly until reduced to no more than ½ a tablespoon. Lift away from the heat, lower the flame and when the liquid has cooled slightly beat in the egg yolk, stirring until it thickens a little. Add the crab butter to the pan, beating it well into the egg, then the chilled butter cut into small cubes, a few at a time, until all the butter is incorporated and the sauce is thick and glossy. Check the seasoning, adding a little pepper if necessary. Take the crab-filled artichokes out of the oven and pour the sauce over them. Serve at once. *Serves 4.*

CRAB-BUTTERED MUD CRAB

1 large live mud crab
1 clove garlic

50 ml (2 tablespoons) dry
vermouth
black pepper, freshly ground

Chill the crab to kill it. Crack the legs and claws and twist them off the body. Lift off the top shell, scrape out the brown, semi-fluid 'crab butter' that sticks to it and put into a saucepan large enough to hold the whole crab. Scrub the top shell, boil it to make sure it is completely clean, and break off the brittle side parts underneath to give a shallow bowl. Remove and discard the gills and guts, break open the body and pile all the meat into the top shell.

Peel the garlic and mash it into the crab butter. Pour in the vermouth, put the saucepan over a low heat and stir until the sauce is smooth and creamy. Put the claws and legs into the pan, balance the meat-filled top shell on top (this is not as difficult as it sounds, for the claws create good bases), sprinkle with freshly ground black pepper, put on the lid and steam for 5–10 minutes, depending on the size. If the crab is really quite large and the claws will take longer to cook, don't add the top shell until halfway through the process, for the exposed flesh will take no more than 5 minutes to be cooked through.

To serve, place the crab on a pre-heated serving dish, pour the sauce over it, and make sure there are table napkins and finger bowls close at hand. This is a feast for two people and adequate for four, but then there are bound to be squabbles over who doesn't get a claw, or, even worse, opportunities for moral victories by those who like being martyred. So perhaps it's better to keep it as a feast for two. *Serves 2–4.*

CHINESE MUD CRAB

1 large live mud crab
1 small piece fresh ginger
1 spring onion
2 tablespoons soy sauce
2 tablespoons rice wine or dry
sherry

1 tablespoon rice wine vinegar
or 1 tablespoon white wine
vinegar plus 1 teaspoon
sugar

Chill the crab and kill it, then lift off the top shell, discard the guts and gills, rinse the body under cold running water very quickly and dry. Break open the inner carapace exposing the flesh and crack the legs and claws, opening the shell as much as possible. Put the crab on a shallow fireproof dish. Grate the ginger, chop the spring onion and mix them together with the soy sauce, rice wine and rice wine vinegar. Pour over the crab, making sure some of the mixture gets into every crack and set the dish aside for at least 1 hour so that the flavours of the marinade have time to permeate the meat.

To cook, simply place the dish in a steamer over boiling water and steam for 5–10 minutes, depending on size. It can be served with boiled or steamed rice, or just on its own.

Another method is to par-cook the crab and remove all the flesh from the body, legs and claws, keeping a nipper on each claw as a handle. Pile the meat into the top shell, pour over the marinade, and leave for 20 minutes, then steam over boiling water for no more than 2 minutes. *Serves 2–4.*

MUD CRAB IN COCONUT SAUCE

1 large live mud crab
300 ml (1¼ cups) coconut
*   milk*
1 piece fresh ginger
pinch chilli powder

1 teaspoon garam masala
juice 1 lime
1 thin slice coconut cream
lime slices for garnish

Chill the crab to kill it, place in a saucepan of cold water, bring to the boil and simmer for 8–10 minutes. Plunge it into cold water to stop the cooking and as soon as it's cool enough to handle take out all the flesh.

Put the coconut milk into a saucepan with the grated ginger and chilli. Simmer for 5 minutes. Add the garam masala, lime juice and crab flesh, lower the heat and cook for another 2 minutes.

Lift out the crab with a slotted spoon, divide it between pre-heated soup plates and return to the oven to keep warm. Raise the heat under the pan, put in the coconut cream, stir to dissolve, and allow to bubble for a minute or so until the sauce is thick and smooth. Check the seasoning, adding some more chilli powder if necessary, and pour over the crab. Decorate with thin slices of lime (they add a spark of fresh green taste as well as colour) and serve at once. *Serves 2–4.*

DRESSED MUD CRAB

1 large cooked mud crab
2 tablespoons dry
*   breadcrumbs*

1 teaspoon cream
½ teaspoon mustard

Lift off the top shell, scrape out the pale butter-yellow creamy material into a bowl and mix the breadcrumbs (a few at a time, as each crab varies in the amount of brown meat it carries and the amount given could be too much), cream and mustard into it to give a thick, pale, rich consistency.

Rinse the top shell, break off the brittle side parts of the undershell so that a shallow container is formed. Wipe it with a little butter. Discard the gills and guts and take out all the meat from the body, legs and claws.

Arrange the brown meat in a line down the centre of the shell and pile the white meat on either side. Place the shell on a large dish, surrounded by lettuce and slices of cucumber, and serve with mustard-flavoured mayonnaise and brown bread and butter. *Serves 4.*

MUD CRAB AND LYCHEE SALAD

1 large cooked mud crab
1 lettuce
8 lychees
60 g (3 tablespoons) unsalted
   macadamia nuts

juice ½ lemon
2 tablespoons light, tasteless
   vegetable oil
black pepper, freshly ground

Lay the rinsed, dried lettuce leaves on four salad plates. Remove all the flesh from the body, legs and claws of the crab, keeping the pieces as large as possible. Peel and halve the lychees and arrange them with the crab on top of the lettuce.

Keep aside 6–8 of the macadamia nuts and chop them roughly. Put the rest into a blender, grind them finely, then pour in the lemon juice and oil, add a couple of grinds of pepper and blend to a smooth sauce, adding a little more lemon juice or water if the mixture seems too thick (it should have the consistency of mayonnaise). Pour the sauce over the crab, scatter the chopped macadamia nuts on top, and serve. *Serves 4.*

MUD CRAB WITH MANDARIN AND GINGER

1 large live mud crab
1 piece ginger

juice of 2 mandarins and the
   grated rind of 1
pinch chill powder

Chill the crab, remove the top shell, discard the gills and guts and crack the legs, claws and carapace, opening up holes so that the marinade can be poured in.

Grate the ginger, mix it with the juice and shredded rind of the mandarins and a pinch of chilli powder, and pour it into the holes in the shell so that the crab meat is impregnated with the flavour. Put the crab into a fireproof dish and set it aside to marinate for at least 1 hour.

Bring a pan of water to the boil, put the dish of crab into a steamer over the top, and steam for 5–8 minutes, depending on size.

This dish can be served with rice, but it really is much better on its own. *Serves 4–6.*

MUD CRAB SOUP

1 large live mud crab	*70 ml (3 tablespoons) dry*
1 leek	*vermouth*
1 potato	*chopped chives for garnish*
butter	

This is a soup to make when cooking a mud crab for other dishes, such as Crab and Artichokes.

Place the crab in cold water to cover, bring to the boil and simmer for 5 minutes. Take out the crab, put it into cold water to stop the cooking and cool, leaving the stock still simmering, uncovered. Remove all the flesh from the body, legs and claws and set it aside to be used for another dish. Return all the shell to the simmering stock, cook for another 15–20 minutes, then strain the liquid into a clean saucepan through a fine sieve.

Bring the stock back to the boil and continue to simmer, uncovered, until it has reduced to about 1 cupful. Take the pan off the heat and allow the liquid to cool.

Clean the leek. Peel it and the potato and chop or grate them both finely. Melt some better in a shallow pan, put in the leek and potato and cook them slowly until the potato is soft. Turn up the heat, pour in the vermouth, let it come to the boil and bubble for a minute or so, then remove the pan from the flame and cool. Pour the crab stock and the leek and potato mixture into a blender and blend until smooth. Pour into pre-heated soup bowls, sprinkle with a few chopped chives and serve.

There is an almost overwhelming temptation to add something to this soup—cream, perhaps, or crab meat, a little mustard, a spot of chilli. Don't. Resist. The flavour is delicate, subtle and elusive. The potato and leek are there to soften the saltiness of the stock rather than add bulk or taste, and the soup should be quite thin. *Serves 2.*

Crayfish

Crayfish are freshwater crustaceans. 'Yabby' is the Aboriginal name given to the species found in south-eastern Australia and scientifically known as *Cherax destructor*. At first sight this seems a rather grandiose name for what is after all quite a small animal, but disregard those claws at your peril, for the yabby is an aggressive eater and a finger isn't much of a challenge to a creature that can happily rip through the carapace of a fellow yabby if necessary.

With its large claws, heavily armoured head and segmented thorax and tail, the yabby looks like a miniature northern hemisphere lobster, and indeed the two are distantly related. There are many species of crayfish around the world, although in Europe overfishing and pollution has reduced the population so severely that Thailand now supplies much of that market. Crayfish are usually a vivid blue-black in colour, with almost iridescent claws, but they can be brown, green, pink or even purple. Usually sold when around 12 cm to 15 cm long, they can grow to 25 centimetres. The marron, *Cherax tenuimanus*, is a big species. Its body length can reach 35 cm and its weight two kilograms. One of the problems with crayfish is that the ratio of flesh to shell is small (four yabbies will yield only about 60 g of flesh, excluding claws), so they aren't very economical. But the taste is delicate and subtle, the texture firm and smooth, and they look wonderful when served in their shells.

Like crabs and lobsters they should be chilled before boiling so that they die painlessly (but they take just as long as a much larger crustacean, as they seem more capable of withstanding extremes of heat and cold), then placed in a pan of cold water, brought to the boil, and simmered for 5 to 8 minutes depending on size. To shell them, cut along either side of the underside membrane, lift it away, and carefully ease out the flesh. Like sand and rock lobsters, the flesh clings tightly to the shell, so it's much easier to peel them after cooking than before.

CURRIED CRAYFISH SALAD

4–6 live crayfish
½ teaspoon each cumin and
*   coriander seeds*
1 teaspoon garam masala

¼ teaspoon each chilli powder
*   and turmeric*
2 tablespoons plain yoghurt
lemon juice
1 bunch fresh coriander

Grind the cumin and coriander seeds, and place in a saucepan with the garam masala, salt, turmeric and chilli powder. Heat gently to release the full flavour, then mix with the yoghurt and season with lemon juice to taste.

Poach the crayfish for 5–8 minutes depending on their size, and shell them quickly while they are still warm. Cut the membrane on the underside of the tail along the edges on each side and lift it away. Loosen the flesh from the shell with the fingers, remove the gut, and put the meat back in the shell. Spoon a little of the curry-flavoured dressing over them and set aside to marinate for at least 1 hour.

Spread two salad plates with fresh coriander leaves, drizzle the dressing over them in wavy, wiggly lines, and arrange the crayfish in their glowing, deep-red shells (wipe them with a little oil to make them glossy) on top. *Serves 2.*

CRAYFISH SOUP

4 live crayfish
250 ml (1¼ cups) water
1 onion
1 carrot

1 small leek
4–6 celery leaves
unsalted butter
1 tablespoon dry sherry

Only the crayfish shells are needed for this soup. Use the flesh for recipes such as Crayfish and Red Cabbage Salad.

Put the crayfish into the cold water, bring to the boil, simmer for 5 minutes, and take them out. Shell as soon as they are cool and set aside. Crush the shells and return to the water to continue cooking for another 10 minutes. Remove from the heat and cool slightly.

Peel the onion and carrot, clean the leek and slice them all thinly. Heat some butter and cook the vegetables until the onion softens. Add the sherry.

Place the crushed shells with the stock in a blender and whizz until the shells are broken down. Line a fine sieve with muslin and pour the stock through it into the vegetables, pressing down on the shells to extract all the flavour. Bring to the boil and simmer for 5–10 minutes. Cool and blend once more. Sieve again, so that no grit from the shells remains, and check for seasoning. Add the celery leaves to the soup bowls at the last minute and serve. *Serves 2.*

CRAYFISH AND PARSLEY SOUP

4 live crayfish
100 ml (½ cup) dry white
* wine*
400 ml (2 cups) water

2 tablespoons heavy cream
pepper
1 generous handful parsley
* stalks and leaves*

Put the crayfish into a deep saucepan with the wine and water. Bring to the boil, lower the heat and simmer for about 5 minutes until the shells turn red. Remove the crayfish from the water, shell them, and return the shells to the stock. Continue to boil the stock for another 20 minutes, then discard the shells.

Cool the stock a little, then pour it into a blender with the cream, pepper, parsley and the flesh of two of the crayfish. Blend to a smooth, pale green soup and strain back into the pan to reheat. Chop the remaining crayfish into pieces and garnish the soup with them. *Serves 2.*

CRAYFISH AND WALNUT SOUP

crayfish soup (see previous
* recipe)*
60 g (2 oz) walnuts, plus extra
* for garnish*

50 g (1½ oz) fresh cream
* cheese*

Place all the ingredients in a blender and whizz until smooth. Chill and serve garnished with coarsely chopped walnuts.

This is one of the easiest and most delicious soups and beautiful as well, the colour of the underside of very young mushrooms, pale pinky-brown, soft and velvety in both taste and texture. It can be served hot as well as cold, but I think it tastes best when chilled. A spoonful of yoghurt or sour cream can be stirred into the plateful of soup just before serving, but it really needs no extra garnish except for the walnuts. *Serves 2.*

CRAYFISH FRA DIAVOLO

6–8 live crayfish
1 tablespoon olive oil
1 onion
1 clove garlic
2 ripe red tomatoes
1 bay leaf

3–4 leaves basil
1 sprig oregano
1 sprig rosemary
70 ml (3 tablespoons) dry
   white wine
2 dried chillies

Place the crayfish in cold water, bring to the boil and simmer for only as long as the shells take to turn dark red. Drain them, rinse under cold running water to stop the cooking process, and remove the shells. Discard the carapaces but keep the large claws, cracking them so that the flesh can be easily extracted. Set them aside with the meat.

Heat the oil in a frying pan and cook the thinly sliced onion and garlic gently until soft. Peel and seed the tomatoes and add to the pan with the bay leaf, oregano, basil and rosemary. Stir for a few seconds, then pour in the wine and turn up the heat so that it bubbles briskly. Shake the seeds from the chillis, chop them finely and add to the sauce. Turn down the heat, put on the lid and continue to cook for 5–10 minutes.

Return the crayfish flesh and claws to the pan, stir in the sauce and continue to cook for another 2–3 minutes. Arrange them in the middle of a pre-heated serving dish and surround with the sauce. *Serves 2.*

CRAYFISH WITH CIDER AND GINGER SAUCE

6–8 live crayfish
100 ml (½ cup) dry cider
30 g unsalted butter

1 small leek
1 slice fresh ginger
black pepper, freshly ground

Chill the crayfish, place in a pan with the cider and just enough water to cover. Bring to the boil and simmer until the carapaces turn red, then immediately remove them from the stock. Shell the crayfish and return the shells to the pan, setting the flesh aside. Simmer the stock for 20 minutes. Remove and discard the shells.

Melt the butter in a saucepan and cook the cleaned, thinly sliced leek until soft. Grate the ginger and add to the pan. Pour on the stock, grind in the pepper, turn up the heat and continue to cook, uncovered, until the sauce has greatly reduced and the edges are just beginning to caramelise (be careful—from here to a burnt and evil-smelling mess is merely a blink of an eyelash). Return the crayfish to the pan, stir in the sauce for a few seconds to reheat them, and serve at once, with freshly grated ginger scattered over the top. *Serves 2.*

CRAYFISH WITH DILL

6–8 live crayfish	*6 black peppercorns*
1 litre (5 cups) water	*1 clove*
1 onion	*4 juniper berries*
1 carrot	*¼ teaspoon each coriander*
1 clove garlic	*and fennel seeds*
1 stem dill	*pinch mustard*

Put the crayfish in the freezer for an hour, or until they stop moving. With a hammer or meat mallet, lightly crack the tops of the shell and claws. Put all the rest of the ingredients into a deep saucepan and bring to the boil, then cover, lower the heat and simmer for at least 30 minutes. Add the crayfish and remove the pan from the heat.

Leave them to cool in the liquid. When cold serve them with brown bread and butter, mayonnaise, slices of lemon, and plenty of dill.

Somehow, the crayfish become imbued with the fragrance of the cooking liquid, and have a subtle, spiced, perfumed flavour. But make sure to crack the shells lightly so that the vapour only is let in, otherwise they will become soggy and watery. *Serves 2.*

CRAYFISH IN CHOU BALLS

4 live crayfish	*1 tablespoon fresh cream*
65 g (3 oz) chou pastry	*cheese*
100 ml (½ cup) water	*1 leek*
	unsalted butter

Divide the dough into 8 balls and place on an ungreased baking sheet with plenty of room between each ball. Cook in a hot (200°C, 400°F) oven for 20 minutes, then turn the tray around, lower the heat to cool (95°C, 200°F) and leave the balls in the oven for a further 10 minutes. Take out and place on a rack to cool, cutting off the tops so that the steam trapped inside can escape. Reheat in a medium oven for 5 minutes before serving time.

Put the crayfish in the freezer for at least 1 hour, then place them in a pan of cold water and bring to the boil. Simmer for 5 minutes. Remove from the pan, and shell as soon as they are cool enough to handle (take the flesh from the claws as well). Return the shells to the water and continue to boil for another 10 minutes or so, then crush the carapaces with a hammer or meat mallet and whizz with the stock in a blender or food processor. Strain through a muslin-lined sieve, pressing down on the crushed shell. Rinse the blender, pour the stock back in with the cream cheese and blend once more until thick and creamy smooth.

Slice the leek and cook gently in a little butter until soft. Pour in the sauce and bring to the boil. Lower the heat to a simmer, stirring to incorporate the leeks. Cut the crayfish into pieces, fold into the sauce, and allow them to reheat. Arrange the chou balls on a serving dish and carefully spoon the crayfish and their sauce into them. Serve at once.

The sauce should be thick and heavy, not too runny or the fragile cases will quickly become soggy. *Serves 2.*

CRAYFISH AND RED CABBAGE SALAD

4 live crayfish	*pepper*
250 ml water	*2 inner leaves red cabbage*
1 tablespoon lemon juice	*1 small apple*
3 tablespoons olive oil	*2 medium, white mushrooms*
pinch mustard	*soft lettuce leaves*

Put the crayfish in the freezer for at least an hour, then place into cold water and bring to the boil. Simmer for 5 minutes and strain (keep the stock to make crayfish soup with). Shell them as soon as they are cool enough to handle and set aside.

Mix together the lemon juice, olive oil, mustard, and a little freshly ground pepper and pour a little over the crayfish. Shred the red cabbage and blanch in boiling water for 5 minutes. Drain, and return to the dry pan to toss over a low heat for a few moments to drive off the water. Moisten with some of the vinaigrette and set aside. Slice the apple thinly, turn the slices in the vinaigrette and slice the mushrooms into the same size pieces.

Arrange the lettuce leaves on salad plates. Place the crayfish in the middle and surround with the red cabbage, apple and mushrooms. Pour over the vinaigrette and serve. *Serves 2.*

Cuttlefish

The floppy, mud-coloured creatures piled in forlorn heaps on the ink-stained ice of the fishmongers' trays give no hint of the voracious appetite, large brain, high-speed galvanic movement and spectacular colour displays of the living cuttlefish. Belonging mainly to the family Sepiidae, they are members of that remarkably successful group of molluscs, the cephalopods. They have tentacles and finned oval hoods or mantles which enclose (with their internal organs and ink sacs) the honeycombed 'cuttles' which give their bodies both buoyancy and stiffening. Like squid, cuttlefish swim by jet propulstion, and also like squid (and octopus) they can change not only the colour but even the pattern on their skins with astonishing speed, something that has fascinated marine biologists and sea-creature-watchers since before Aristotle first commented on it.

Cuttlefish are found everywhere—in warm seas and cold ones, in shallow waters and ocean depths—and are fished mainly by trawling, although they are solitary creatures not given to hunting in great shoals like squid. The razor-sharp, incredibly light cuttles are washed up on beaches all round the world, but the creatures themselves, regardless of their own predatory prowess, are usually consumed by other, larger predators before reaching shore.

Small varieties are fat, almost circular in shape, but the larger ones are usually elongated, flattened ovals. They have ten arms, two of which are longer and thinner than the rest, with flat, paddle-like endings, presumably for scooping in their prey. These two legs have suckers only on the paddles, but the rest are suckered throughout their length. The skin is soft and slippery but heavy, and is difficult to strip off as it keeps sliding out of one's grasp, and the cuttle is extremely sharp, especially at the point. Because of this, the first thing to do when cleaning the creature is to cut out and discard the cuttle, then remove the organs from the inside of the hood, including the ink sacs unless they are needed for the dish in hand. Cut off the tentacles just below the eyes so that they are still attached to each other by the rim of flesh surrounding the central mouth. Press out and discard the beak in the middle, rub off what skin you can from the tentacles and set them aside. Rinse the hood, grasp the skin firmly at one end, and pull it slowly and steadily away from the flesh. Regardless of how firmly and slowly and steadily you do all of these things, the stuff will slip and slide and break, slithering about until the easiest thing to do seems to be giving the whole lot to the cat and going out to dinner. But having come this far it is worth pressing on, for finally all the skin will come away. Turn the hood over, strip off the transparent inner lining (mercifully this is much easier) and pinch out the two tiny, hard, ear-shaped protuberances near the top (wide) edge of the hood. The cuttle fish is now finally ready to be cooked.

One last word on the dreadful subject of cleaning cuttlefish. The same treatment applies regardless of the size of the creature, and anyone who tells you it's easier with a large specimen is prevaricating to say the least. But all the trauma is worthwhile for cuttlefish have intensely white, dense flesh, perhaps a little tougher or chewier than squid, but with a beautiful flavour and texture so long as it's not overcooked. Even the largest specimen should take no more than five minutes poaching to become tender. And compared to some other species of shellfish, cuttlefish have a reasonable proportion of edible meat to gross weight—about 45 per cent.

CUTTLEFISH IN DASHI

350 g (12 oz) cuttlefish,	*2 spinach leaves*
cleaned and skinned to give	*250 ml (1 cup) dashi stock*
150 g (5 oz) hood flesh	*½ tablespoon light soy sauce*

Score the inner face of the cuttlefish hood in a diamond pattern, then slice into long thin strips. Drop the strips into boiling water and simmer for about 1 minute. Drain, and place in warmed soup bowls.

Boil some more water in a shallow pan. Dip the spinach leaves in and immediately back out so that they soften. Dry on absorbent paper. Cut them into thin strips and add to the cuttlefish.

Bring the dashi to the boil and remove it instantly from the heat.

Stir in the soy sauce, check the seasoning and pour over the cuttlefish and spinach strips, which will float in the amber-coloured liquid. Serve at once. *Serves 2.*

DEEP-FRIED CUTTLEFISH

*180–200 g (6–7 oz) cuttlefish
   hoods, cleaned and skinned
60 g (3 tablespoons) self
   raising flour*

*pinch salt
150 ml (½ cup) beer
oil for frying*

Cut the cuttlefish into strips, and drain them on kitchen paper so that they are completely dry.

Just before cooking put the flour, salt and beer into a blender and whizz until amalgamated into a smooth batter. Heat some tasteless oil for deep frying until a piece of bread takes about 1 minute to brown. Dip the cuttlefish in the batter and drop the strips, a few at a time, into the hot oil. Cook them until they puff up and turn pale gold and crisp. Drain on absorbent paper.

Serve them at once, with slices of lemon and dipping sauces such as baba ghanoush or fresh tomato sauce. The best accompaniment is a salad like tabbouli.

They should be cooked very quickly—too long and the flesh will toughen. *Serves 2.*

CUTTLEFISH IN ITS OWN INK

*180 g (6 oz) cuttlefish, cleaned
   and skinned but retaining
   ink sacs and tentacles
70 ml (3 tablespoons) dry
   white wine
black pepper, freshly ground*

*2 onions
1 clove garlic
1 bay leaf
sprig each basil and oregano
1 tablespoon olive oil
1 tomato*

Cut the hoods into 3 cm squares (unless they are very small) and leave the tentacles whole. Put into a bowl, cover with the wine and a good grinding of black pepper and leave to marinate for at least 1 hour.

Peel the onions and garlic and chop them both finely. Heat the oil in a frying pan and add the onion, garlic and herbs. Lower the heat and cook slowly until the onion is very soft but not browned.

Peel, seed and chop the tomato, retaining the juice. Strain the marinade from the cuttlefish into the frying pan, add the tomato and its juice and the ink sacs, pricking them to release the ink (but carefully: the ink can spurt for startling distances and is extremely difficult to remove from clothes and carpets). Bring to the boil and simmer, uncovered, for 15–20 minutes, or until the sauce is rich and dark and heavy.

Stir the cuttlefish into the sauce, cover and simmer for no more than 1–2 minutes until the squares are tender. Serve at once.

. Polenta is a good accompaniment, its bland thickness offering a good foil to the strong-tasting, rich, dark stew. *Serves 2.*

CUTTLEFISH WITH PEAS

400 g (14 oz) small cuttlefish
200 g (7 oz) fresh peas
1 leek
1 clove garlic
60 g (3 tablespoons) unsalted
* butter*

70 ml (3 tablespoons) dry
* white wine*
100 ml (½ cup) white fish
* stock*
1 tablespoon crème fraîche
parmesan cheese, freshly
* grated, for garnish*

Clean and skin the cuttlefish, discarding everything except the hood and tentacles. Rinse away any grit or sand under cold running water and dry on absorbent paper. Shell the peas, cook them for 5 minutes in boiling water, pour them into a colander and run cold water into it to stop them from cooking further. Drain and set aside.

Peel, clean and slice the leek into short, thick rounds and chop the garlic finely. In a frying pan melt the butter and cook the leek gently until soft, then add the garlic and continue cooking for a minute or so. Cut the cuttlefish hoods into strips, leaving the tentacles whole, and toss them in the butter for 1 minute until the pieces are all coated with butter and lightly browned. Add the peas, white wine, fish stock and crème fraîche and continue to cook until the cuttlefish is tender, about 2 minutes or so.

Transfer the cuttlefish, peas and leek to a heated dish. Raise the heat beneath the pan and reduce the sauce by about half so that it thickens. Pour over the cuttlefish, sprinkle with plenty of freshly grated parmesan and serve at once.

Again, this is a good dish to go with polenta, or with gnocchi made from either potato or semolina and baked in the oven until bubbling and golden on top. *Serves 2.*

RISOTTO NERO

400 g (14 oz) small cuttlefish
500 ml (2 cups) water
70 ml (3 tablespoons) dry
   white wine
1 bay leaf
sprig rosemary
30 g (1½ tablespoons) unsalted
   butter

1 tablespoon olive oil
1 tomato
1 onion
2 cloves garlic
200 g (¾ cup) round Italian
   rice
parsley and grated parmesan
   cheese for garnish

Skin and clean the cuttlefish, carefully reserving the ink. Rinse the hood thoroughly to get rid of any grit and pat dry. Bring the water, wine and bay leaf to the boil and blanch the cuttlefish hoods and tentacles for 1 minute. Lift them out of the stock with a slotted spoon, rinse under cold water to stop the cooking process, then drain and dry the pieces on absorbent paper. Cut the hoods into thin strips, leaving the tentacles whole.

In a wide, heavy-based pan melt the butter and oil together. Add the cuttlefish and toss them for a minute or so until lightly browned, then set aside once more. Peel, seed and chop the tomato, reserving the juice. Peel the onion and garlic, grate them finely and add with the rosemary to the butter to cook until the onion is soft. Pour in the rice and stir until all the grains are coated and shining.

Mix a cupful of the stock with the ink and the peeled, seeded tomato with its juice and stir this into the rice, turning it with a wooden spoon until all the liquid is absorbed. Add another cupful of stock and continue to cook, stirring occasionally until this is absorbed in turn. Check to see if the rice is cooked—it should be soft and creamy in texture—and if the grains are still hard in the centre, add more stock a spoonful at a time (no more, otherwise you could end up with a sloppy mixture instead of a creamy one) until the rice is ready. Return the cuttlefish to the pan, stirring gently so the fish is incorporated but the grains of rice are not broken or mashed.

Pour the risotto into a pre-heated bowl, add some butter, sprinkle over some finely chopped parsley and plenty of fresh grated parmesan. Serve at once. *Serves 2.*

CUTTLEFISH WITH SILVER BEET

400 g (14 oz) cuttlefish
400 g (14 oz) silver beet leaves
1 onion
1 stalk fennel

1 stick celery
1 handful parsley
3 tablespoons olive oil
black pepper, freshly ground

Clean and skin the cuttlefish, rinsing to release any sand or grit. Drain, dry and cut the hoods into small squares, leaving the tentacles whole or chopping them into short lengths depending on the size.

Swish the silver beet in plenty of cold water to release any grit in the folds of the leaves and discard the thick, white central stems. Drain and slice the leaves into thin ribbons. Peel the onion, string the fennel and celery, and grate or mince them all with the parsley. Heat the oil, cook the onion, celery, fennel and parsley until soft, put in the ribbons of silver beet, grind on some black pepper, cover the pan and simmer for 5 minutes.

Add the cuttlefish, stirring it into the vegetables. Continue to cook for 2–5 minutes depending on the thickness of the cuttlefish meat. Check the seasoning, adding more pepper if necessary. Spoon into a pre-heated bowl and serve at once. *Serves 2.*

CUTTLEFISH WITH STIR-FRIED VEGETABLES

180–200 g (6–7 oz) cuttlefish
   hood, cleaned and skinned
1 small piece fresh ginger
2 tablespoons soy sauce
1 tablespoon water
1 tablespoon dry sherry
1 onion
1 clove garlic

1 carrot
1 stick celery
½ each small red and green
   capsicums
1 zucchini
200 g (½ head) broccoli
1 tablespoon sesame oil

This dish needs to be started 24 hours beforehand.

Score the underside of the hoods in a diamond pattern, then cut into long strips and place them in a bowl. Grate the ginger, mix with the water, soy sauce and sherry, pour over the cuttlefish, cover the bowl with plastic film or a lid and place in the refrigerator for at least 24 hours. Strain and reserve the marinade before cooking.

Peel the onion and slice into thin rings. Crush the garlic. Peel the carrot, string the celery, seed the capsicums and slice them all with the zucchini into slender batons. Peel the broccoli stems of their tough outer skin and separate into little flowers. Heat the oil in a wok or frying pan and cook the onion until soft, then add the carrot and broccoli. Stir-fry for a minute and add the celery and the garlic. Stir over a high heat for 1 minute longer, taking care not to break up the broccoli, and put in the cuttlefish. Continue to stir with the vegetables for no more than a minute longer then pour in the marinade and bring to the boil. Remove from the heat and serve at once with rice.

The cuttlefish takes on an extraordinary gelatinous texture with the long marinade and is a wonderful balance to the crispness of the vegetables. *Serves 2.*

CUTTLEFISH AND TOMATOES

200 g (7 oz) cuttlefish tentacles   *1 clove garlic*
2 ripe tomatoes   *olive oil for frying*
1 onion   *chilli sauce*
1 carrot

The tentacles from a large cuttlefish are good for this dish, perhaps with some of the mantle flesh to make up the required weight if necessary. Poach the tentacles in water for just as long as it takes to make them tender (it depends on the size of the cuttlefish but should never take more than 2–3 minutes). Remove them with a slotted spoon, and as soon as they are cool enough to handle skin and slice them into short lengths. Reserve the liquid and let it cool.

Skin, seed and chop the tomatoes, reserving the juice. Peel and slice the onion, carrot and garlic. Heat the oil in a frying pan, cook the onion until soft, then add the carrot, garlic, one of the tomatoes and the tomato juice. Continue to cook for another 5 minutes, cool slightly and pour into a blender with a cupful of the cuttlefish stock and blend to a smooth sauce. Return it to the saucepan, bring back to simmering point, put in the cuttlefish tentacles and the rest of the chopped tomato, stir them around (to heat but not to cook) and serve. *Serves 2.*

Mussels

The mussel is an edible member of the family Mytilidae. It is housed in a hinged bivalve shell, usually coloured blue-black to brown on the outside and streaked with blue inside (the very large New Zealand mussel is brown with a wide border of vivid green). Mussels live in intertidal zones in huge colonies, attaching themselves to rocks and wharf piles and each other by the coarse, harsh 'beard' of the byssus, which clings like glue to hard surfaces and stops the creatures from being torn from their moorings by the action of the sea.

Early humans, according to some pre-historians, were carnivorous creatures, but about 20 000 years ago a population explosion occurred in what is now Turkey. To extend the dwindling supply of game, the people began to collect mussels from the shores and rivers, along with crabs and small turtles. At a fascinating excavation in Eastern Europe of a much later Neolithic site, the midden revealed a layer of fish bones concentrated at one level, with those of forest animals underneath, and below that again a layer of freshwater mussels some 30 cm thick.

The inference drawn is that the community ate seasonally—fish in summer, forest animals in autumn and winter, and shellfish in spring. Or maybe they were just confirmed binge eaters. Whatever the conclusion, it shows that humans have exploited and enjoyed mussels for many thousands of years.

Jupiter, it was reported, grew bored with the everlasting ambrosia and wanted to swap it for mussels. The Romans considered the molluscs worthy of their greatest feasts, no doubt because they could eat enormous amounts without stuffing themselves to a standstill. But later, mussel popularity seemed to go into a decline. In China, Marco Polo commented on the Hangchow restaurants 'for the poorer people' which sold oysters, mussels and bean curd, while the rich feasted on shrimp and silkworms (the latter seems a bit like eating the goose that laid the golden egg) and in 19th-century Europe they were also considered to be food only for the poor. But then, so were salmon and oysters and look what happened to them. Luckily for us, however, mussels have remained cheap and plentiful, and seem to be making a comeback on the top-pop mollusc charts.

Mussels have been cultivated for hundreds of years; indeed, in 19th-century Britain farming was so intense that port authorities complained about the choking of harbour and river mouths. In Lancashire the rich mussel beds were estimated to produce 80 times more meat per acre than corresponding land grazed by cattle. While this may have as much to do with lack of feed for the cattle as with the productivity of the mussel beds, it's nonetheless an astonishing comparison.

Like oysters, mussels filter water through their systems and if the water they live in becomes polluted they can pass on the poisons to the eater without themselves being affected. For this reason it's better to buy cultivated or commercially harvested mussels. Don't go out and collect your own unless you are very sure the water isn't polluted (again, commercial ones are passed under infra-red lights which makes them sick, disgorging sand and mud, as well as spending time in purification tanks), especially as the very places which are their natural habitat, such as inlets and estuaries, rock shelves and wharf piles, are the very places most likely to become contaminated by sewage and oil.

I have a sneaking suspicion that one of the reasons some people disliked mussels was because they were often so overcooked that they became small, tough pellets of pink or cream (the colour varies according to sex) muscle, having been boiled for far too long in far too much water. Mussels toughen very quickly, and should be removed from the heat as soon as the shells start to open, which can take as little time as a minute. The longer they cook, the tougher and nastier they become.

The New Zealand green mussel, currently enjoying a universal vogue, is a very large, green-shelled variety with an enormous amount of flesh. It is stronger in taste and tougher in texture than the smaller, blue-black creatures most of us are used to, and is therefore better suited to recipes using stronger flavours—green peppercorns or chilli sauce, for instance. The outer rims of flesh which attach themselves to the edges of the shell come away easily from the rest of the body and should be discarded, as they toughen even more quickly than the rest of the meat, acquiring the consistency of rubber bands. Although New Zealand mussels are so much larger, they take no longer to cook, and should open in 2 to 3 minutes. They are cleaned and prepared in the same way as other varieties.

Mussels are bought alive, and should be dealt with as soon as possible after purchase, although they can be kept in a cool, dark, damp place (not the fridge) for a few hours. The only time I ever tried to keep them overnight, they died. The byssus, the hairy tufts protruding from the shells, bind them to each other as well as rock faces and wharf piles, so the mussels are frequently fixed together in a tight jumble. Drop them into a sink of cold water, tumbling them about vigorously so that they eject any sand or grit and the shells close together tightly. Discard any that gape open or are broken, and scrape off the barnacles from the rest, scrubbing the shells with a hard brush to loosen and dissolve the fine grit that clings like a film. Pull away the beard, rubbing it against the edges of the shells with a seesawing action until it comes away, and rattle the creatures about in clean water again until all the sand has gone (it can take a few changes of water) and drain.

There are various methods of opening them. Some people suggest putting them in a single layer in a large, shallow, dry pan with a tight-fitting lid, jamming the lid on and shaking the pan over a high heat for a couple of minutes. Others drop them into boiling water; others lay them in a fireproof dish, setting it in a hot oven for five minutes or so. I find the simplest method is to steam them open over a small amount of boiling liquid; if the steamer is lined with muslin the juices can be strained into the pan below when the mussels are taken out. Whatever method is chosen, the most important thing is to remove them from the heat as soon as the shells start to part so that they don't overcook and become tough.

Once opened, they can be served still in the shell with their sauce or soup, but even then they should be checked to make sure all the beard has been removed, and to take out the hard neck inside with its tough if tiny tendons. The ligaments which attach the flesh to the shell are very strong, especially in the large New Zealand species, and the meat should be loosened, breaking the tendons, before serving. Unless both shells are specifically required (for moules marinières perhaps, or paella), twist off the top ones, prepare the mussels as explained above, and return them to the half shell. Arrange on a flat dish with a little mussel juice dribbled into each to stop them from drying out.

Covered with plastic film, the prepared mussels can be refrigerated until they are ready to be used, even overnight if necessary. If they are to be eaten cold, remember to take them out of the fridge at least two hours before they are to be served so that they have plenty of time to reach room temperature.

Mussels are usually eaten cooked, although they can be eaten raw like oysters, with a squeeze of lemon juice and some ground black pepper; but they are at their best simply steamed open and served cold.

Mussels taste marvellous. They have a subtle, salty, almost smoky flavour, and a texture not unlike that of oysters: plump and smooth and silky.

They can be served as an elegant entree, no more than 5 or 6 arranged on a plate, with a sauce spooned into the shell; or as the main course for a summer Sunday lunch, tightly packed in a single layer on a huge, flat serving dish and surrounded by bowls of salads and sauces. And they look wonderful. Framed by their triangular, round-edged, indigo-washed shells, their colours range from the palest cream to bright orange, glossy from their own juice.

When purchasing mussels, always buy a few more than you need as often there are some dead or broken in the batch.

MUSSELS CLUB 200

12 mussels
1 stick celery
1 carrot
1 spring onion
1 tablespoon sour cream

1 tablespoon fresh tomato
  puree
few drops Tabasco
black pepper, freshly ground

Scrub, beard and steam open the mussels. Prepare them in the half shells, and arrange on two salad plates. String the celery, peel the carrot and chop them both with the spring onion. Mix them together, with a little freshly ground pepper, and pile small spoonfuls on top of 3 of the mussels on each plate. Blend the sour cream, fresh tomato puree and Tabasco thoroughly and pour over the others. The contrast of the crisp vegetables and the smooth sauce is very effective. *Serves 2.*

COLD MUSSELS

2.5–3 kg (5½ –6½ lb) mussels
selection of sauces for dipping

fresh bread

As the centrepiece of a Sunday lunch for six, this is a lot of shellfish to scrape, scrub and beard. About halfway through the task the thought that something—anything—would be a better bet will undoubtedly slide into one's mind. This is why it's a good idea to prepare them well ahead of time—even the day before—so that the tediousness of the task fades from the memory and only the anticipation of eating them remains.

Serve them in their half shells, with plenty of good, fresh, crusty bread (mussels taste marvellous piled on bread and butter like prawns), salads, and a variety of sauces. Mussels can tolerate surprisingly strong flavours. Indeed, the richness and depth of such sauces as nut-based tarators, and the aubergine-and-tahina mixture of baba ghanouch can turn a plate of mussels into a grand feast. And aioli, saffron-tinted mayonnaise, pesto and a good red wine vinaigrette all add their extra flavours and textures to the molluscs. New Zealand mussels can take much hotter and spicier tastes. Add some curry paste to 2 tablespoons of mayonnaise; or mix a teasponful of chilli sauce with some sour cream or yoghurt; blend green peppercorns with a lemon-juice vinaigrette and a tablespoon of crème fraîche; or grate a piece of ginger and mix it with a pinch of chilli powder and some coconut milk. All of these sauces go well with the smaller blue-black varieties of mussel as well, but any really volcanically hot taste will overpower them. The best way to find the nicest sauces for cold mussels is by having at least four or five different ones on the table for everyone to try. *Serves 6.*

MUSSELS IN CREAM AND SAFFRON

500 g (1 lb) mussels	*150 ml (¾ cup) cream*
1 onion	*3–4 strands saffron*
1 clove garlic	*black pepper, freshly ground*
butter for frying	

Scrape, scrub and beard the mussels. Peel the onion and garlic and chop them finely.

Melt some butter in a saucepan. Cook the onion and garlic until soft, then pour into a blender with the cream and blend until smooth. Return to the saucepan and bring to the boil.

Line a steamer with muslin and put in as many mussels as will fit in one layer (it may be necessary to cook them in 2 or 3 batches, depending on the size of the steamer). Set the steamer over the saucepan, cover and cook for 1 minute before checking to see if any of the shells have parted. Remove each mussel as it opens, straining its juice through the muslin into the sauce below. Loosen the flesh in the shells, pulling it away from the tendons and the edges, and check that all grit and beard has been removed. Put them in a deep, pre-heated bowl to keep warm until all of them are cooked.

Continue to boil the sauce, uncovered, for 2–3 minutes; grind in the pepper, crumble in the saffron threads, stir quickly and pour over the mussels. Serve at once. *Serves 2.*

Variation 1   Remove the mussel meat from the shells and divide it between 2 warmed soup plates. Reduce the sauce a little, stir in the saffron so that it creates swirls of deep yellow, and pour over the mussels. *Serves 2.*

Variation 2   Add 1 beaten egg yolk to the sauce, arrange the mussels in the half shell on an oven-proof dish, and pour the sauce on the mussels. Place under a hot grill for no more than a minute, until the top crusts and cracks slightly. Serve at once. *Serves 2.*

MUSSELS IN CURRY SAUCE

500 g (1 lb) mussels
1 onion
1 stick celery
1 handful fresh coriander
   leaves
clarified butter for frying

200 ml (1 cup) water
1 teaspoon garam masala
¼ teaspoon chilli powder
juice ½ lime
1 egg yolk

Scrape, scrub and beard the mussels. Peel the onion, string the celery and chop them finely with the coriander. Melt some clarified butter in a saucepan and cook the onion, celery and coriander until the onion softens. Add the water, bring to the boil, and simmer for 2–3 minutes.

Put a muslin-lined steamer over the pan, add the mussels in a single layer and steam them, removing each one as soon as it opens and tipping the liquid from the shells through the muslin into the sauce below. Twist off the top shells, remove the meat and check to make sure all grit and beard has been removed, and discard the hard neck. Return to the half shell, place them on a pre-heated dish and keep warm in the oven.

Add the garam masala and the chilli powder to the sauce. Simmer for 2–3 minutes, then withdraw the pan from the heat and squeeze in the lime juice. Break the egg yolk into a cup, beat a little and pour in a spoonful of the sauce. Mix them well together and whisk back into the saucepan, continuing to beat until the sauce thickens and becomes glossy and smooth. Pour it over the mussels, spooning it in the shells, and serve at once, with rice. *Serves 2.*

DEEP-FRIED MUSSELS

8 New Zealand green mussels
* or 16 black mussels*
50 g (2 tablespoons) plain
* flour*
70 ml (¼ cup) beer

40 g (2 tablespoons) unsalted
* butter*
1 egg white
oil for frying
pepper, freshly ground

Blend together the flour and the beer, add a little freshly ground black pepper, and leave the batter to expand for at least 1 hour.

Scrape, scrub and beard the mussels. Steam open and remove the flesh from the shells (if you are using the large, green New Zealand mussels, discard the tough outer rims of flesh which cling to the edges of the shell. Set the mussel meat aside and throw away the shells.

Melt the butter and pour it into the batter. Whisk the egg white to stiff peaks and fold it in as well. Heat enough oil for deep-frying in a saucepan until a piece of bread turns golden brown in about 1 minute. Dip the mussels into the batter and drop them, a few at a time, into the hot oil, lifting them out with a perforated spoon as soon as they turn pale gold and crisp. Skim the oil all the time to remove any floating bits of batter which could burn. Drain the mussels on kitchen paper and serve at once, with a sharp, acidic sauce such as sauce tartare. *Serves 2.*

MUSSELS WITH FENNEL

500 g (1 lb) mussels
1 stalk fennel
100 ml (½ cup) dry white
* wine*

1 tablespoon brandy
peppercorns
2 tablespoons water
100 ml (½ cup) cream

Scrape, scrub and beard the mussels. Put the fennel stalk (reserve some of the feathery leaves for a garnish) into a saucepan with the wine, brandy, a few peppercorns and 2 tablespoons of water and bring to the boil. Simmer for 5 minutes, then place a muslin-lined bamboo steamer on top and put in the mussels. Steam for 1 minute. Check to see if any of the shells have parted, and take out each mussel as soon as it opens, tipping the juice through the muslin into the simmering broth below. When all the mussels are ready, remove the steamer from the pan and leave the liquid to simmer, uncovered, until reduced by about half. Take out the fennel stalk, pour in the cream, and continue to simmer.

 In the meantime, shell the mussels, checking carefully to see that no grit or beard remains and removing the hard neck inside. Twist the shells apart and put the mussels back into the better-looking halves. Place them in wide, shallow bowls, cover with lids or foil, and put into the oven to keep warm.

Cut the fennel leaves into sprays, check the sauce for flavour and consistency (it should resemble thin cream), pour it over the mussels and decorate with the sprays of fennel. Serve at once, either alone as a soup or with rice. *Serves 2.*

MUSSELS AND FETTUCINE

300 g (10 oz) mussels
1 small onion
2 cloves garlic
olive oil for frying

70 ml (3 tablespoons) dry white wine
250 g (8 oz) fettucine
1 handful parsley

Peel and finely chop the onion and garlic and cook in olive oil until the onion is soft. Add the wine, bring to the boil and simmer for 5 minutes.

Scrape, scrub and beard the mussels. Steam them over the wine and onion in a muslin-lined steamer, removing them from it as soon as they open and tipping the liquid from the shells through the muslin into the pan below. Shell them, setting the flesh aside. When all the mussels are cooked, remove the steamer and continue to simmer the stock, uncovered, while the fettucine is prepared.

Bring a large saucepan half full of water to the boil, add some salt and a little olive oil, and cook the fettucine. Drain thoroughly, transfer to a warmed bowl and mix in the mussels, plenty of finely chopped parsley and the simmering sauce and serve at once.

The amount of liquid always seems to be enormous, and the temptation is to lower the amount—reduce it by boiling, or not use all of it. But the pasta soaks it all up in a most greedy manner, and there never seems to be enough in the bottom of the bowl to spoon up at the end. If you are still worried about the quantity of sauce, pour some of it over the pasta and serve the rest in a sauceboat or bowl on the side. *Serves 2.*

MUSSELS IN GARLIC BUTTER

*8 New Zealand green mussels
    or 12 black mussels
2 tablespoons fresh white
    breadcrumbs*

*50 g (2 tablespoons) unsalted
    butter
juice ½ lemon
pepper
1 handful parsley*

Scrape, scrub, beard and steam open the mussels, and twist off the top shells. Check for any trace of beard or grit and put them back into the half shell. Butter a shallow fireproof dish, put in the mussels in a single layer and sprinkle them with the breadcrumbs.

Peel and chop the garlic finely, and put into a small saucepan with the butter, lemon juice and pepper. Stir over a low heat until the butter is melted and all the ingredients are mixed together. Pour the sauce over the mussels, making sure each shell gets its share. Sprinkle with some finely chopped parsley and place in a hot oven for 5 minutes, or until sizzling. *Serves 2.*

GRILLED MUSSELS (1)

*8 New Zealand green mussels
    or 12 black mussels
½ red capsicum*

*2 tablespoons olive oil
1 dried chilli, seeded*

Scrape, scrub, beard and steam the mussels. Twist off the top shell, detach the meat from the ligament which attaches it to the shell and, if using the New Zealand mussels, discard the outer rim of flesh. Lay each mussel in one half shell. Grill the red capsicum to remove the skin, discard the seeds, and put into a blender with the olive oil and the seeded chilli. Blend to a thick paste, adding a little water if necessary.

Heat the grill to very hot. Butter a shallow fireproof dish, arrange the mussels in a single layer and pour or spoon the sauce over them so that they are thickly covered. Put the dish under the griller for 2–3 minutes, until the sauce is sizzling and bubbling. *Serves 2.*

GRILLED MUSSELS (2)

8 New Zealand green mussels
  or 12 black mussels
50 g (2 tablespoons) fresh
  tomato puree

2 tablespoons cream
salt
black pepper, freshly ground

Scrape, scrub, beard and steam open the mussels and put them in their half shells in a buttered fireproof dish.

Reduce the tomato puree with the cream by rapid boiling until the consistency becomes thick and smooth. Grind in a little salt and plenty of black pepper and pour over the mussels. Grill as in the previous recipe. *Serves 2.*

MUSSELS WITH POULETTE SAUCE

500 g (1 lb) mussels
1 shallot
100 ml (½ cup) dry white
  wine
30 g (2 tablespoons) plus extra
  20 g unsalted butter

30 g (2 tablespoons) plain
  flour
1 egg yolk
30 ml (2 tablespoons) cream
juice ½ lemon
grated nutmeg
black pepper, freshly ground

Scrape, scrub and beard the mussels. Peel the shallot, mince or chop it very finely, and cook in the wine for 5 minutes. Steam open the mussels in a muslin-lined steamer on top and strain their liquid into the wine below. As the mussels open, remove them from the steamer and twist off the top shells. Check that no beard is still attached, remove the necks and return the flesh to the half shells. Arrange the mussels on a pre-heated, flat serving dish, cover with foil or a lid, and keep them warm in a low oven while the sauce is prepared.

In a clean saucepan, melt the butter and sieve in the flour. Cook over a low heat, stirring all the time, for a minute or so to cook the flour. Add the pepper, wine and mussel liquid. Bring to the boil, stirring constantly, then lower the heat and simmer for 10 minutes. Mix the egg yolk and cream together in a bowl, stir in 2 or 3 tablespoons of the sauce, beat them well together and return to the pan, stirring constantly over a very low heat so that the mixture thickens but doesn't boil. Add the lemon juice and a little grated nutmeg, swirl in the rest of the butter and pour over the mussels. Serve at once with a fresh green vegetable (such as broccoli sprinkled with lemon juice) as a side dish. *Serves 2.*

MUSSELS IN RED WINE

500 g (1 lb) mussels
1 spring onion
½ small red capsicum
1 sprig each parsley, mint,
  oregano
1 clove garlic

1 tablespoon light, tasteless
  cooking oil
100 ml (½ cup) red wine
1 tablespoon red wine vinegar
pepper
sugar
extra parsley for garnish

Scrape, scrub and beard the mussels. Peel the spring onion, seed the capsicum, and chop them finely with the parsley, mint, oregano and garlic. Heat the oil in a saucepan and cook them all gently for 5 minutes. Add the red wine and red wine vinegar and turn up the heat. Steam open the mussels over the stock, straining their liquid through a muslin liner into the pan, and removing them to a pre-heated bowl as soon as they open. Loosen the flesh in the shells, discard the tough necks and any traces of grit or beard that may remain and pile them into a pre-heated serving dish, returning it to the oven to keep warm while the sauce is finished.

Turn up the heat under the pan and continue to cook the sauce, uncovered, until reduced by half. Season with pepper, sprinkle with a pinch of sugar if necessary, and pour over the mussels. Scatter a handful of chopped parsley over the top and serve at once, with crusty brown bread to mop up the rich sauce. *Serves 2.*

MUSSEL AND SCALLOP FEUILLETTES

10 mussels
10 scallops
250 g (8 oz) puff pastry dough
beaten egg for glaze
1 shallot
70 ml (3 tablespoons) dry
  white wine

1 leek
unsalted butter
50 ml (2 tablespoons) thick
  cream
pepper

Roll out the pastry to an oblong twice as long as it is wide and cut into 4 rectangles. Place these on a buttered baking tray and chill for 30 minutes, then brush the tops with beaten egg glaze and bake in a hot oven (200°C, 400°F) for 15–20 minutes until well-risen and golden brown. Cool on a wire rack, then split them open lengthways and scoop out any uncooked paste. Put the halves on top of each other and return to the oven on a low heat to keep warm.

Scrape, scrub and beard the mussels. Peel and mince the shallot. Bring the wine and shallot to the boil and steam open the mussels over the top in a muslin-lined steamer, removing them from the pan and straining their liquid into the stock as soon as they open. Shell the mussels, check them for any remaining beard or grit, remove the hard necks and set aside. Lower the heat so that the liquid is barely moving. Poach the scallops for no more than 1 minute, or until they turn opaque. Set them aside with the mussels.

Clean the leek, discarding the outer leaves and tough tops, and slice thinly. Heat some butter in a separate pan and cook the rings gently until soft. Meanwhile, raise the heat under the stock and reduce it to about 2 tablespoons. Pour in the thick cream and return to the boil, then add the leek and remove from the heat. Stir in the mussels and scallops, check the seasoning, and pile into half the pastry cases, spooning over the sauce. Place the other pastry pieces over the top like hats, and serve at once. *Serves 2.*

MUSSEL BROTH

12 mussels
100 ml (½ cup) dry white
   wine
black pepper, freshly ground

2 strands saffron
100 g (3 oz) very thin Chinese
   noodles

Scrub and beard the mussels and lay them in a muslin-lined steamer. Bring the wine to the boil with some pepper and the saffron, place the steamer on top, and cook until the shells open (check after 1 minute). As the shells part, take them out of the steamer, straining the liquid through the muslin into the pan below. Loosen the flesh from the shell and connecting ligaments. Check that all the beard has been removed, take out the hard neck and attendant tendons, and put the mussels into a pre-heated soup tureen to keep warm in the oven.

Add the noddles to the saucepan. Boil until they soften—no more than 2–3 minutes—and pour them with the soup over the mussels. Serve at once. *Serves 2.*

MUSSEL SOUP

12–14 black mussels	*unsalted butter*
1 shallot	*150 ml (¾ cup) dry white*
1 clove garlic	*wine*
1 leek	*50 ml (2 tablespoons) cream*
½ stalk fennel	*pinch saffron*
½ stick celery	*pepper*

Scrape, scrub and beard the mussels. Peel the shallot, garlic and white part of the leek, string the fennel and celery and slice them all thinly. In a saucepan, cook them in some butter for a few minutes, then add the wine and bring to the boil. Place a steamer on top, put a folded piece of muslin on the slats and add the mussels. Remove them from the heat the moment they open, tipping the juices from the shells into the liquid below through the muslin.

Take the stock from the heat, cool slightly and pour in the cream. Shell the mussels, put half of them into a blender with the stock and vegetables and blend to a smooth, creamy soup. Strain it back into the saucepan through a fine sieve, discarding the fibrous residue. Return to the boil and check the seasoning. Divide the remaining mussels between 2 pre-heated soup plates and pour on the hot soup. Crumble over a couple of threads of saffron, or sprinkle with a pinch of powdered saffron, stir once, and serve. *Serves 2.*

MUSSEL AND LING CHOWDER

300 g (10 oz) mussels	*1 tablespoon unsalted butter*
200 g (7 oz) ling fillets	*1 sprig each basil and parsley*
1 clove garlic	*150 ml (¾ cup) milk*
1 leek	*black pepper, freshly ground*
1 medium potato	*2 tablespoons thick cream*

This is a substantial dish, for a main course rather than an entree, but this amount would serve 6 or 8 as a first course.

Scrape, scrub and beard the mussels and remove any bones from the ling fillets. Peel the garlic and the leek and slice them finely. Skin the potato and cut into small cubes.

Melt the butter in a saucepan, put in the leek and cook gently until soft. Add the garlic, basil and parsley, the milk and the diced potato and bring to the boil. Place a muslin-lined steamer over the pan. Steam the mussels until the shells just start to open, and remove them, straining their liquid into the pan below. Shell them and set aside.

Take off the steamer, lower the heat under the pan so that the stock barely bubbles, and poach the ling for about 2 minutes, or until the flesh turns opaque. Lift it out, cut into cubes and set aside with the mussels.

Continue to simmer the chowder, uncovered, for another 5 minutes, until the potato is soft, then season with plenty of pepper. Stir in the cream, return the ling and the mussels, and ladle into pre-heated soup plates. Serve at once. *Serves 2.*

MUSSEL AND RICE SOUP

24 black mussels
400 ml (2 cups) water
1 cup long-grain rice
1 ripe, red tomato

1 clove garlic
1 handful parsley
1 tablespoon olive oil
pepper (optional)

Scrape, scrub and beard the mussels. In a deep saucepan bring the water to a fast boil and put in the rice. Place a muslin-lined steamer over the top and steam open the mussels, straining their liquid into the pan below as they open. Shell them and put the meat into a pre-heated soup tureen, then return it to the oven to keep warm. Cover the saucepan and continue to cook until the rice is ready.

Meanwhile, peel the tomato, skin the garlic and chop them roughly with the parsley. Heat the oil in a frying pan and add them to it, stirring until heated through. Stir into the rice, taste for seasoning (it could need pepper) and pour over the mussels. Serve at once. *Serves 4.*

MUSSEL AND TOMATO SOUP

24 black mussels
1 ripe, red tomato
1 stalk fennel

200 ml (1 cup) water
100 ml (½ cup) dry white
wine

Scrape, scrub and beard the mussels. Peel, seed and dice the tomato. Strip the feathery leaves from the fennel. Pour the water and wine into a saucepan, bring to the boil and simmer for 5 minutes. Put a steamer over the boiling liquid, line it with a muslin cloth and lay the mussels on top. Cover and steam for 1 minute. Check to see if any have opened, removing them from the heat the instant they do so, tipping the juice from the shells into the stock through the muslin.

Twist off the top shells, pull the flesh away from the ligaments which bind them both together and check that all the beards have been discarded. Place the mussels on their half shells and divide them between two pre-heated shallow bowls, arranging them in a circle, leaving the centre open. Return the bowls to the oven to keep warm.

Heat the diced tomato gently in a little of the liquid in a separate pan and spoon into the centre of the mussels, arrange the fennel fronds on top, and carefully pour the boiling soup over the mussels. Serve at once. *Serves 2.*

MOULES MARINIÈRES

500 g (1 lb) mussels
1 clove garlic
1 shallot or 1 onion
1 handful celery leaves

unsalted butter
70 ml (3 tablespoons) dry
 white wine
black pepper, freshly ground

This is the archetypal mussel soup, the simplest and easiest of them all.

Scrape, scrub and beard the mussels. Peel and chop finely the garlic and shallot. Shred the celery leaves.

Melt the butter in a large saucepan, cook the shallot and garlic until soft, and pour in the wine. Bring to the boil and let bubble for a few moments. Put in the mussels, cover the pan and cook, shaking the pan for a few minutes until all the mussels are open. Grind over some black pepper, scatter the chopped celery leaves on top, and serve. *Serves 2.*

GREEN MUSSELS WITH CHILLI SAUCE

12–14 green mussels
½ red capsicum
1 ripe, red tomato

2 tablespoons water
1 teaspoon chilli sauce
 or ½ teaspoon chilli powder

Scrape, scrub and beard the mussels. Peel and seed the capsicum and tomato, reserving the tomato juice.

Heat the water to boiling in a saucepan and steam the mussels open over it in a muslin-lined steamer, removing them from the pan and straining their juices into the pan as soon as they open. Twist off the top shells, loosen the meat from the ligaments, discarding the tough outer rims of flesh at the edges of the shells. Arrange the mussels in their half shells on two pre-heated plates and put them in the oven to keep warm.

Add the tomato, tomato juice, capsicum and chilli sauce or powder to the mussel stock in the pan. Turn up the heat and boil rapidly for 5 minutes, or until the sauce has thickened a little, spoon some over each mussel in its shell and serve. *Serves 2.*

GREEN MUSSELS AND GREEN PEPPERCORNS

12–14 green mussels
1 tablespoon dry white wine
1 teaspoon peppercorn liquid

150 ml (¾ cup) cream
1 tablespoon green
   peppercorns

Scrape, scrub and beard the mussels. In a saucepan, bring the wine and peppercorn liquid to a fast boil and place the mussels over the top in a muslin-lined steamer. Remove them as soon as they open, pouring their liquid into the pan below. Arrange them in their half shells on two pre-warmed plates and return them to the oven to keep warm.

Add the cream and the peppercorns to the pan. Turn up the heat and boil until the sauce is thickened slightly, then pour over the mussels and serve at once. *Serves 2.*

Octopus

The octopus is descended from ammonites, cephalopods with external spiral shells, which were immensely prolific about 30 million years ago. At some stage in its evolution the octopus successfully left the security of its shell and put its faith in aggression and intelligence instead. Like the squid it can change colour with amazing speed, not only to suit its environment but also perhaps as a method of communication, and can be quickly trained to react to certain stimuli in laboratory tests (but the octopus is a voracious feeder, and would make an unsettling pet). Most species are non-toxic, although the small blue-ringed octopus that lives beneath the ledges of rock pools around the coasts of Australia is a lethal affair and its poison works quickly and efficiently.

In Samoan mythology the primeval octopus gave birth to fire and water and the breaking of its ink sacs created the oceans. In the Herakleion Museum in Crete a vase, dated about 1400 BC, is decorated with a Minoan octopus swimming among seaweed and shells. A Greek vase of about 480 BC shows a boy fishing, and among the various creatures swimming about in the water below is an octopus hiding under the overhanging rock on which the child stands. A Carthaginian gold coin shows an octopus with a horse, and another wriggles sinuously across the mosaic floor of a Roman villa.

The Ancient Greeks and Romans didn't just portray them on vases and mosaics, however. They ate them with the same enjoyment their descendants do now. Philoxenus of Cythera, a playwright who lived around 436 to 380 BC, wrote a play called *The Supper*, and in it describes a banquet where the first course was fish, including eels and swordfish, cuttlefish and 'the long, hairy polypus', a variety with particularly long and slender tentacles. (It was Philoxenes, according to Alexis Soyer's *Pantropheaon*, who, when told by his doctor that he would die from indigestion caused by overeating a particular—unnamed—fish dish, calmly replied, 'Before I go, allow me to finish the remainder'. Soyer, unfortunately, doesn't say whether he died or recovered.)

The Ancient Romans apparently served the octopus whole, its tentacles overflowing the serving dish, and cut it into pieces at the table to be served with the ubiquitous sauce of garum and pepper. The Maoris caught small octopus by the simple and efficient method of plunging an arm into a rock pool and pulling it back out with the octopus clinging to it (obviously there are no blue-ringed octopus in New Zealand) and baked it on stones by the fire.

Baked, boiled, grilled or steamed, certain basic rules cover the initial preparation, for tough octopus remains tough, regardless of how long or carefully it is cooked. First of all it must be tenderised by beating or pounding until the tentacles become relaxed and floppy; this process is almost always done by the fishmonger before sale, so check the tentacles to feel how soft they are before buying.

Large specimens are often sold with the head and organs already removed, and this is a good way to buy them as it's the tentacles that are the important part. If they have been really well tenderised they can be skinned without prior blanching. Grasp the heavy, slippery outer tissue, strip it downwards towards the ends of the tentacles and cut off the suckers with a sharp knife. The flesh is then ready to be cooked but, unblanched, it is very salty and I prefer to simmer it for a few minutes to lower the salt content somewhat. If the skin is removed and the flesh chopped into 3-cm segments before being poached in plenty of water for five minutes, the segments will bulge at the ends, turning them into little balls.

Some small octopus have short arms—with only one row of suckers instead of two—which curl up in tight coils rather than hanging limply. These little ones are the best for grilling and frying as they don't need to be skinned at all, just cleaned and gutted. The organs of all octopus are inside the head mantle, and the beak, curved and pointed just like that of a parrot, is in the very centre of the body. To clean the creature, carefully turn the hood inside out and remove the organs, rinsing throughly as sand and grit can be trapped at the bottom. Cut out the beak and the eyes and turn the hood right way out again (and if you think cutting out the eyes a good reason for only buying specimens which have already been dealt with by the fishmonger, I have a tendency to agree).

The Japanese method of tenderising an octopus is to knead it with grated daikon (Chinese radish) until the daikon turns grey and the octopus turns soft; but in practice the Japanese cook buys it not only already tenderised but also already blanched, and then just carries it home to take it from there.

The majority of recipes for octopus in the Western world come from the Mediterranean, for although the creatures are found in the colder waters of the north Atlantic, they were not considered as fit to eat by the great chefs of 19th-century Paris (or by northern fishermen, who used to throw them back if they caught them in their nets). But this is not a reasonable attitude for octopus is delicious if properly treated and not overcooked. Most cookbooks advocate simmering for three hours, which is far too long—a properly tenderised octopus, even one weighing a kilo or more, will take no more than 40 minutes to poach, and even less if it is first blanched and then steamed. It has a delicate flavour and rich texture and can be prepared in various ways: in a cream sauce like lobster; in vinegar, as the Japanese often serve it; in curries, casseroles and stews; or wrapped in spinach or leek leaves and steamed. Octopus is nutritious, cheap, readily available and delicious. The only drawback I can think of is the large amount they lose once the skin and suckers are removed—almost two-thirds of the total body weight. But the flesh is rich and dense in texture, so a little goes a long way.

OCTOPUS CAKES

200 g (8 oz) raw, skinned octopus tentacles	*1 piece fresh ginger*
2 slices bread	*2–3 celery leaves*
1 onion	*½ zucchini*
	clarified butter for frying

Discard the crusts from the bread and blend the slices into fine crumbs. Peel the onion and the ginger and cut the octopus into pieces. Mince or process the octopus, celery, ginger, onion, zucchini and half the breadcrumbs together. Take small spoonfuls of the mixture and roll into little balls about the size of a walnut, flatten them to form little green-flecked cakes, and cover them with the rest of the breadcrumbs.

Melt some clarified butter in a shallow pan and fry over a moderate heat for 3–4 minutes on each side until the coating is golden-brown and crisp and the octopus is cooked. *Serves 2.*

OCTOPUS CASSEROLE

750 g (1½ lb) small octopus
2 tablespoons olive oil
2 onions
1 small carrot
2 cloves garlic
1 red capsicum

1 stick celery
½ teaspoon cumin seeds
1 bay leaf
1 sprig each basil and
   rosemary
4 tomatoes

Slit the octopus hoods and discard the guts, ink sacs, eyes and beaks. Skin the hoods, slice them into small squares and set aside.

Put the tentacles in a saucepan of cold water, bring to the boil, and remove from the heat at once. Leave for 5 minutes, then drain and rub off the skin (and the suckers if they are large). Set aside the tentacles with the hoods.

Heat the oil (if you store grilled, skinned capsicums in olive oil, this is the best kind to use, or the oil from a jar of dried tomatoes) in a frying pan and cook the thinly sliced onions and carrot until the onion softens. Chop the garlic, skin and slice the capsicum and celery and add them to the pan with the cumin and herbs. Cover and simmer for 5 minutes. Add the octopus and stir in the oil for another minute or so.

Peel and seed the tomatoes, chop them roughly and add to the pan. Lower the heat, put on the lid and continue to cook very gently for about 10 minutes until the octopus is tender. Serve with plenty of bread and a salad. *Serves 2.*

TOMATO-COVERED OCTOPUS

300 g (10 oz) tiny, curled
   octopus
olive oil
2 ripe, red tomatoes

black pepper, freshly ground
1 large handful parsley
2 tablespoons fresh tomato
   puree

Clean the little octopus by turning the mantles inside out, pulling away the guts and ink sac and cutting out the beaks and eyes. Divide them between two small, oiled casseroles.

Peel, seed and chop the tomatoes and pile on top, sprinkle with freshly ground pepper and finely chopped parsley and put into a medium oven for 30 minutes or until the octopus is tender, checking every so often to ensure there is enough liquid to keep the sauce simmering. If it becomes too dry, add the fresh tomato puree, but it depends on the juiciness or otherwise of the tomatoes themselves. Serve these little casseroles with bread to mop up the salty tomato sauce. *Serves 2.*

FRIED OCTOPUS

*300 g (10 oz) tiny, curled
 octopus*
*100 g (5 tablespoons) plain
 flour*

175 ml (¾ cup) beer
1 tablespoon unsalted butter
1 large egg white
oil for frying

Clean the little octopus and cut out the guts, ink sac, beak and eyes. Drain and dry thoroughly on kitchen paper.

Meanwhile, make the batter. Sift the flour into a deep bowl, then make a hole in the centre and pour in the beer, whisking from the centre outwards to incorporate the flour and stopping as soon as the mixture is smooth. Leave to rest for at least 1 hour at room temperature. Just before using, melt the butter and beat the egg white until it forms peaks. Mix the butter into the batter, then fold in the egg white.

Heat a deep pan of oil until a piece of bread will turn golden brown in 1 minute. Dip the little octopus into the batter and fry until crisp and gold and puffy. Drain on kitchen paper and serve on their own, with plenty of lemon. They should be eaten before they have time to cool, while the batter remains puffy and crisp.

These little fried octopus are delicious, but they must be really small. The little tightly-curled ones which cook very quickly can be eaten suckers and all.

SMALL OCTOPUS SALAD

2 small, curled octopus
lemon juice
olive oil
black pepper, freshly ground
½ small aubergine

1 zucchini
1 stick celery
½ red capsicum
1 ripe, red tomato

Clean the octopus, removing the guts, ink sac, beak and eyes. Simmer in water for 5 minutes, or until the flesh can be easily pierced with a fork, then drain and cool. Chop the head and tentacles into short pieces and sprinkle with oil and lemon juice and a little freshly ground pepper.

Slice the aubergine into rounds and drop into boiling water for 1 minute, then drain and plunge into cold water. Drain thoroughly on plenty of kitchen paper for a few minutes. Cook in olive oil until browned on both sides. Drain again, reserving the oil, and sprinkle the slices with lemon juice. Slice the zucchini into long, slender batons and cook for 1 minute in boiling water, drain and turn in the oil in which the aubergine was cooked for a minute or so.

String the celery, seed the capsicum and slice it into slender strips. Lay the tomato, cut into rounds, in a shallow dish. Pile on the aubergine, zucchini, celery, and capsicum and top with the octopus. Pour over the oil and lemon juice, sprinkle with pepper and serve. *Serves 2.*

OCTOPUS WITH CAPSICUM

400 g (14 oz) octopus tentacles	*1 onion*
20 g (1 tablespoon) clarified butter	*1 red capsicum*

Strip the skin and suckers from the tentacles, cut into chunks and drop into boiling water for 1 minute to get rid of the excess salt. Drain and dry.

In a shallow pan, heat a tablespoonful of clarified butter and cook the peeled, thinly sliced onion until soft. Skin the red capsicum, cut it into long, thin strips and add them to the pan with the octopus. Cook over a gentle heat for about 5 minutes stirring constantly until the octopus is tender. Serve with aubergine slices fried in olive oil and sprinkled with lemon juice, black pepper and finely chopped parsley. *Serves 2.*

SPINACH-STEAMED OCTOPUS

400 g (14 oz) octopus tentacle	*6 large spinach leaves*

This recipe needs the tentacle part of an octopus only, preferably in one piece and about the same thickness throughout. Peel off the skin and slice away the suckers with a sharp knife. Bring a pan of water to the boil and drop the octopus in to blanch for 1 minute (the water should be just below boiling while the octopus is in it). Drain and cool.

Clean the spinach carefully and remove the central stem from the leaves, taking care not to split them. Boil some water in a shallow frying pan, and with a slotted spoon drop each leaf separately into the water, removing it instantly as it will soften as soon as it hits the water. Drain the leaves on kitchen paper, spreading them out flat and being careful not to tear them, then lay them on a board so that they overlap to form a wrapping wide enough to enfold the length of the tentacle, and long enough to wrap round and enclose it.

Roll the spinach round the octopus so that it looks like a dark green cylinder, cut it into 4 cm lengths, and place it in a muslin-lined bamboo steamer, making sure the edges where the spinach ends are underneath (spinach attaches itself to itself in much the same way as cling wrap does, and just as infuriatingly, but it can become detached if the joins are not underneath during cooking). Bring a saucepan of water to a steady boil, place the steamer on top, and cook, covered, for 10–20 minutes. Serve the rolls with a dipping sauce of soy sauce, or a saffron-flavoured warm mayonnaise, or with a Japanese vinegar sauce.

Octopus tentacles can also be wrapped in leek leaves and steamed in the same way. Cook the cleaned leek in simmering water for 10 minutes and drain thoroughly. As soon as it is cool enough to handle separate the leaves and spread them out flat, overlapping if necessary to form a wrapping large enough to hold the octopus. Roll up in the same way as the spinach and steam for the same amount of time. *Serves 2.*

OCTOPUS IN WHITE WINE

400 g (14 oz) octopus tentacles
olive oil
150 ml (¾ cup) dry white
  wine

1 clove garlic
1 bay leaf
1 sprig each thyme, parsley,
  tarragon

Clean the octopus and blanch for 1 minute in simmering water, then rinse and cool it until it can be handled. Strip off the skin and suckers and chop the flesh into chunks.

Heat a little olive oil in a saucepan with the crushed, peeled garlic, add the octopus, cook for 1–2 minutes, then add the wine and herbs and poach very gently for 5–10 minutes or until tender. Remove the octopus to a heated serving dish and keep warm while the wine is reduced by about half. Strain off the herbs, pour the wine over the octopus and either serve it hot with lots of fresh bread to soak up the sauce, or allow it to cool at room temperature and leave to marinate for at least 24 hours to serve cold. *Serves 2.*

TUNISIAN OCTOPUS

400 g (14 oz) octopus tentacles
2 tablespoons olive oil
2 tablespoons fresh tomato
*　puree*
1 teaspoon hot chilli sauce
*　or ½ teaspoon chilli powder*
200 ml (1 cup) water
2 teaspoons ground cumin

Clean and blanch the octopus, discard the skin and suckers and chop into short lengths. Heat the olive oil in a frying pan, stir in the octopus, and add the tomato puree, hot chilli sauce (or powder), water and cumin. Bring to the boil, lower the heat and poach for 5–10 minutes, until the octopus is tender.

Take out the octopus and pile it into a heated dish, then put it into the oven to keep warm while the liquid is reduced by about half to become a warm, rich, aromatic sauce. Pour over the octopus and serve with couscous or rice. *Serves 2.*

OCTOPUS RICE

400 g (14 oz) octopus tentacles
200 ml (1 cup) red wine
2 cloves garlic
1 onion
2 tablespoons olive oil
2 ripe, red tomatoes
½ green capsicum
1 teaspoon hot chilli sauce
*　or ½ teaspoon chilli powder*
200 g (7 oz) long-grain rice
black pepper, freshly ground

Blanch the octopus for 1 minute in simmering water and drain. When it has cooled strip off the skin and suckers, cut the tentacles into short lengths and poach for 5 minutes in the red wine. In the meantime, cook the onion until soft in a little olive oil with garlic. Peel, seed and roughly chop the tomatoes. Seed the capsicum, cutting out the white pith and slice it into pieces the same length as the octopus.

Add the tomatoes and capsicum strips to the onion, with some freshly ground black pepper. Cook for 2–3 minutes. Add the hot chilli sauce or a dash of chilli powder, and the octopus with its stock.

Pour in the rice, stir so that it is well covered with the sauce, cover and cook over a low heat for 20–30 minutes, or until the rice is tender. Check the liquid level occasionally to ensure it doesn't dry out and burn, adding spoonfuls of water if necessary. *Serves 2.*

POACHED OCTOPUS

1 octopus, weighing about 700 g (1 ½ lb)	*1 onion*
	1 clove garlic
100 ml (½ cup) dry white wine	*1 bay leaf*
	1 handful parsley

If the octopus still has its mantle, turn it inside out, rinse thoroughly, discard the guts and ink sacs, and cut out the beak and eyes.

Bring a large pan of water to the boil, then add the wine, onion, garlic and herbs. Simmer for 5 minutes and put in the octopus. Cover with the lid and cook for 10 minutes on a very low heat, making sure the water doesn't boil. After 10 minutes test the tenderness by piercing the thickest part, where the tentacles join, with a fork. If it meets no resistance the octopus is ready. If the flesh is still resilient, leave it to cook for another 5–10 minutes, or until tender.

Drain the octopus, thread a piece of string through the middle, and hang it up over a sink or basin for an hour or so with the tentacles dangling. This will tenderise it even further. Then take it down, strip off the skin and suckers, and chop it into chunks. This is the most basic method of dealing with octopus. It can then be presented in all manner of ways, both cold and hot. The following are suggestions for *tapas*, to be served with drinks.

• Pour good olive oil over the pieces and marinate for at least 24 hours. Serve drained of the oil, sprinkled with lemon juice, parsley and freshly ground black pepper.
• Finely chop a small onion or shallot, and put into a saucepan with 100 ml (½ cup) of red wine. Boil until the wine is reduced to about 1 tablespoonful, then add a clove of finely chopped garlic and a piece of dried tomato, also finely chopped. Let the mixture cool and put

in the octopus pieces to marinate for at least 24 hours, but preferably longer.

• Blend together 1 red capsicum, peeled and seeded, 2 tablespoonfuls of olive oil, a dash of chilli pepper, and enough water to make a thick, smooth sauce, and serve with the octopus pieces.

• In north-western Spain the tapas bars serve 'pulpo': octopus straight from deep, steaming cooking pots. The tentacles are roughly chopped into thick slices, put into earthenware bowls with a ladleful of the dusky, salty, pink liquid, and served with thick chunks of crusty bread.

AVOCADO AND OCTOPUS SALAD

100 g (½ cup) poached,
  skinned octopus
1 small leek
lemon juice
olive oil
black pepper, freshly ground

1 tablespoon ginger wine
1 teaspoon vinegar
60 g (3 tablespoons) unsalted
  butter, chilled
soft-leaved lettuce leaves
1 ripe avocado

Clean and peel the leek, discard the outer leaves and the tough, fibrous tops, and cook in lightly salted, simmering water for 10 minutes. Drain thoroughly and chop into thin rounds. Sprinkle with lemon juice and a little olive oil, grind over some pepper and set aside.

In a small saucepan, boil the ginger wine and the vinegar until reduced by half. Start beating in the chilled, cubed butter, removing the pan from the heat and putting in the little cubes in batches, waiting until the first lot has incorporated before adding the next. When all the butter has amalgamated with the ginger wine to create a smooth, rich, dark-gold sauce, fold in the octopus, cut into small pieces—the more slender parts of the tentacles are best for this—and sprinkle on a little lemon juice.

Arrange some soft-leaved lettuce on two plates. Peel and halve the avocado, slice diagonally across each half to produce long, curved sections, and spread like a fan over the lettuce. Put spoonfuls of the octopus at the apex of each fan, spoon the rest of the sauce over the avocado, decorate with the leek rounds, and serve.

Ginger wine is not only powerful, it's also very sweet, and this sweetness needs to be cut by either the vinegar or by dry white wine.

A little lemon juice added right at the last minute brings out the hot, gingery flavour. *Serves 2.*

OCTOPUS SALAD WITH POTATOES

100 g (½ cup) poached,
*   skinned octopus*
1 medium potato
1 white onion
3 tablespoons olive oil

1 tablespoon lemon juice
salt
white pepper, freshly ground
mayonnaise

Boil the potato in its skin until just tender, then drain, peel and cut into cubes while it is still warm. Peel the onion and cut into thin rings. Simmer for 5 minutes, drain and dry on kitchen paper. Mix together the onion rings and potato cubes, keeping aside 4–6 of the best rings for decoration. Blend the oil and lemon juice and pour over the vegetables, adding some salt with descretion and freshly ground pepper with a fairly lavish hand. Cut the octopus into short lengths and fold into the potato mixture.

Arrange the salad on plates, put a spoonful of mayonnaise on the side of each, decorate with the reserved onion rings, and serve.

This salad is subtle in taste and beautiful to look at, with the smooth, shiny pearly octopus and the grainy whiteness of the potato set off by the green-lined transparency of the onion rings. Against their paleness, the mayonnaise seems positively vivid. *Serves 2.*

OCTOPUS IN WHISKY CREAM

300 g (1½ cups) poached,
*   skinned octopus*
1 tablespoon unsalted butter

2 tablespoons whisky
200 ml (1 cup) cream

Chop the octopus into thick slices, heat the butter and toss in the melted butter until warmed through. Pour in the whisky, bring to the boil and remove the octopus at once to a heated serving dish. Add the cream to the pan and continue to boil until reduced and thick. Pour over the octopus and serve at once, surrounded by brown rice and sugar snap peas. *Serves 2.*

OCTOPUS IN SAUCE AMERICAINE

300 g (1½ cups) poached,   *2½ tablespoons cognac*
*   skinned octopus*   *2 medium ripe, red tomatoes*
1 onion   *1 sprig tarragon*
2 shallots   *salt*
1 clove garlic   *pepper, freshly ground*
butter
70 ml (3 tablespoons) dry
*   white wine*

Peel the onion, chop finely and cook in a little butter until soft. Mince the shallots and garlic and add them to the onion. Cook for 1 minute more. Add the wine, 1 tablespoon of the cognac, the peeled and seeded tomatoes (and their juice) and the tarragon. Cover and continue to cook for 20 minutes, then take off the lid, raise the heat and reduce the sauce until it thickens.

Chop the octopus into thick slices and add it to the pan. Pour in the rest of the cognac, grind in some pepper, and swirl a knob of butter into the sauce. Pile it all into the centre of a pre-heated serving dish, surround with steamed white rice and serve at once. *Serves 2.*

JAPANESE OCTOPUS

The Japanese don't beat octopus to tenderise it but instead knead it with finely-grated diakon until it becomes soft and flexible. This takes about 20 minutes of hard work, and I find the grated daikon stings my hands just like nettles except that there are no weals to show for it and the tingling sensation dies away quite quickly once the hands are removed from the bowl.

For an octopus weighing between 700 g and 1 kg, grate a medium-sized daikon finely and put into a large, deep bowl. Clean the octopus, removing the ink sacs, eyes and beak, and put it into the bowl with the daikon, pressing it down with the hands. As the kneading progresses, it softens and the radish turns a sludgy, watery grey. Finally the octopus is soft and smooth, the bowl full of dark-grey water, and the hands and shoulders of the kneader feel as though they have been through a wringer.

After this, the creature is rinsed thoroughly and a large pan of water brought to the boil. Hook a long spoon or handle into the mantle so that the tentacles hang down and dip the octopus two or three times into the water, then leave it in and put on the lid. Let it simmer for five minutes. Lift it out again and hang it up over a sink or basin, tentacles dangling free, for at least an hour so that the flesh tenderises even more. Take it down and slice the tentacles into slender slices, still with the skin and suckers intact.

It must be said, however, that although it's well worth while trying out this method in the interests of science (for it really does produce very tender and succulent octopus), in Japan it is usually bought from the fishmonger already prepared and boiled and all the cook has to do is prepare the sauce.

VINEGARED OCTOPUS

200 g (1 cup) cooked octopus
25 ml (1 tablespoon) mirin
75 ml (4 tablespoons) rice vinegar or 75 ml white wine vinegar plus a teaspoon of sugar

1 tablespoon soy sauce
100 ml (½ cup) dashi
1 lemon, quartered

If you decide not to try the Japanese method, poached octopus will do just as well. I must admit to a prejudice against the skin and suckers and always remove them but that's a purely personal choice. Anyway, slice the tentacles into thin diagonal strips and arrange round a large dish.

Mix together all the other ingredients, bring to the boil and remove the pan from the heat at once. Allow to cool at room temperature. Pour into a bowl, put into the middle of the dish of octopus slices, and serve with quarters of lemon. *Serves 2.*

OCTOPUS SOUP

100 g (½ cup) cooked octopus
200 ml (1 cup) dashi
100 ml (½ cup) sake or dry sherry

1 tablespoon light soy sauce
pinch sugar
1 small square piece Japanese dried seaweed

Make up the dashi according to the instructions on the packet if there are any. If not begin by adding 1 tablespoon to 250 ml (1 cup) boiling water and tasting the result. If the taste is not strong enough, add more until the flavour is correct. Bear in mind that the taste should not be overpowering, but rather subtle and elegant. Add the sake, soy sauce and a pinch of sugar and simmer with the lid on for 5 minutes. Cut the seaweed into thin strips, slice the octopus into thin diagonal slices, put them both into the soup, bring back to the boil and serve.

The amber-coloured soup and the pale slices of octopus are counterpointed by the dark-green strips of seaweed, and the flavour is magical—full of freshness and the sea. *Serves 2.*

RED-COOKED OCTOPUS

200 g (1 cup) poached octopus
4 tablespoons fish stock
3 tablespoons light soy sauce
3 tablespoons dry sherry

1 piece fresh ginger
2 spring onions
1 teaspoon sugar

Bring to the boil the stock (light chicken stock can be used if you have no fish stock), soy sauce and sherry. Add the ginger and sugar, and simmer with a lid on for at least 30 minutes. Put the octopus pieces into a deep heat-proof dish, slice the spring onions into short lengths and arrange them on top. Pour the stock into the dish, place it in a steamer and steam for 15–20 minutes. Serve with plenty of rice. *Serves 2.*

Oysters

'I think oysters are more beautiful than any religion', wrote 'Saki' in *The Match Maker*, going on to praise their 'sympathetic unselfishness' when about to be eaten. Which seems a little unfair to the oysters—after all, nobody asked them whether they wanted to be eaten or not.

Oysters have probably had more words expended on them than any other shellfish. Aristotle, Homer, Horace and Cicero, Apuleius and Apicius all wrote about them—and ate them. Doctor Johnson wrote about them too, but didn't like them; and Oliver Goldsmith considered them much the same as mussels, but stupider. Brillat-Savarin tells of a friend who ate 32 dozen at the beginning of a dinner party, and then proceeded to eat everything else presented to him with unflagging appetite. Dickens, in the *Pickwick Papers*, has Sam Weller remark on the fact that oysters and poverty always seem to go together.

This is no longer the case, however, and hasn't been for many years. Pollution and imported diseases, sudden weather changes and various predators (other than humans) have made major inroads into oyster populations, even though they have been farmed for at least 2,000 years, in places as far apart as China and Europe. Oysters are found in all seas, both hot and cold, and have been eaten enthusiastically by all races. Captain Cook, on arrival in New Zealand, found that the local people ate mainly oysters, mussels and cockles which they collected from the rocks and mud banks of the seashore; and from America to Australia excavated middens reveal their shells in vast numbers.

There are various different types of oyster, and people usually consider their local species as the best. The Americans are jealous of the reputation of blue points, the English of Whitstable and

Colchester natives, the French of Belons and Arcachons, and the people of New South Wales of the Sydney rock oyster. The oysters of cooler seas are smaller than those of the tropics, and the Pacific oyster which ranges from Japan to New Zealand can be very large indeed.

Oysters are bivalves, but unlike scallops they cement themselves to rocks or sticks some time between two hours and two weeks after spawning (depending on the species) and never move again. They are left-handed (or -sided) always attaching themselves to their habitat with the left shell.

Oysters are farmed in estuaries and sheltered bays, growing from microscopic spat to adulthood on rafts or beds of sticks. Pacific and some tropical species can be ready to eat in about eight months, but colder water varieties may take as long as two or three years to mature.

In China a large part of the produce is dried for distribution throughout the country, and oysters are considered as just another ingredient rather than something to be treated with great respect. In the West they are usually served on their own, with little accompaniment except lemon juice and perhaps brown bread, but historically this hasn't always been the case. In 19th-century Britain, for instance, they were used in all sorts of ways, even put into steak-and-kidney puddings (since I have never tasted a steak-and-kidney pudding with oysters in it I can't judge as to whether they would enhance the dish or not).

Oysters are hermaphrodites, starting off as males and changing to females at least once in a lifetime. They are at their best (for eating, that is) just before spawning, which takes place when the water temperature becomes warm emough, during the summer months.

Fresh oysters can be purchased unshelled, but they are usually sold on the half shell. Unshelled, they will keep for a few days in a dampened hessian bag set in a cool (not cold) dark place; but unless one is a dab hand with an oyster knife it's much easier to buy them already opened. Look for those that sit glistening plumply in their shells, and bypass the ones that seem shrunken and dried around the edges. Make sure they are packed into their cardboard boxes so that all the shells are upright, or the liquid will spill from them.

Oysters can also be bought in tins, smoked and packed in oil for eating with biscuits or toast; canned in brine; or bottled in fresh water. These last are fresh, not cooked, and can be used for soups and sauces and for Chinese stir-fried dishes, or for mixing with other ingredients (even, perhaps, for putting into a steak-and-kidney pudding).

But there is no doubt that top quality, freshly opened oysters are at their best almost completely unadorned. Well-cooled and arranged in the half shell on large flat plates, they need no other garnish than plenty of juicy quarters of lemon. The only other requirements are pepper grinders close to hand, perhaps some brown bread and butter, and dry white wine (or, even better, champagne).

However, not everyone likes oysters naturel, and a few alternative methods of dealing with them follow.

ANGELS ON HORSEBACK

12 oysters　　　　　　　　*lemon juice*
4 rashers bacon　　　　　　*black pepper, freshly ground*

Cut the rind from the bacon, and stretch the rashers with the flat of a knife so that 3 pieces can be cut from each. Sprinkle the oysters with lemon juice and freshly ground black pepper. Roll each one in a strip of bacon, press the ends down so they don't come undone, and secure them with toothpicks. Chill for 10 minutes or so, then place under a very hot grill to cook until the bacon is crisped, which should take no longer than 2–3 minutes on either side. Serve very hot. *Serves 2.*

OYSTER AND ASPARAGUS SALAD

12 oysters on the half shell　　　*4 tablespoons olive oil*
12 fresh asparagus spears　　　　*black pepper, freshly ground*
1 orange　　　　　　　　　　　*1 soft-leaved lettuce*

Prepare the asparagus by snapping off the tough ends, peeling the spears, and steaming them for 5 minutes. Drain.

Cut the orange in half lengthways. Peel the segments from one half and set aside. Squeeze the juice from the other half, beat it together with the olive oil to make a vinaigrette, and grind in some black pepper.

Lay the lettuce on two large plates and arrange the asparagus, orange segments and oysters on their half shells on top. Pour the dressing over and serve. *Serves 2.*

OYSTER AND COCKLE SALAD

12 oysters on the half shell   *1 handful parsley*
12 cockles   *3 tablespoons olive oil*
1 shallot   *pepper, freshly ground*
1 tablespoon red wine vinegar

Soak the cockles for at least 6 hours to rid them of sand and grit, then scrub the shells thoroughly. Steam them open, discard the top shells, and arrange on two plates with the oysters.

Mince the shallot finely, cook it in the red wine vinegar until soft. Cool. Chop the parsley finely and whisk it with the olive oil, vinegar, freshly ground pepper and shallot until thick. Pour the dressing over the oysters and cockles and serve. *Serves 2.*

FRIED OYSTERS

12 oysters   *100 g (½ cup) dried*
pepper   *breadcrumbs*
lemon juice   *tasteless vegetable oil for frying*
1 egg

Sprinkle the oysters with pepper and lemon juice and set aside. Beat the egg, season with pepper, and dip the oysters first into the beaten egg and then into the breadcrumbs, rolling them around so they are well covered. Put on a plate and refrigerate for at least 30 minutes, turning them after a while so that the surfaces dry evenly on all sides.

In a deep saucepan heat a tasteless vegetable oil to the point where a piece of bread will brown in 1 minute. Drop in the oysters and cook until golden brown and crisp—they will only take about 1 minute. Drain on kitchen paper and serve at once, with slices of lemon and a sauce. Tartare is good, but even better, baba ghanoush or walnut tarator.

If oysters must be eaten hot, this is one way to cook them. Encased in the egg and breadcrumbs and deep-fried very quickly, the oysters themselves are protected from the heat and have no time to overcook. *Serves 2.*

JAPANESE OYSTERS

12 oysters on the half shell
1 tablespoon lemon juice
1 tablespoon rice vinegar
1 tablespoon mirin or dry
  sherry

2 tablespoons soy sauce
½ stick celery
1 small carrot
1 piece daikon
1 piece fresh ginger

Mix the lemon juice, rice vinegar, mirin and soy sauce together as far in advance as possible (the day before is good) so that all the flavours have time to amalgamate and expand.

String the celery, peel the carrot and discard the woody inner core, and shred both into long, curling slivers. Grate the daikon and the ginger.

Lay the oysters on large plates, arrange the daikon, carrot, celery and ginger in little mounds about them and pour the dressing carefully into the shells. *Serves 2.*

OYSTER OMELETTES

12 oysters
3 eggs
1 tablespoon vegetable oil
1 tablespoon soy sauce
½ tablespoon sesame oil
1 tablespoon rice wine or dry
  sherry

1 teaspoon rice vinegar
pinch sugar
1 piece fresh ginger
1 spring onion
2–3 water chestnuts

Mix together the 3 eggs and the tablespoon of oil and set aside. In a small pan, bring the soy sauce, sesame oil, rice wine, vinegar and sugar to the boil. Lower the heat and keep hot.

Grate the ginger and spring onion finely and mix with the oysters and the water chestnuts, thinly sliced. Put them in a small pan, bring just to boiling point and remove from the heat.

Heat a small omelette pan to very hot and pour in a little of the egg mixture (the bottom should set almost as soon as it hits the heat). Spread a spoonful of the oyster filling on top, flip over one side and slide it onto a hot plate to keep warm. Repeat until all the eggs and the oysters are used up, piling the little omelettes on top of each other as they are cooked (all this must be done over a very high heat, as quickly as possible, so that neither the oysters nor the eggs dry out or overcook). Pour the sauce over the top and serve at once, very hot. *Serves 2.*

OYSTERS WITH ORANGE BUTTER

24 oysters on the half shell
1 orange
1 tablespoon dry white wine
  or vermouth

60 g (3 tablespoons) unsalted
  butter
pepper

Grate the rind of the orange and squeeze out the juice. Bring the white wine to the boil with the orange juice, most of the shredded peel (keep some back to garnish the oysters), and the liquid from the oyster shells and simmer, uncovered, until the amount is reduced to about 1 tablespoonful.

Chill the butter and cut into small cubes. Whisk them into the pan a few at a time, adding the next batch as soon as the last is incorporated. When all the butter is used up and the sauce is thick and smooth, pour it over the oysters and sprinkle with shreds of orange peel. *Serves 2.*

OYSTERS IN ORANGE AND GINGER

24 oysters on the half shell
juice and peel of ½ orange

1 piece fresh ginger
black pepper, freshly ground

Grate the orange peel and the ginger, mix with the juice and freshly ground pepper, and pour over the oysters. Cover with plastic wrap and put into the fridge to marinate for at least 1 hour. Just before serving, grind over some black pepper. *Serves 2.*

OYSTERS IN ROLLS

12 oysters on the half shell
2 small round bread rolls or 2
  little brioches

clarified butter
4 tablespoons tartare sauce
pepper

Slice the tops off the rolls, scoop out the crumbs, and butter the inside of the crust cases. Place them in a hot oven (200°C or 400°F) for 10 minutes or so to crisp.

Shell the oysters, then poach them in the liquid from their shells over a very low heat for a few seconds—they should be heated through but not cooked.

Take the crust cases out of the oven. Mix the tartare sauce with the oysters, pile into the cases, and serve at once as a first course. *Serves 2.*

OYSTER SOUP

1 small jar oysters   *2 tablespons sour cream*

Oyster soups are easy and very good. The easiest and quickest method is to pour the contents of a jar of oysters into a blender with the sour cream. Blend until smooth, transfer to a small saucepan, and heat, stirring all the time, until almost boiling. Pour into pre-heated soup plates and serve at once. A couple of the oysters can be kept back from the blending if you like to garnish the soup. Add them just before serving. *Serves 2.*

OYSTER CHOWDER

12 oysters in the shell   *100 ml (½ cup) milk*
1 onion   *2 tablespoons thick cream*
1 potato   *black pepper, freshly ground*
1 carrot   *1 handful parsley*
1 stick celery

Peel the onion, potato and carrot, string the celery, and cut them all into small dice. Cook the onion in butter until soft, then add the rest of the vegetables, stirring until they are all well coated with butter. Pour in the milk, bring slowly to the boil and strain in the liquid from the oyster shells (but not the oysters themselves) and continue to cook until the potatoes are soft. Stir in the cream and the shelled oysters. Grind over some black pepper. Pour into pre-heated soup bowls, scatter chopped parsley over the top, and serve. *Serves 2.*

SPICY OYSTER SOUP

1 small jar oysters
100 ml (½ cup) milk
100 ml (½ cup) cream
50 g (2 tablespoons) cooked,
   drained spinach

1 clove garlic
few drops Tabasco
black pepper, freshly ground
2 tablespoons whipped cream

Drain off and discard the liquid from the jar. Place the oysters with the milk, cream, spinach, garlic, Tabasco and black pepper in a blender. Blend until smooth, then pour into a saucepan and bring to the boil. Simmer for 1–2 minutes, taste for seasoning (it may need more pepper or Tabasco) and pour into two pre-heated, oven-proof bowls. Put a tablespoon of whipped cream on top of the soup in each bowl. Place them under a hot grill, until the cream puffs and browns like toasted marshmallow. Serve at once. *Serves 2.*

VODKA MARINATED OYSTERS

24 oysters on the half shell
4 tablespoons vodka

2 tablespoons sour cream
1 jar salmon eggs

Pour a little vodka into each shell and put the oysters in the fridge to marinate for at least 1 hour. Arrange them on two large plates, spoon some sour cream on top of each oyster and garnish with a few golden, glowing salmon eggs. *Serves 2.*

WOK-FRIED OYSTERS

12 oysters
2 tablespoons light soy sauce
1 tablespoon rice wine or dry
   sherry

pinch sugar
1 tablespoon sesame oil

Mix together the soy sauce, rice wine and sugar and marinate the shelled oysters in the mixture for 1 hour. Drain them on absorbent paper, reserving the liquid.

Heat the oil in a wok (or a frying pan if you don't have one) and stir-fry them for no more than 30 seconds. Pour in the marinade, bring to the boil, and serve the oysters at once, very hot, with Chinese vegetables. *Serves 2.*

Periwinkles

The word 'Periwinkle' covers a variety of species, most of them having a spiral, turban-shaped, snail-like shell that has its mouth stopped with a flat disc of mother-of-pearl. Periwinkles can be turban shells (Turbinidae), top shells (Trochidae) and winkles (Littorinidae) among others. They live in colonies on rocks and wharf piles around the edges of the high-water mark; some of them are capable of living out of water for days on end.

In Britain, winkles were once one of the great delicacies of the Londoner, along with jellied eels and other no-longer-cheap specialities. Winkles were served with a pin to pull them out of their shells, some vinegar to dip them in, and bread and butter. In Australia, however, they are only occasionally available in fish markets, and to tell the truth they are pleasant to eat rather than earth-shaking. Because they are small, they are best served in conjunction with other shellfish rather than on their own, although a small dish of winkles is a good addition to the tapas table.

To clean winkles, soak them in fresh water to remove all the sand and grit from the shells. Changing the water frequently, leave them to soak for an hour or so, then bring some salted water (or, traditionally, sea water if you can get it) to the boil and drop in the winkles to cook for 5 minutes. Drain them, and as soon as they are cool enough to handle, take off the stoppers from the mouths and carefully draw out the flesh with a pin. In theory, the flesh should come out in one piece, to lie in a tightly curled spiral, tapering from the thick black head to the tiny, pale tail in the centre of the circle. Often, however, the meat breaks up as it comes out of the shell so that it has to be served in several pieces. Make a vinaigrette of 1 part red wine vinegar to 4 parts olive oil and mix together with a crushed garlic clove and plenty of black pepper. Pour the vinaigrette over the winkles and leave to marinate for 2–3 hours before serving.

Prawns, Shrimps or Crevettes

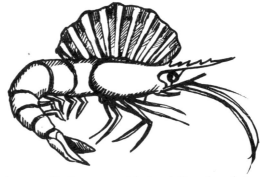

North Americans call all prawns 'shrimp' ('jumbo shrimp' they term even the largest ones); Australians call all shrimps 'prawns' ('tiny prawns' they say); in Britain 'shrimps' are the small, curled, lolly-pink or brown members of the family Crangonidae, while 'prawns' are any of the larger and heavier varieties (including Dublin Bay prawns which aren't prawns at all but *Nephrops norvegicus*, colloquially known as scampi). There are hundreds of different species, some widespread, others confined to specific localities, so the best way to avoid argument is to say that they all belong to the class Decapoda, and that most of the commercially-caught varieties found in the warmer waters of the world belong to the family Penaeidae.

Their life-cycle begins in the open sea when they hatch out in millions, starting their migration towards the coast almost at once. They move into lakes and inlets and estuaries where they find food on the muddy, sandy bottoms and grow quickly, until at last they start their return journey to the sea to begin the whole cycle again.

Small (school) prawns are netted inshore, in shallow bays, lagoons and rivers, but the larger species are usually caught in the deeper waters above the continental shelf, where the prawns return to spawn.

Prawns range in size from the transparent crustacea of plankton to very large tropical species measuring 30 cm or more in length. They are abundant in almost all seas and while most of them go through some kind of sea-coast-sea migration, not all do so. This fact hasn't escaped the attention of countries such as Thailand and Taiwan, where brackish-water-breeding varieties have been cultivated for a long time. There, prawn farming has expanded to become a vast aqua-business which exports technology and equipment to other countries as well as the prawns themselves. While prawns don't have the same enormous productivity of meat-per-hectare that mussels do, they are nonetheless a very high protein crop, with a much better flesh-to-shell ratio than most other crustaceans. This makes them extremely important for both local food production and for valuable foreign currency earnings.

All along the coastlines of South-East Asia prawns are caught, cleaned and strung on bamboo racks set up on the beaches to dry. Leached of their moisture by the heat of the sun they become rock-hard, and can be ground or grated to a powder for adding to curries and other dishes; or, as in China, soaked to reconstitute to their original form if not their original flavour.

The same region also uses prawns to make the sharp, spicy, salty pastes which are such an essential part of cooking from Indonesia and Malaysia to Thailand and Burma. These pastes must bear a close relationship to the 'garum' of Rome, that essential ingredient which seems to have been incorporated in every Roman dish (or those that have come down to us anyway). Garum, apparently, was originally made of prawns, salt and water. The mixture was packed in layers in jars or vases, sealed, and allowed to ferment for two months or more before being mixed with vinegar and parsley. Later, fish intestines, blood and gills were used instead of prawns, but the mixture retained its original name, derived, according to Pliny, from the Roman word for prawns—garos. The Romans used garum in everything, and added everything to it. Vinegar, garlic, herbs, wine, oil, even honey, dates and raisins, all went in at different times and for different dishes. Some decades ago, the very idea of such a paste was greeted with a shudder by many if not most European commentators, who managed to conveniently forget such local passions as anchovy paste when raising their hands in horror at the barbarity of Roman tastes. But a growing interest in, and predilection for, cusines such as Thai and Malaysian, has made these spiced, fermented fish sauces part of modern international cooking.

As well as the coastal and brackish-water species, there are also deep-water prawns which live off the continental shelf at depths of 400 m or more, and have soft flesh which is bright pink even when uncooked. Coming up from such depths they can easily arrive at the surface crushed and flattened, with their shells torn or broken, and it's possibly for this reason that they are usually sold peeled but still uncooked. Deep-sea prawns, called 'Red' or 'Royal Red' prawns, can be used for dishes where the prawn taste and texture isn't of prime importance as well as in dishes which make use of their particular qualities. But for a prawn feast of the classic sort one of the firm-fleshed varieties should be used.

Most prawns are sold already cooked, but it's much better to buy 'green' or uncooked ones if possible, always bearing in mind that prawns must be *fresh*. Their tails should glow with bright colours, and the flesh show translucent through firm shells, with no discolouration at the base of the heads. They should neither look nor feel soggy, and shouldn't be sitting in pools of water in the plastic bins of the fish markets for then they will probably have been frozen, and freezing doesn't suit prawns regardless of the fact that much of the catch is usually processed in this fashion. That's why the best prawns are always the freshly caught local ones, wherever you are. The taste difference between these and frozen specimens, regardless of how fashionable they may be, bears no comparison.

Because there are so many different local varieties, the best way to classify prawns from the point of view of cooking them is by size. The smallest ones available commercially are usually school prawns. They average 6–10 cm in length, are pale grey-green when raw and pink when cooked. They are trawled and netted in creeks and estuaries during the summer months. Because of their small size they are considered fiddly to peel, but are no more difficult than the larger ones, it's just that there are more of them, so it takes longer. Any fiddliness is made up for in sweetness and delicacy in taste and texture.

Like all other shellfish, prawns should never be overcooked. When raw, both flesh and shells are translucent, fragile yet resilient. As they cook, they turn pink or pink-and-white striped; the flesh loses its translucence and becomes firm; and the tails curl up towards the abdomen, springing back when pulled straight. The longer they cook the tougher they become, until finally they collapse into a mushy mess.

Prawns lend themselves to almost any method of cooking and presentation, and it's always worthwhile looking at the varieties available before deciding how to cook them. Large species can be barbecued or grilled, medium-sized ones fried in oil, and small ones tossed in butter, but the best way to cook (and eat) fresh prawns of any size is also the simplest. Bring a large, shallow pan of water to the boil and drop fresh prawns, a handful at a time, into the simmering water. As soon as the shells turn pink and the flesh is opaque and firm, remove the batch from the water and drain on absorbent paper, putting the next lot into the pan. They will continue to cook as they cool, but the amount of time they need in the simmering water depends on the size. Small school prawns take no more than 30 to 60 seconds, but larger, thick-bodied specimens will take a minute or longer.

Serve them with lemon quarters, mayonnaise, and plenty of fresh bread and butter.

ARTICHOKES WITH PRAWN MAYONNAISE

*200 g (7 oz) small green
    prawns
2 tablespoons mayonnaise
2 artichokes*

*½ tablespoon lemon juice
3 tablespoons olive oil
2–4 leaves butter lettuce*

Poach the prawns in a shallow pan of simmering water for 30–60 seconds, or until they turn pink. Drain on absorbent paper and shell as soon as they are cool enough to handle. Fold into the mayonnaise and set aside for the flavours to develop for an hour or so.

Strip off the coarse outer leaves of the artichokes, cut off the tough tops, trim the stems and rub all the cut surfaces with lemon juice. Cook, uncovered, in plenty of boiling, lightly salted water for 15–20 minutes until the bases can be pierced with a fork. Drain thoroughly, turning them upside down on kitchen paper to absorb the water, then cut them in half and remove the chokes. Mix together the oil and lemon juice and pour over the artichokes while they are still warm.

Spread the lettuce leaves on two salad plates, arrange the artichoke halves on top, and spoon the prawn mayonnaise into and over them, filling the cavity in the centre and spilling between the leaves. *Serves 2.*

PRAWNS AND AUBERGINE WITH CHICKEN

*200 g (7 oz) small green
    prawns
1 small, elongated aubergine
200 g (7 oz) chicken breast,
    uncooked
3 water chestnuts*

*1 slice fresh ginger
1 clove garlic
tasteless cooking oil for frying
2 tablespoons soy sauce
3 tablespoons chicken stock*

Cut the aubergine into long, slender batons and put them into a deep container. Pour boiling water over and leave for 10 minutes before draining and drying carefully on absorbent paper. Cut the chicken into the same slender lengths as the aubergine. Peel the prawns, slice the water chestnuts, and grate the ginger and garlic.

Heat a tablespoon of tasteless cooking oil in a wok or frying pan and stir-fry the aubergine, ginger and garlic for 1 minute before adding the chicken and prawns. Continue to stir-fry for 30 seconds or so. Pour in the soy sauce and chicken stock and add the water chestnuts. Bring to the boil and let it bubble for a couple of seconds. Serve at once, with rice. *Serves 2.*

PRAWN BALLS WITH PARSLEY

400 g (14 oz) small green
   prawns
50 g (½ cup) plain flour
70 ml (3 tablespoons) beer
1 egg, separated

1 small onion
1 handful parsley
pepper
oil for frying
1 dessertspoon unsalted butter

Beat together the sifted flour and the beer and set the batter aside for at least 1 hour.

Separate the egg yolk from the white. Peel the onion and the prawns and mince or process them with the parsley, some pepper and the egg yolk. Roll the mixture into small balls and refrigerate for 30 minutes or so.

Heat enough oil for deep frying in a pan until a piece of bread will turn golden brown in 1 minute. Beat the egg white, melt the butter and fold them both into the batter. Dip the little prawn balls into the batter and fry them, a few at a time, until puffed and crisp and golden. Drain them on kitchen paper for a few seconds before serving, very hot, with a tartare sauce. *Serves 2.*

PRAWN AND CAULIFLOWER SALAD

250 g (9 oz) small green
   prawns
300 g (½ small) cauliflower
20 g (1 tablespoon) walnuts

juice 1 lime
pinch ground cinnamon
20 ml (1 tablespoon) plain
   yoghurt

Break the cauliflower into little florets and cook in lightly salted, boiling water for 1 minute. Drain and dry thoroughly. Poach the prawns, peel them, and mix with the cauliflower.

In a blender grind the walnuts finely, then pour in the lime juice, cinnamon and yoghurt and blend to a smooth sauce. Pour over the prawns and cauliflower and serve.

Almonds can be substituted for the walnuts, and fresh cream cheese and cream for the yoghurt. This gives a different texture and a drier, slightly smoother flavour to the sauce. *Serves 2.*

PRAWNS AND AN EGG

*100 g (3 ½ oz) small green
   prawns
1 spring onion
butter*

*½ tablespoon port
½ tablespoon heavy cream
1 large egg
black pepper, freshly ground*

Poach the prawns for 30–40 seconds in a shallow pan. Peel and place in a buttered, fireproof ramekin. Chop the spring onion finely, cook for a few seconds in butter and sprinkle over the prawns. Put the port and the cream into the pan, bring to the boil, spoon into the ramekin, then break the egg over the top. Grind over some black pepper, add the rest of the port and cream and place in a hot oven for 5 minutes, until the egg is cooked. *Serves 1.*

PRAWN FETTUCINE

*150–200 g (5–7 oz) small
   green prawns
200 g (7 oz) fettucine
butter
1 clove garlic*

*1 shallot
100 ml (½ cup) cream
1 large egg yolk
parmesan cheese, freshly
   grated*

Bring a large pan of water to the boil with a teaspoon of oil, and boil the fettucine in it until just cooked. Drain and toss to remove the moisture. Put into a deep bowl, stir in a knob of butter and keep warm.

Meanwhile, peel the prawns. Peel and grate the garlic and shallot, and cook in a shallow pan with a little butter until soft. Stir the prawns into the butter until pink and curled (no more than 30–50 seconds) then take them out and mix into the fettucine.

Beat the cream with the egg yolk and a tablespoonful of freshly grated parmesan cheese and add to the pan. Stir over a low heat until the sauce thickens but don't let it boil. As soon as it is hot and thick and smooth, pour over the fettucine and prawns and serve at once. *Serves 2.*

MARINATED PRAWNS

*250 g (8 oz) small green
    prawns
1 shallot
1 bay leaf
juice ½ lemon
olive oil*

*50 ml (2 tablespoons) fresh
    tomato puree
1 clove garlic
¼ teaspoon chilli powder
½ teaspoon each cumin and
    fennel seeds
1 soft-leaved lettuce*

Peel and slice the shallot and bring to the boil in a little water with the bay leaf. Simmer for 5 minutes then strain.

Combine the lemon juice with 3 times its volume of olive oil then add the shallot and bay leaf with the tomato puree, crushed garlic, chilli powder and ground cumin and fennel seeds. Pour them all into a small pan, bring to the boil, lower the heat and simmer for 1 minute or so.

Peel the prawns and stir them into the mixture. Poach for 30–50 seconds. Remove from the heat and transfer to a bowl. Cool to room temperature, then cover the bowl and refrigerate for at least 12 hours. Take it out of the fridge 1–2 hours before eating so that the prawns return to room temperature.

To serve, arrange on beds of soft-leaved lettuce. Or heat up some taco shells, spoon in the prawns and top with cheese. *Serves 2.*

PRAWNS IN POTATOES

*150 g (5 oz) small prawns,
    cooked and peeled
2 medium baking potatoes
1 tablespoon butter*

*30 g (2 tablespoons or 1½ oz)
    shelled walnuts
1 tablespoon sour cream
black pepper, freshly ground
chives for garnish*

Bake the potatoes until soft. Slice off the tops and scoop out the flesh, leaving behind enough to give the cavity a fairly solid wall.

Cut the scooped-out potato pulp into cubes and turn gently in the butter in a saucepan. Chop the prawns into small pieces if they are very large, halve or quarter the walnuts, and add them both to the butter, turning them gently with the potato cubes until heated through. In a separate saucepan, heat the sour cream and pour it over the potatoes, prawns and walnuts, making sure each piece is well coated.

Grind over some black pepper, sprinkle with chopped chives, and pile into the potato cases. Put the lids back on and serve at once.

This is the most basic recipe, and an enormous variety of flavourings can be added—chilli and tomato sauce, for instance, instead of sour cream, or walnut tarator. A pinch of curry paste will lift the smoothness of the cream. Or, instead of the cream, melt a few cubes of fresh cream cheese over the potato when it's served. *Serves 2.*

PRAWN PUFFS

*100 g (½ cup) cooked, shelled
     small prawns*
2 tablespoons mayonnaise

1 egg white
slice thin toast

Chop the prawns and mix into the mayonnaise. Whip the egg white until stiff, fold into the mayonnaise and prawn mixture, and turn into a bowl. Cover with plastic film or a lid and place in the refrigerator for at least 1 hour so that the mixture firms.

Just before serving, heat the griller to very hot. Pile the mixture onto small squares of thin toast, and place under the heat until puffed and brown. Serve at once as a first course.

Scallops can also be used in the same way, and soy sauce or a few drops of Tabasco can be added to spice up the flavour. *Serves 2.*

PRAWN AND RICE SALAD

*100 g (½ cup) cooked, shelled
     tiny prawns*
100 g (½ cup) long-grain rice
3 tablespoons olive oil
*1 tablespoon white wine
     vinegar*

pepper
1 handful parsley
*100 g (½ cup) fresh peas,
     shelled*
salt (optional)

Cook the rice and drain thoroughly. Mix the oil and vinegar with the pepper and chopped parsley and pour over the rice in a deep bowl while it's still warm. Cook the peas for no more than a couple of minutes. Drain, and fold into the rice with the prawns. Check the seasoning, adding salt and more pepper if necessary, and serve at once. *Serves 2.*

STEAMED MANDARIN PRAWNS

250 g (8 oz) small green
  prawns
1 piece dried mandarin peel

2 tablespoons soy sauce
1 piece fresh ginger
1 tablespoon dry sherry

Soak the mandarin peel for 10 minutes in the soy sauce, then shred.
Grate the ginger and mix with the soy and mandarin peel and sherry.
Peel the prawns, put in a heat-proof dish, pour over the sauce and
marinate for 1 hour. Place the dish in a steamer over boiling water
and steam for 5 minutes until the prawns are curled and pink. Serve
with rice and Chinese vegetables. *Serves 2.*

PRAWN TACOS WITH GUACAMOLE

100 g (½ cup) cooked, shelled
  small prawns
1 small avocado
1 teaspoon lemon juice
pinch salt

1 tablespoon sour cream
½ teaspoon chilli powder
1 tablespoon tasteless oil
2 taco shells

Peel the avocado and mix the flesh with the lemon juice, salt, sour
cream and half the chilli powder. Put the taco shells in a fireproof
dish and set them to warm in a hot oven.

Heat the oil with the rest of the chilli powder and toss the prawns
in it quickly so that they are heated through. Pile into the taco shells,
spoon the guacamole on top and put back in the oven for a minute—
no more or the avocado will go oily and taste unpleasant. Take them
out, scatter shredded lettuce on top and serve at once.

This is delicious but definitely not polite food. The guacamole
slithers out of the taco shells, oozing like brilliant green mud over
hands and fingers and plopping onto plates just as the tongue stretches
out to rescue it. Almost as nice to eat, and much easier to deal with,
are tacos filled with marinated prawns and shredded lettuce. These
tacos are less likely to cover every surface within reach with their
contents. *Serves 2.*

KING PRAWNS

The term 'King' covers various species of medium-sized prawns, changing with habitat and the seasons. King prawns are not only longer, they are also heavier and thicker-bodied than the more fragile school prawns. They range in size from 8 to 15 cm in length, and are usually trawled in deeper water (though still in relatively shallow depths above the continental shelf). They are available throughout the year, although sometimes in limited quantities.

Green king prawns should have undamaged shells, clear colour and vivid tints in their tails with no discolouration about the head, and a firm, resilient texture. Because of their size, the long intestinal tract that runs from the head to the tail along the back showing as a dark line beneath the shell should be removed before serving. It's quite easy to get out, either by gripping the end that is exposed when the head is removed and drawing it steadily through the groove, or after shelling by peeling away the covering flap of flresh and lifting it out. Alternatively, make a cut in the flesh of the back about two-thirds of the way to the tail, and draw it out like a thread through a piece of cloth. If the prawns are to be marinated in their shells, cut a thin groove through the shell along the back and lift out the intestine, leaving a channel for the marinade.

Medium-sized prawns are perhaps the most practical kind to use in most dishes. They can be cooked in various ways, but the rules for choosing remain the same as those for small school prawns. They should be local; they must be fresh; and always buy green ones if they are to be served hot (and even if they aren't, so long as you have the few minutes it takes to poach them).

PRAWNS IN BLACK BEAN SAUCE

250 g (8 oz) green medium-sized prawns
1 slice ginger
1 clove garlic
2 tablespons black beans

2 tablespoons water
2 tablespoons soy sauce
4 tablespoons vegetable oil
1 spring onion

Grate the ginger and garlic and mix into the black beans, crushing them slightly. Stir in the water and the soy sauce. Peel and de-vein the prawns.

Heat the oil in a wok or frying pan. Put in the prawns and stir-fry for 30 seconds, then pour in the black bean mixture and bring to the boil, stirring all the time so that the prawns are coated as they cook. Pile onto a dish, scatter the chopped spring onion on the top, and serve at once, with rice. *Serves 2.*

PRAWNS IN BRANDY WITH TOMATO SAUCE

300 g (10 oz) green medium-sized prawns
2 ripe, red tomatoes
black pepper, freshly ground

butter for frying
1 tablespoon brandy
chives

Skin the tomatoes, scrape out the seeds, and puree the flesh in a blender with a generous amount of black pepper.

Peel the prawns and pull away their intestines. Heat some butter in a frying pan, toss the prawns in it for a few seconds, then pour in the brandy and set it alight, stirring so that all the prawns are coated with the flaming alcohol. Pour in the tomato puree, bring to the boil, stirring all the time, and immediately remove from the heat. Arrange on a heated dish. Sprinkle lavishly with chopped chives, and serve at once. *Serves 2.*

PRAWNS AND CABBAGE

250 g (8 oz) green medium-sized prawns
½ small Chinese cabbage
clarified butter for frying

100 ml (½ cup) coconut milk
1 teaspoon garam masala
pinch chilli powder
juice 1 lime

Shred the cabbage coarsely, blanch in boiling water for 1 minute. Drain and dry thoroughly. Melt some clarified butter in a frying pan and stir-fry the cabbage until soft. Transfer to a pre-heated serving dish and keep warm.

Mix the coconut milk with the garam masala and a pinch of chilli powder. Shell and de-vein the prawns, add them to the pan and stir-fry for a few seconds, then pour in the coconut milk and bring to the boil. With a slotted spoon, transfer the prawns to the dish with the cabbage. Add the lime juice to the pan, bring the sauce to the boil once more and bubble fiercely until rich and smooth. Pour over the prawns and cabbage and serve at once. *Serves 2.*

PRAWNS WITH COCONUT MILK AND ALMONDS

250 g (8 oz) green medium-sized prawns
1 onion
1 clove garlic
1 ripe, red tomato
1 fresh hot chilli pepper
20 g (1 tablespoon) blanched almonds

1 handful fresh coriander leaves
1 spring onion
clarified butter for frying
juice ½ lime
150 ml (¾ cup) coconut milk

Peel the onion and garlic and slice thinly. Skin and seed the tomato, shake the seeds from the chilli and chop them both roughly. Grind the almonds, and chop the coriander and spring onion. Peel and de-vein the prawns.

Heat some clarified butter in a frying pan and cook the onion until soft, then add the garlic, chilli and tomato. Stir to mix, remove from the heat and cool slightly. Put in a blender with the almonds, coconut milk and lime juice and blend to a smooth sauce (the sauce becomes a startingly pretty pale pink).

Return to the pan, bring to the boil, lower the heat to barely simmering and put in the prawns and chopped coriander. Stir the prawns in the sauce for 50 seconds or so, until they are just pink and firm (remember that they will go on cooking in the hot sauce) and pour into a pre-heated serving dish. Scatter the spring onion over the top and serve at once, with sweet potatoes baked in their jackets.

This dish can be expanded to become an even more substantial casserole with the addition of fillets of a firm-fleshed, white fish such as leatherjacket, and some crab meat and claws. *Serves 2.*

PRAWN AND GRAPEFRUIT SALAD

6–8 green medium-sized prawns
1 butter or mignonette lettuce
1 small, ripe grapefruit

3 tablespoons olive oil
juice ½ lime
black pepper, freshly ground
1 tablespoon cream (optional)

Wash and dry the lettuce and arrange on salad plates. Poach the prawns in simmering water in a shallow pan for about 50 seconds until they are just pink and firm, then shell and de-vein them. Peel the grapefruit, separate the segments and arrange on top of the lettuce with the prawns.

Blend the oil and lime juice with the freshly ground black pepper (and a tablespoon of cream if the sauce seems a little too sharp) and pour over the grapefruit and prawns.

There are endless variations to these simple and pretty salads. For instance, kiwi fruit or watermelon could replace the grapefruit and scallops be used instead of prawns. *Serves 2.*

GRILLED PRAWNS

*350 g (12 oz) green medium-
    sized prawns
1 tablespoon each parsley and
    basil leaves*

*pinch chilli powder
2 cloves garlic
olive oil*

Chop the parsley and basil finely and mix with a little chilli powder and the minced cloves of garlic. Peel and de-vein the prawns and rub the mixture into them. Place in a single layer in a fireproof dish and pour in enough olive oil to moisten them. Cover with plastic film or a lid and refrigerate for at least 1 hour, or overnight if possible, turning them every so often to make sure they are impregnated with the flavours.

Heat the grill to very hot. Place the dish under it and cook the prawns, turning once, for about a minute on each side.

Serve at once, with plenty of fresh bread to mop up the garlic marinade. *Serves 2.*

PRAWNS WITH OKRA

*250 g (8 oz) green medium-
    sized prawns
100 g (½ cup) fresh okra
1 green banana or, preferably,
    plantain
1 tomato*

*1 fresh hot chilli
1 handful fresh coriander
    leaves
olive oil
juice 1 lime*

Trim the stems of the okra close to the top of the pods but don't split them open. Peel the banana and cut into thick slices. Peel the tomato, remove the seeds from both it and the chilli and slice them roughly. Chop the coriander leaves finely. Peel and de-vein the prawns.

Heat some olive oil in a shallow pan. Stir-fry the okra in it for a couple of minutes, then add the banana or plantain with the tomato, chilli and lime juice. Simmer, covered, over a low heat for 5 minutes, then add the prawns and continue to cook for another 50–60 seconds, until the prawns are pink and just firm. *Serves 2.*

PRAWNS IN ORANGE CASES

8 green medium-sized prawns   *100 ml (½ cup) dashi*
2 large oranges   *1 teaspoon light soy sauce*
1 teaspoon gelatine

Shell and de-vein the prawns, leaving the tails on. Poach them in simmering water for 50 seconds or until they are just pink and firm. Drain and dry on absorbent paper.

Slice off the top one-third of the oranges and carefully scrape out all the pulp from both parts into a sieve over a bowl. Drop the orange skins into boiling water and simmer for 5 minutes. Drain, dry inside and out, and set upright in a flat dish (if they have problems standing up, slice a thin layer from the bases, but be careful not to pierce the cases).

Press the orange pulp in the sieve to release the juice into the bowl below. Discard the pulp and spinkle the gelatine over the orange juice to soften it. Bring the dashi and the soy sauce to the boil, stir in the orange juice, and immediately remove from the heat, stirring until the gelatine is completely dissolved.

Divide the prawns between the orange skins, arranging them so the tails curl over the sides, then carefully spoon the dashi and orange stock into the cases so that it reaches almost but not quite to the top. Put the orange lids on the top and transfer the dish to the fridge to chill for at least 3 hours before serving. *Serves 2.*

PRAWN, PAWPAW AND AVOCADO SALAD

8 green medium-sized prawns
1 soft-leaved lettuce
1 small ripe avocado
¼ small pawpaw, preferably
   Fijian
2 tablespoons mayonnaise

1 tablespoon light sour cream
   or plain yoghurt
1 teaspon fresh tomato puree
½ teaspoon French mustard
few drops Tabasco

Wash the dry the lettuce and arrange on two salad plates. Poach the prawns for 50 seconds until they are just pink and firm, then peel and de-vein them as soon as they are cool enough to handle.

Halve the avocado, remove the seed and peel, and slice the flesh into thin diagonal slices. Cut the pawpaw into cubes and arrange the prawns, avocado and pawpaw on top of the lettuce. Mix the mayonnaise, sour cream or yoghurt, tomato puree, mustard and Tabasco together and pour over the salad. *Serves 2.*

SESAME-SPICED PRAWNS

300 g (10 oz) green medium-
   sized prawns
1 hot fresh red chilli
100 ml (½ cup) rice wine
   or 50 ml (¼ cup) dry white
   wine and 50 ml (¼ cup)
   dry sherry

chilli sauce or chilli powder to
   taste
2 tablespoons sesame oil
1 tablespoon sesame seeds

Remove the seeds from the chilli and put it into a saucepan with the rice wine or wine-and-sherry mixture. Simmer for 15–20 minutes. Take the chilli out and reduce the liquid by half. Add the chilli sauce (or chilli powder with a teaspoon or so of water) to taste (this should be hot), cover with a lid and continue to simmer gently.

Remove the heads and legs of the prawns. Pull out the intestinal tract but leave the shells on. In a wok or shallow pan, heat the sesame oil until very hot. Add the prawns, stir-fry for 1 minute, then put in the sesame seeds and stir for a few seconds longer, until the seeds start jumping and the prawns are crisp and golden brown. Transfer them to a pre-heated dish and shake the seeds over the top. Pour the sauce into a bowl and serve on the side as a dipping sauce for the prawns. *Serves 2.*

PRAWNS ON SKEWERS

10–12 green medium-sized
prawns
juice 1 lemon

olive oil
1 handful parsley, chopped
black pepper, freshly ground

Peel and de-vein the prawns and marinate in the lemon juice for at least 1 hour. Thread them onto skewers, bending each prawn into a U-shape and piercing it with the skewer at both ends. Brush with oil, place the skewers over hot coals (or under a very hot grill) and cook until the prawns are pink and firm, turning them once. Chop the parsley finely, roll the prawns in it, and grill for a minute longer. Serve at once with more lemon juice and black pepper. *Serves 2.*

PRAWNS AND SNOW PEAS

250 g (8 oz) green medium-
sized prawns
1 tablespoon rice wine or dry
sherry
1 tablespoon light soy sauce
2 tablespoons sesame oil

1 onion
1 clove garlic
2 spring onions
1 piece fresh ginger
100 g (8–10) snow peas

Mix together the rice wine, soy sauce and 1 tablespoon of the sesame oil. Remove the central sections of the prawn shells, leaving on the heads and tails, and hook out the intestinal tract. Cut a thin slit along the back to deepen the groove a little. Pour over the soy sauce mixture and marinate for at least 1 hour. Drain and pat dry, reserving the marinade.

Peel the onion and garlic and chop them both finely. Cut the spring onions into matchstick lengths. Grate the ginger and string the snow peas.

Heat the rest of the sesame oil in a wok or frying pan. Cook the onion with the garlic and ginger until the onion is soft, then add the prawns and the spring onions. Stir-fry for a few seconds, add the snow peas and stir for a few moments more, then pour in the marinade and bring to the boil. Let the sauce bubble for a minute then transfer the prawns and snow peas to a pre-heated serving dish to keep warm. Reduce the sauce a little, pour over the prawns, and serve at once, with boiled or steamed rice. *Serves 2.*

PRAWNS WRAPPED IN SPINACH

12 green medium-sized prawns	*2 tablespoons mayonnaise*
1 bunch spinach	*(made with lemon juice, not*
butter	*vinegar)*
black pepper, freshly ground	*pinch saffron*

Clean the spinach thoroughly in lots of cold water to get rid of all sand and grit, and pinch out the central stems. Set aside 12 large, unbroken, unblemished leaves and chop the rest finely. Put into a saucepan without any extra water and cook over a low heat for 5 minutes, until soft and wilted. Drain through a sieve, and as soon as it's cool enough to handle, squeeze out as much moisture as possible with the hands. Put a tablespoon of butter in the pan and return the spinach to it. Grind over some black pepper, put on the lid, and let it continue to cook gently.

Bring a wide shallow pan of water to the boil and dip each large leaf into it one by one, lifting out immediately with a slotted spoon. Lay each out flat on absorbent paper to drain.

Peel and de-vein the prawns and sprinkle with pepper. Wrap each one in a spinach leaf, rolling it up like a cigar and tucking the ends in so that the whole package is sealed (spinach clings to itself with much the same obduracy as plastic wrap, so they don't need to be tied or skewered). Melt some butter in a shallow frying pan and cook the little dark-green packages for 2 minutes on each side over a medium heat.

Spread the chopped spinach on a flat serving plate, arrange the wrapped prawns on top, and put into the oven to keep warm while the sauce is finished.

In a small saucepan, warm the mayonnaise very, very gently (it will separate if it gets too hot) to about the same heat as a Bearnaise or Hollandaise is served at. Sprinkle in some freshly ground black pepper and a pinch of saffron. Stir until the colour of the sauce is bright golden yellow, and pour over the spinach-wrapped prawns. Serve at once. *Serves 2.*

PRAWN AND CAPSICUM CASSEROLE

300 g (10 oz) green medium-sized prawns	*½ each small red and green capsicums*
1 onion	*1 tomato*
1 tablespoon olive oil	*pinch cayenne pepper*
1 carrot	

Peel and slice the onion and cook in the olive oil until soft. Peel the carrot, seed the capsicums and slice them all into slender batons. Skin the tomato, scrape out the seeds into a sieve set over a basin, pressing down to push through the juices, and chop the flesh roughly. Peel the prawns, discard the intestines, and set aside.

Cook the carrot and capsicum batons in the olive oil for 1 minute. Put in the prawns and continue to stir until they begin to turn pink. Add the chopped tomato and its juice with a pinch of cayenne pepper. Bring to the boil, remove from the heat and serve immediately.

All the tastes and textures in this dish should be fresh and crisp—the capsicum and carrot batons, the tomato chunks, and most of all the curled, pink prawns themselves, should retain their individual flavours. *Serves 2.*

TIGER AND OTHER LARGE PRAWNS

Many of the very large varieties of prawn come from tropical or semi-tropical regions, trawled in the warm waters over the continental shelves of the Indo-Pacific region and the Americas. But not all giant prawns are tropical in origin: some of the species caught in the deeper waters of the temperate oceans can grow up to 30 cm in length and weigh more than 200 g apiece.

Large prawns are always expensive, so the dishes they are used in should show off their particular attributes. One of the best ways of eating them is simply to grill them on the hot plate of a barbecue, still in their shells, for about 2 or 3 minutes each side, or until the shells are blistered and browned.

They should be eaten as soon as they are cool enough to peel, dipped into spicy sauces or mayonnaise. Fingers and tongues are guaranteed to get burnt, but the prawns themselves are delicious.

CHILLI PRAWNS

4–8 very large green prawns
1 clove garlic
1 handful fresh coriander
    leaves
1 tablespoon dry sherry

3 tablespoons olive oil
1 teaspoon paprika
½ teaspoon chilli sauce or
    good pinch chilli powder
black pepper, freshly ground

Crush the garlic, chop or mince the coriander, and mix them with the sherry, olive oil, paprika, chilli sauce and some ground black pepper.

Remove the central sections of the prawns, leaving the heads and tails intact, and de-vein them, widening the groove along the back by slitting deeper with a sharp knife (but don't cut them in half). Put them in a bowl with the marinade, cover with plastic wrap, and refrigerate for at least 1 hour. Drain and pat dry, reserving the marinade.

Place the prawns in a hinged wire frame and grill them over hot coals for 2–3 minutes on each side, turning once and basting frequently with the marinade. Serve with any left-over marinade as a dipping sauce. *Serves 2.*

TIGER PRAWNS WITH CURRY HOLLANDAISE

4–8 large green prawns
1 teaspoon garam masala
½ teaspoon each coriander, cumin and fennel seeds
¼ teaspoon each chilli powder, turmeric, mustard seeds and peppercorns

4 tablespoons hollandaise sauce
2 large, ripe tomatoes
salt
black pepper, freshly ground
lemon juice
ghee

Remove the centre part of the prawn shells, leaving the heads and tails intact. Take out the intestinal tract that runs along the back, then widen the groove it leaves, cutting into it with a knife so that it forms a trench.

Grind the spices and heat them all in a saucepan over a gentle heat until they smell spicy and warm. Remove from the heat, stir well to mix, and add half to the Hollandaise sauce. Spread the other half of the mixture into and over the prawns, patting it down with the fingers so that it sticks and pushing it into the pocket in the back. Cover the prawns with plastic wrap and refrigerate for at least 1 hour.

Peel, seed and chop the tomatoes into cubes, and arrange them in a ring around the edges of a flat dish. Sprinkle with salt, pepper and a little lemon juice and place in a warm oven to heat gently.

Melt some ghee in a shallow pan and cook the prawns for 2–3 minutes on each side, turning them carefully so that the spice stuffing remains intact. When the flesh is firm and pink, arrange them in the centre of the dish, and cover them with the curried hollandaise, spreading it like a glaze over each prawn. Serve warm, rather than hot, as the sauce could separate. *Serves 2.*

PRAWNS AND PEANUTS

4–8 large green tiger or
* banana prawns*
juice 1 lime
1 dried chilli
1 onion

1 clove garlic
1 tablespoon peanut oil
30 g (2 tablespoons) unsalted
* roasted peanuts*

Peel the prawns, leaving on the heads and tails but removing the intestinal tract from the backs. Sprinkle them with a little of the lime juice and set aside for at least 30 minutes.

Split the chilli, discard the seeds, and mince or chop it finely with the peeled onion and the garlic. Heat the peanut oil and cook the mixture gently until the onion is soft. Crush the peanuts, add them to the onion with the rest of the lime juice, stir so that all the flavours are amalgamated, then withdraw from the heat and cool.

Oil a shallow fireproof dish. Lay the prawns in it in a single layer, and spread the onion and peanut mixture over the top. Place the dish under a hot grill and cook for 3–4 minutes until the prawns are cooked through.

Serve with a satay peanut sauce, with fried aubergines or a warm ratatouille. *Serves 2.*

SZECHUAN-STYLE PRAWNS

4–8 large green tiger or
* banana prawns*
2 dried chillies
2 cloves garlic
1 piece fresh ginger
1 spring onion
2 tablespoons soy sauce

2 tablespoons rice wine
2 tablespoons water
½ teaspoon Szechuan pepper
1 tablespoon oil
1 onion
4 ears baby corn
8 snow peas

If you can get the Szechuan pepper, put the berries in a tin and roast them in the oven for a few minutes until they become crisp and hard, then cool and grind them coarsely.

Seed the chillies, mince the garlic and the ginger. Mix with the soy sauce, rice wine, water and Szechuan pepper. Shell and de-vein the prawns and marinate them in the mixture for 30 minutes. Drain and dry, reserving the marinade.

Heat the oil in a wok or frying pan and cook the peeled, sliced onion until soft and pale brown. Stir the baby corn in the oil for 1 minute, then put in the snow peas, stir for 30 seconds longer and put in the prawns. Stir-fry for a minute, pour in the marinade and bring to the boil. Allow to bubble gently for 1–2 minutes. Remove the prawns to a pre-heated serving dish and arrange the vegetables around the edge. Boil the sauce a little longer to reduce by one-third and pour over the prawns. Cut the spring onion into 2 cm lengths and scatter over the top. Serve at once. *Serves 2.*

BRANDY-FLAMED PRAWNS

4–8 large prawns
unsalted butter
2 tablespoons brandy

2 tablespoons thick cream
pepper, freshly ground

Peel the prawns, leaving on the tail sections, and de-vein them. Heat some butter in a frying pan and cook the prawns for 1 minute. Pour in the brandy and set it alight. Shake the pan until the flames die down, then pour in the cream, grind in the pepper and bring to the boil. Cook the prawns for another minute or so, until they are pink and just firm. Remove them to a pre-heated serving dish and turn up the heat under the pan to reduce the sauce to a thick, smooth consistency. Pour over the prawns and serve at once, with puff pastry feuilletes and sugar snap peas.

This is simple and luxurious and one of the nicest ways to eat large prawns—or any other prawns, for that matter.

DEEP-SEA PRAWNS

Deep-sea prawns are marketed as 'Royal Red' or 'Red' prawns, and are usually sold uncooked but already peeled. They are bright pink even in that state, and they have soft flesh that doesn't stiffen much in cooking. They don't have as much flavour as other prawns, but can be used to advantage in patés and mousses.

PRAWN MOUSSE IN ARTICHOKES

100 g (½ cup) uncooked Royal
*   Red prawns*
2 artichokes

1 tablespoon dry white wine
2 tablespoons double cream
1 egg, separated

Peel off the tough outside leaves of the artichokes, cut off the tops and trim the stems. Cook for 20–25 minutes, uncovered, in lightly salted boiling water until the stems can be pierced with a fork. Drain, and as soon as they are cool enough to handle take out the centre leaves and scrape out the chokes.

Bring the wine and cream to the boil. Simmer for 5 minutes. Remove from the heat and cool. Separate the egg, place the yolk in a blender or food processor with the prawns, wine and cream and process to a smooth puree. Beat the egg white until it forms stiff peaks, fold into the prawn puree and pile into the artichokes. Brush with melted butter, place on a fireproof dish and cook in a hot oven for 10 minutes, until puffy and golden. *Serves 2.*

PRAWN PATÉ

200 g (1 cup) cooked Royal Red prawns
½ cucumber
salt
200 g (1 cup) fresh cream cheese

1 tablespoon mayonnaise
chives
paprika
black pepper, freshly ground

Peel and seed the cucumber and sprinkle with salt. Leave to drain in a colander for 1 hour. Rinse under cold water, dry thoroughly, and chop into small dice.

Beat the cream cheese with the mayonnaise until smooth and mix in plenty of chopped chives, paprika and ground black pepper. Stir the diced cucumber and the prawns into the cream cheese mixture and turn into a terrine that has been lined with lightly oiled foil or greaseproof paper. Smooth the top flat, cover with more foil, and chill for at least 3 hours or preferably overnight.

To serve, unmould the paté onto a dish and surround it with lemon wedges and cucumber slices. *Serves 4.*

PRAWN-STUFFED MUSHROOMS

200 g (1 cup) cooked Royal Red prawns
2 water chestnuts

4–6 medium mushrooms
1 egg white
oil for frying

Put the prawns and water chestnuts in a food processor or blender and process until finely ground.

Remove the stems from the mushrooms and spoon the prawn mixture into the cavities, pressing it in firmly. Beat the egg white until stiff, dip the mushrooms into it, and deep-fry in oil until crisp and golden. *Serves 2.*

PRAWN KILLERS

The Prawn Killer or Mantis Shrimp belongs to the family Squillidae and is a strange creature with a long, soft, semi-transparent body and praying mantis-like forelimbs. As its name implies, the animal is commonly believed to attack prawns, and is certainly a voracious feeder, grabbing at anything it sees.

Prawn killers are not a sought-for catch but come up in the nets of prawn trawlers and find their way to the fish markets from there. They have very little flesh, but make marvellous sauces and soups.

PRAWN KILLER SAUCE

300 g (10 oz) prawn killers
500 ml (2½ cups) boiling
  water

1 tablespoon dry vermouth or
  white wine
pepper to taste

This is a good sauce for pasta. Put the prawn killers in the boiling water and simmer for 1 minute then take them out, leaving the water still simmering uncovered. Peel off the shells from what little flesh there is. Place this in a blender with the vermouth or wine and blend to a smooth puree. Return to the stock in the pan and continue to cook until the sauce has reduced to about 1 cup.

Check for seasoning (it will be salty, but may need pepper), and pour over the pasta.

Extended with cream and an onion softened in butter, or a potato simmered in the stock, this can easily be turned into a very good soup.

PRAWN SOUPS

Not only mantis shrimps make good soups; ordinary prawns do too, and a whole chapter could be written on these alone. There is an enormous repertoire, embracing the bisques of France and northern Europe, the satisfying stew-like chowders of North America and the potages of South America, as well as the more delicate clear stocks of China, Japan and South-East Asia.

The following recipes are no more than an indication of what can be done. One of the simplest is the first, a Chinese soup which makes use of the shells from prawns used for other dishes.

PRAWN AND LEEK SOUP

shells from 200 g (8 oz)
  prawns
500 ml (2 cups) water
1 leek

1 spring onion
1 tablespoon rice wine or dry
  sherry
2 tablespoons soy sauce

Simmer the shells in 2 cups of water for 20 minutes. Strain, and discard the shells. Skim the stock and continue to simmer.

Peel the leek and slice into slender rings. Cut the spring onion into matchstick lengths and drop them both into the stock. Simmer for another 5–10 minutes, until the leek is cooked, then add the rice wine and soy sauce. Stir, boil for 1 minute more, and serve. *Serves 2.*

PRAWN AND COCONUT SOUP

250 g (9 oz) small green
  prawns
100 ml (½ cup) water
1 onion
unsalted butter

150 ml (¾ cup) coconut milk
30 g (2 tablespoons) coconut
  cream
black pepper, freshly ground

Bring the water to the boil in a shallow pan and cook the prawns a few at a time, removing them from the water as soon as they turn pink. Peel them and return the heads and shells to the pan, and continue to simmer, uncovered, for 20 minutes.

Peel and finely chop the onion and cook with a little butter in a deep saucepan until soft. Strain the prawn stock into the pan through a fine sieve and discard the shells. Add the coconut milk, bring to the boil and simmer, uncovered, for 10–15 minutes. As the soup starts to thicken, put in the piece of coconut cream and stir to dissolve. Add the prawns, bring back to the boil, then immediately withdraw the pan from the heat. Grind in some black pepper to taste, and serve. *Serves 2.*

PRAWN AND POTATO SOUP

*200 g (7 oz) small green
   prawns*
1 ripe, red tomato
1 onion
1 clove garlic

1 small fresh hot chilli
olive oil
1 potato
*30 g (2 tablespoons) coconut
   cream*

Bring the water to the boil in a shallow pan and cook the prawns, a few at a time, until they turn pink—about 30–60 seconds. Peel them, set aside, and return the shells and heads to the water to simmer for 20 minutes with the tomato.

Peel the onion and garlic, seed the chilli, chop them all finely and cook gently in the oil until the onion is soft. Peel and cube the potato and stir in the oil with the onion for 5 minutes. Pour on the prawn stock through a fine sieve, pressing down on the residue to extract all the flavour.

Bring the soup to the boil, lower the heat and simmer with the lid on for 15–20 minutes, or until the potato is cooked. Remove from the heat and allow to cool a little. Pour into a blender or food processor and process to a smooth, rich consistency. Pour it back into a clean saucepan and bring to the boil once more. Stir in the coconut cream, adding the prawns when it has melted and amalgamated with the soup, and serve. *Serves 2.*

PRAWN AND PEA SOUP

*250 g (9 oz) small green
   prawns*
1 tablespoon brandy
150 ml (¾ cup) water
*100 g (½ cup) fresh green
   peas, together with their
   shells*

1 sprig mint
6–8 black peppercorns
100 ml (½ cup) cream
salt (optional)

Bring the water to the boil with the brandy in a shallow pan and cook the prawns a few at a time, fishing them out as soon as they turn pink. To the water add the pods from the peas, the shells and heads from the prawns, the mint and the peppercorns. Cover and simmer for 20 minutes. Remove from the heat and cool.

Put the peas and half the prawns into a blender, strain in the stock (pressing down on the pea pods and prawn shells to extract all the flavour), and puree until smooth and brilliantly green. Return to the heat in a clean saucepan with the cream, bring to the boil, check the seasoning (cream can have a very flattening effect on other flavours, so salt as well as pepper may be needed), put in the rest of the prawns and serve. *Serves 2.*

PRAWN AND BLACK BEAN SOUP

*200 g (8 oz) small green
   prawns
200 g (8 oz) Mexican black
   beans
½ teaspoon ground cumin
1 bay leaf
1 sprig oregano*

*1 ripe, red tomato
150 ml (¾ cup) water
1 tablespoon tasteless oil
1 onion
1 clove garlic
1 tablespoon brandy*

Put the beans into a saucepan, barely cover with water, bring to the boil and turn off the heat. Leave them to soak for 1 hour, then strain and cover with fresh water. Add the cumin, bay leaf, oregano and the peeled, seeded tomato (seed it over a sieve so that all the juices can be retained and pressed into the saucepan). Bring to the boil once more. Cover and cook on the lowest possible heat for 1–2 hours, or until the beans are soft.

Bring 150 ml water to the boil in a shallow pan. Cook the prawns a few at a time just until they turn pink, then peel them and return the shells to the water. Cover and simmer for 20 minutes. Add the sieved stock to the black beans, pressing down on the sieve to extract all the flavours.

In a clean saucepan heat the oil. Peel the onion and garlic, chop them finely and cook until soft. Put the onion and garlic mixture into a blender, add the beans and tomato and blend to a rich, dark, smooth soup. Pour into a clean saucepan, return to the boil, add the brandy and the prawns and serve. *Serves 2.*

Rock Lobsters

Rock lobster, spiny lobster, saltwater crayfish—what to call the beast is a thorny problem before one even gets down to the task of defining what it is. What it isn't is a lobster, which is interesting because the English word comes from the Latin 'locusta', meaning lobster (or locust, just to confuse matters even further). And the Roman lobster would most likely have been the clawless variety, because the 'true lobster' *(Homarus vulgaris)* is fairly rare in the Eastern Mediterranean. Even more fascinating—to me at any rate—is the obvious family resemblance of the words 'aragosta', 'langouste' and 'langosta' to 'lobster', and they are all words that describe the spiny version, *not* the clawed number, which is called variously Homard, Astice and Bogavante. Quite where this excursion into the murky waters of etymology leads is unclear, except I think I have managed to prove (to myself, if to nobody else) conclusively that the clawless variety should be dignified with the name Lobster and the clawed one something else—something in between Homard and Hummer, perhaps.

As the word has been usurped in English the most practical thing to do would be to take over the French name and say 'langouste'. Then there would be no confusion anywhere. For it isn't a crayfish, either. A crayfish is a freshwater creature, and crawfish just another way of spelling it. Yabbies and marron are crayfish. These creatures are not. Practically, however, the term 'rock lobster' seems to be universally understood, so using it would appear to be the most sensible solution.

So, *rock lobsters* are members of the families Palinuridae and Panuliridae. Unlike the true lobster, which isn't found anywhere in the southern hemisphere, rock lobsters are caught in many places around the world, both in warmer waters and, to a lesser extent, in temperate ones. Most of them look much the same, and while some are green, others range in colour from yellowish-brown through to almost purple. The carapaces are armed with plentiful knobs and bumps and other protuberances which make up for the lack of claws. They have long feelers which wave like antennae as they move, and spindly legs with which they stalk across the reefs and rocks of the shallower waters along the coast and the continental shelf. They are caught commercially in lobster pots, and are the source of a large and lucrative export industry in frozen tails.

In fish markets, rock lobsters are sold frozen, cooked or live. In the latter case they are kept in tanks where they clamber and heave over each other, frequently ending up in a great heap in one corner of the tank. There the ones underneath haul themselves out of the tangle at the bottom of the pile, only to climb back up to the top and start the whole process all over again. Togetherness taken to extremes.

Rock lobsters are available throughout the year, although not always in large quantities. Much of the catch is processed by discarding the heads and packing the tails in individual plastic bags to be sold from the deep freezers of fish markets and food halls around the world (and, of course, locally) as 'crayfish tails'. While the flesh doesn't have the same texture (it's softer and spongier) or the same intensity of flavour as a live specimen freshly cooked, frozen crayfish tails are nonetheless extremely useful things, and can be used for most of the recipes in this section.

Only a small part of the rest of the catch is sold live; most of it is cooked either on board the lobster boat or on arrival at the fish markets. If it's to be eaten cold with salad—and that's one of the best ways—then buying a ready-cooked one is a convenient way to proceed, especially if you ask the fishmonger to split the creature in half lengthways (most kitchen utensils are totally inadequate to this task). Then all you have to do is make the mayonnaise, arrange the lettuce and wait for the applause.

For serving rock lobster hot, however, a live and lively specimen is required. I must admit that, faced with an active crustacean, I tend to become an instant vegetarian, though whether from pity for a fellow creature or from cowardice I'm not too sure. The latter is probably closer to the truth. There is something extremely unnerving about the way the legs and antennae click and rustle when the creature of your choice has been removed from the tangled mass of its fellows and placed into a plastic bag, to be twisted securely into a parcel. If you loosen the bag a little, you can feel the body flex. In particular, yabbies—with their disproportionately huge claws—can be quite frightening, especially when you thought you had managed to lull them safely to sleep in the freezer.

The instructions in most cookery books, usually those written by professional chefs, tell one to throw the creature live into boiling water; or, even worse, to cut it into pieces while still alive. This is definitely the stuff to make one think longingly of ratatouille. But there is no need to treat the poor creature in such a barbaric fashion. Chill in the freezer for an hour or so before dealing with it. The cold, we are informed by the RSPCA, will send it to sleep and it will die painlessly. Don't forget it's in there though—freezing the creature is not the plan.

If the rock lobster is to be served still in its shell, the next part is another problem usually glossed over in cookery books. 'Split the lobster in half lengthways' they instruct grandly. This sounds extremely simple—until you try it. The underside of a rock lobster is covered by a thick, tough membrane, banded at close intervals by a bone brace. The carapace itself is heavy, hard, knobbly and curved. And in between them is the transparent and tender flesh. Somehow or other the tail, which naturally curves inwards towards the body, must be straightened out and the whole thing deftly parted into two equal halves.

As usual, when in doubt, cheat. Pull the armoured head away from the tail (don't cut it off, as much of the flesh is inside it) and set it aside to be dealt with later. Hold the tail straight, underside upwards, and either cut straight through the membrane with a single blow from a very sharp meat cleaver or heavy knife, or snip the centres of the bone bands with chicken shears. Point a very sharp knife along the middle line and, holding it down, hit it with a hammer, tip end first, so that it cuts through the membrane, flesh and carapace. This will cut the flesh cleanly, although it mightn't do much for your favourite knife. Discard the gritty stomach sac and guts. If the head is needed for the dish, get rid of the gills before rinsing it out, then cut it in half with the chicken shears. From the body, remove the intestinal tract that runs along the centre of the back (bits of it will be found in both halves) and loosen the flesh from the shell to make it easier to deal with when the time comes to eat it.

If, however, the carapace isn't required, then the whole procedure is much easier and far less traumatic. Remove the head as before, and cut along each edge of the underside membrane with chicken shears. Lift the membrane away and, with the fingers, carefully ease out the translucent, pink-tinged flesh in one piece, to be cut into medallions. A creature weighing 1 kg will give around 200–250 g of flesh, but this is very dense, high-protein meat and is enough for two servings. Even more than other shellfish, rock lobster becomes tough with over-cooking, turning into indigestible india-rubber in seconds.

BRAISED ROCK LOBSTER

1 live rock lobster
1 slice fresh ginger
1 clove garlic
2 cloves
1 tablespoon rice wine

2 tablespoons soy sauce
light, tasteless vegetable oil
pinch chilli powder
1 spring onion, finely chopped

Chill the rock lobster to kill it, then remove the flesh in one piece from the shell by cutting along the edges of the under-membrane so that it can be lifted out cleanly. Discard the shell and slice the rock lobster into medallions. Grate the ginger and the garlic, and mix them with the cloves, rice wine and soy sauce. Marinate the medallions in the mixture for at least 30 minutes before straining them carefully and draining for a moment on absorbent paper. Set the marinade aside.

In a wok or frying pan heat a tablespoon of light, tasteless vegetable oil, and turn the medallions carefully in the oil (don't stir-fry them with vigour, or the fragile flakes of the flesh will come apart) for a minute or so, until the flesh loses its transparency. Mix the chilli powder with the marinade, pour into the pan, bring to the boil and immediately remove the pan from the heat. Arrange the medallions on a pre-heated serving dish and keep warm in the oven while the sauce continues to bubble for a minute more, then pour over the rock lobster, scatter the chopped spring onion over the top, and serve. *Serves 2.*

ROCK LOBSTER WITH CUMQUATS

1 live rock lobster
1 strip dried orange peel
butter
1 tablespoon orange liqueur

4 tiny cumquats
150 ml (¾ cup) cream
black pepper, freshly ground

Soak the orange peel in the cream for at least 1 hour, then discard it. Chill the lobster to kill it, take out the flesh and cut into medallions. Melt some butter in a shallow pan, add the medallions, grind over a little black pepper and cook for 30 seconds, turning each piece.

Add the orange liqueur and set it alight, shaking the pan so that all the pieces are coated with the alcohol. Remove the rock lobster medallions to a pre-heated serving dish to keep warm in the oven (put the cumquats on the dish too so that they will heat through gently).

Pour the cream into the pan, turn up the heat and reduce to a rich, smooth consistency. Return the rock lobster to the pan, turn the medallions in the sauce, then arrange them on the serving dish. Pour the sauce over the top, and decorate with the cumquats.

Serve with wild rice or very thin pasta tossed in a little butter. *Serves 2.*

ROCK LOBSTER WITH FENNEL

1 live rock lobster	*1 head fennel*
½ pod vanilla	*unsalted butter*
150 ml (¾ cup) cream	*black pepper, freshly ground*

Soak the vanilla pod in the cream for an hour or so, then remove it and discard. Chill the rock lobster, ease the flesh from the shell and slice into medallions. Trim the fennel, peeling away the toughest strings and cutting into quarters, or even eighths if it's big enough. Simmer in plenty of water for 5 minutes. Drain thoroughly and return to the pan with a little butter to continue to cook for another 5 minutes or so until softened but still crunchy. Arrange in a ring on a pre-heated serving dish and keep warm in the oven.

Melt some butter in a shallow pan. Put in the rock lobster, grind over some black pepper, and turn the medallions carefully until the flesh loses its fragile transparency and becomes dense and white, with pink-tinged edges. Arrange the pieces inside the ring of fennel and return the dish to the oven once more.

Pour the vanilla-flavoured cream into the pan, turn up the heat and bubble until the sauce thickens, turning a rich creamy yellow in colour. Pour over the medallions and serve at once, with nothing else to distract from the subtle combination of fennel, vanilla and rock lobster. *Serves 2.*

ROCK LOBSTER WITH GREEN SAUCE

1 live rock lobster   *1 handful chervil*
butter   *1 sprig tarragon*
black pepper, freshly ground   *100 ml (½ cup) dry white wine*
1 handful parsley   *2 tablespoons brandy*

Freeze the lobster for an hour to kill it, then split it down the middle, laying it underside up on a board, pulling the tail flat and cutting through the membrane with a sharp, heavy knife or cleaver. Discard the guts and gills from the head and the intestinal trail that runs along the back (bits will be in both sides). Loosen the flesh in the shell, cutting it into sections so that it will be easy to remove when the time comes to eat it, then press it back into shape. Cover thickly with butter, grind on plenty of black pepper, cover with foil and bake in a medium oven for 10 minutes.

In the meantime, chop or mince the parsley, chervil and sprig of tarragon very finely. Bring the wine and brandy to the boil in a shallow saucepan and bubble until reduced to no more than 2 tablespoons. Mix in the herbs, stir for a few seconds and remove from the heat.

Discard the foil, put the rock lobster halves on pre-heated dinner plates, pour the sauce into the shells and over the flesh, and serve at once. *Serves 2.*

GRILLED ROCK LOBSTER

1 live rock lobster   *unsalted butter*
lemon juice   *oil (optional)*
black pepper, freshly ground

Chill the lobster, split in half lengthways and remove the guts and gills from the head and the intestinal tract that runs along the back. Loosen the flesh in the shell, cutting it into chunks and then pressing back into shape (so that the flesh is easy to eat, but won't fall out while cooking). Sprinkle it with lemon juice, grind over some black pepper, and spread with a little butter. Press a piece of foil on the flesh side, and put the rock lobster, shell side uppermost, on the grid of a pre-heated griller. Wipe the shell with oil or butter and put the grid under a medium heat for about 5 minutes, until the shell turns bright red.

Turn the two halves over. Arrange them on the grid so that they will remain stable (scrunched up foil packed around them helps), discard the foil covers and spread more butter over the flesh, this time quite thickly. Put the pan back under the grill and continue to cook for another 3–5 minutes, until the flesh is white and tender.

This is the basic recipe for grilling lobster, and there are endless variations. One of the best is to pour dry sherry over the halves, marinating the meat for an hour or so before cooking. Bacon, placed on the cut side and grilled at the same time, is a good addition, and of course breadcrumbs, or sauce mornay, or even just grated cheese. You could add a tablespoon of thick cream (or whipped cream, which will puff up like marshmallow, burning on the top to a golden crust), or some brandy or orange liqueur, or soy sauce and rice wine. *Serves 2.*

HOT ROCK LOBSTER

1 live rock lobster
1 piece fresh ginger
1 clove garlic
½ teaspoon chilli oil
1 teaspoon tasteless vegetable oil

2 tablespoons light soy sauce
1 tablespoon rice vinegar
2 tablespoons rice wine
1 teaspoon fresh tomato puree
fresh coriander for garnish

Kill the rock lobster by placing it in the freezer for an hour or so, then cut away the underside membrane, take out the flesh and cut it into medallions. Grate the ginger and the garlic.

In a wok or frying pan, heat the chilli oil and the vegetable oil together and stir in the ginger and garlic for a few moments. Add the rock lobster medallions, stirring them gently in the oil for no more than 1 minute. Remove them from the wok and place on a pre-heated serving dish to keep warm. Pour the soy sauce, vinegar, rice wine and tomato puree into the wok, bring to the boil and let it bubble fiercely for a minute. Lower the heat and return the lobster pieces to the pan. Turn them in the sauce for a minute more, then arrange on the serving dish. Pour the sauce over them, and serve at once, sprinkled with fresh coriander. *Serves 2.*

ROCK LOBSTER AND ORANGE SALAD

200 g (1 cup) cooked rock
  lobster meat
6 pink peppercorns
2 tablespoons mayonnaise

4–6 leaves soft-leaved lettuce
1 orange
mint for garnish

Put the peppercorns into the mayonnaise at least 1 hour before serving, so that the flavour has plenty of time to infuse.

Lay the washed, dried lettuce leaves on two salad plates and arrange the rock lobster, cut into thick slices, on the top. Grate the orange skin so that you have long, thin strands of peel, then remove all the pith, peel and membrane from the orange, catching the juice in a basin, and arrange the segments with the rock lobster medallions.

Sieve the mayonnaise into the orange juice, pressing down on the pink peppercorns to extract all the flavour. Beat the juice and mayonnaise together (it should have a consistency of thin cream) and spoon some onto each plate, to one side of the main arrangement. Scatter the strands of peel over the dressing, strew a few leaves of mint on top of the orange segments, and serve. *Serves 2.*

POACHED ROCK LOBSTER

1 live rock lobster
1 carrot
1 leek
150 ml (¾ cup) dry white
  wine

bay leaf
handful parsley
12 peppercorns

This is the classic way to cook a rock lobster for eating cold.

First, measure how much water is needed by putting the chilled lobster into the pan with the other ingredients and add just enough to cover it. Take it out again, bring the liquid to the boil and simmer for 10 minutes. Put the rock lobster into the boiling water, lower the heat, put on the lid, and simmer for about 15 minutes, until the shell is bright red (this happens quite quickly. It isn't a sign that the meat inside is completely cooked, just that it's well on the way).

If the creature is to be eaten hot, take it out of the stock, split in half lengthways and clean out the guts and gills in the head as quickly as possible so that it doesn't cool too much. Place a piece of foil over the flesh so that it doesn't dry out and put the rock lobster on a pre-heated dish in the oven. Ladle some of the stock into a small saucepan, boil rapidly to reduce to about ½ cup, beat in some thick cream, boil once more and pour over the lobster. Alternatively melt some butter and pour it over, with plenty of black pepper.

Much the nicest way to eat poached lobster is cold. Rather than leave the stock simmering for 15 minutes, turn it off after 10, and allow the creature to cool in the liquid. Take it out, split it open lengthways, clean it, and serve with mayonnaise and salad. *Serves 2.*

ROCK LOBSTER WITH RED CURRANTS

1 *live rock lobster*	2 *tablespoons water*
2 *tablespoons dry sherry*	*sugar (optional)*
50 *g (2 tablespoons) red*	1 *bunch watercress*
currants	*black pepper, freshly ground*

Chill the rock lobster until it dies, then remove the flesh from the shell and cut into thick medallions. Sprinkle them with sherry and set aside to marinate for about 30 minutes.

Poach the red currants for 1 minute in 1 tablespoon of sherry and 2 tablespoons water (add a little sugar if you like, but the taste should be tart rather than sweet). Lift the currants out of the liquid with a slotted spoon and drain them on absorbent paper, carefully handling them so they don't get squashed.

On a pre-heated serving dish, spread the rinsed and dried watercress as a bed and put the dish in the oven to warm (put the red currants on one side as well to reheat).

Reheat the liquid in which the red currants were cooked, bring to boiling point, then lower the heat until the liquid is just moving and poach the rock lobster medallions in it for about 1 minute on each side, grinding a little black pepper on them as they are turned. Arrange the medallions on the watercress, decorate with the red currants, and pour the juices over the top.

This can be served either hot or cold (in the latter case, don't warm the watercress), and is equally good either way. The bitterness of the watercress, the sweet-sour clarity of the red currants and the rich density of the lobster combine in an unusual but very effective way. *Serves 2.*

ROCK LOBSTER WITH BEURRE BLANC

*200 g (1 cup) cooked rock
lobster meat
1 bunch watercress*

*60 g (3 tablespoons) unsalted
butter
1 tablespoon dry white wine
small jar salmon roe*

Rinse and dry the watercress and arrange as a bed on two small salad plates.

Cut the rock lobster meat into rounds. Melt a little of the butter in a small saucepan and turn the medallions in it until just heated through, adding the white wine at the first turn. Take out the lobster and arrange on top of the watercress. Boil the wine briefly, remove from the heat, and beat in the rest of the butter, chilled and cut into small cubes. Whisk until all the cubes are incorporated and the sauce is smooth and glossy.

Pour the beurre blanc over the lobster medallions. Decorate with the golden eggs of the salmon, and serve warm. *Serves 2.*

ROCK LOBSTER IN SPICED GINGER WINE

*1 live rock lobster
1 piece fresh ginger
1 clove garlic*

*200 ml (1 cup) ginger wine
1 dried chilli
unsalted butter*

Chill the rock lobster to kill it, then cut away the underside membrane and carefully lift out the flesh. Cut into thick rounds.

Grate the ginger and the garlic, mix with the ginger wine and whole dried chilli, and marinate the rounds in the mixture for at least 1 hour. Drain the medallions (reserve the marinade, but discard the chilli), and cook for about 1 minute each side in some butter. Transfer to a pre-heated serving dish and keep warm in the oven.

Pour the marinade into the pan, raise the heat and boil until the sauce is reduced to 2–3 tablespoons, is dark brown and starting to become sticky (be careful or it can become caramel very quickly, as ginger wine is sweet). Pour it over the rock lobster and serve at once.

A warm salad of carrots and celery, cooked in lemon juice and either butter or olive oil, goes well with the hot, spicy sweetness of the sauce. *Serves 2.*

STUFFED ROCK LOBSTER

1 live rock lobster
1 onion
1 handful parsley
1 sprig lemon thyme
1 sprig oregano

4 tablespoons fresh
  breadcrumbs
unsalted butter
juice ½ lemon
oil

Chill the rock lobster to kill it, then cut in half lengthways and clean out the guts and gills from the head. Loosen the flesh from the shell and slash it diagonally in 4 cuts on each half.

Mince the onion and herbs finely and mix with the breadcrumbs. Melt some butter in a small saucepan and stir the mixture until the butter is absorbed by the breadcrumbs. Cool slightly and pack some of it into the diagonal slashes in the rock lobster flesh. Rub with a little lemon juice and mix the rest with the remaining stuffing.

Oil the shells, cover the cut side with buttered foil, and place the lobster halves on a grid under a medium-hot grill, shell sides uppermost. Grill for about 5 minutes, then turn them over. Remove the tinfoil (pack it round the shells if they won't stand upright), pack the rest of the stuffing on top of the meat, dot with more butter and return to the grill, meat side up, for another 5 minutes, or until the stuffing is bubbling and the meat is cooked. Serve still bubbling. *Serves 2.*

Sand Lobsters

Shovel-nosed lobster, Balmain bug, slipper lobster, Moreton Bay bug, flat lobster, sand lobster, flapjack... these wedge-shaped, heavily-armoured creatures seem to have accumulated an enormous number of names in Australia alone. There are a variety of different species, most of them found in the warmer seas from the Mediterranean to the Pacific. They range in size from the small Balmain bug *(Ibacus peroni)* and Moreton Bay bug *(Thenus orientalis)* which are usually sold commercially when they are between 10 cm and 20 cm, to the slipper lobster or flapjack *(Scyllarides squammosus)*, which can grow up to 26 cm in length, weigh 500 g, and is altogether a much larger and heavier creature.

Unlike their more accommodating relatives the rock lobsters, sand lobsters cannot be trapped in lobster pots, but instead are caught in the nets of prawn trawlers, along continental shelves. They have a fairly wide distribution, but because they are caught mainly as a subsidiary to prawn fishing, they are not always available (and when they are, are all too often already cooked) in large quantities. As with all shellfish, it's better to buy green ones if possible, even if they are to be eaten cold—and definitely if they are to be served hot.

While there are various species, they are linked by the common characteristics of flattened heads, attenuated feelers and short, spindly legs. From the point of view of the cook the major distinction is that of size.

BALMAIN BUGS AND MORETON BAY BUGS

The Balmain bug is a bright gold-brown, with a wide, flat, frilly-edged head and a correspondingly short thorax and tail. At first glance it looks hardly worth buying, for there seems to be very little flesh with the great armoured head taking up more than 60 per cent of the total size. But in fact they are deceptive, and will yield about 35 per cent flesh to total weight—not as good as prawns, but better than scallops. Moreton Bay bugs are more streamlined—darker, slimmer, more of a classic wedge shape, not so prehistoric-looking—with a better flesh-to-weight ratio (40 to 50 per cent), as well as tasting just as good. Both creatures have a delicate sweetness which is delicious.

Because of their smaller size bugs are much easier to deal with than rock lobsters, or even slipper lobsters. The tail shells can be detached and split open without damge to life and limb—although they have some very sharp edges. To shell bugs, cut along the edges of the underside tail membrane and around the join where the legs are attached to the head and gently loosen the meat from the shell with the fingers, taking care that it doesn't stick and tear inside the head. The soft, translucent flesh should come away in one piece, bringing with it one or two sections of pinky-orange coral, but neatly leaving the intestinal tract still attached to the shell.

If the bugs are to be served cold, one way to cook them is in their shells. Bring a shallow pan of water to the boil. Lower the heat so that it is no longer bubbling, and put in the bugs, a few at a time, to cook for 3 to 5 minutes depending on size. Really large ones can take up to 7 minutes, but it's always best to err towards under- rather than over-cooking. The shells retain the heat for a surprising amount of time, and during that time the flesh goes on cooking unless they are dropped into cold water as soon as they are removed from the pan.

Once cooked, the bugs can be served still in their shells or removed from them, depending on the party. While they are delicious either way, it's easier on the eaters to serve them shelled, as they can be pretty messy otherwise.

BUG AND APPLE SALAD

4–6 green bugs   *pepper*
1 orange   *1 tablespoon mayonnaise*
1 small, sweet, juicy red apple   *1 tablespoon crème fraîche*

Grate the orange skin, keeping the shreds as long as possible, and squeeze out all the juice. Shell the bugs and poach them in a shallow pan in water just below boiling point for 1 minute, or until the flesh is no longer translucent. Drain them on kitchen paper. Put into a bowl and sprinkle with a little of the orange juice.

Core the unpeeled apple and cut into thin slices. Turn each slice in orange juice and arrange them on two salad plates, then pile the bugs in the centres. Sprinkle with pepper, mix the rest of the orange juice with the mayonnaise and crème fraîche, drizzle some over the bugs, decorate with the orange fronds and serve. *Serves 2.*

BUGS WITH APRICOTS

4–6 green bugs
2–3 ripe, fresh apricots
1 tablespoon brandy

2 tablespoons heavy cream
sugar (optional)

Shell the bugs and cut the flesh in half lengthways. Halve the apricots, remove the stones, and poach the fruit in the brandy for about 5 minutes, or until the skins slip off easily but the fruit retains its shape.

Transfer the apricot halves to a pre-heated serving dish and keep warm. Put the bug tails into the brandy and poach for about 1 minute, or until the flesh firms and whitens, turning the pieces gently so that all sides are cooked. Arrange them on the serving dish with the apricots and return to the oven to keep warm.

Pour the cream into the brandy, turn up the heat and boil until the sauce becomes thick and smooth. Check for seasoning (it's possible the sauce may need a little sugar if the apricots aren't fully ripe), pour over the bug tails and serve at once, with brown rice. *Serves 2.*

BUGS IN CABBAGE

4–6 green bugs
4–6 inner leaves of a Chinese
  cabbage
70 ml (3 tablespoons) dry
  white wine

1 tablespoon brandy
2 tablespoons crème fraîche
black pepper, freshly ground

Cabbage is one of those vegetables that suffer from a bad press— slums and tenements are often characterised in novels as smelling of bad drains and cooked cabbage. Autobiographies recalling tormented childhoods in horrible boarding schools describe grey, slimy, watery, evil-smelling cabbage to evoke the image of ghastly food. And even Juvenal in the *Satires* writes of the wretched man who will surely be killed by the constant repetition of reheated cabbage.

But as always (or almost always) it's the cooking that's at fault rather than the plant itself. There are, of course, many different varieties, and some are coarser and sourer than others, so choosing the right kind for the right dish is important. The long-cooking stuffed-cabbage dishes of northern Europe require white or Savoy types, while the quick stir-fried cooking of Asia needs the looser-leaved, lighter textured Chinese varieties.

For this dish too the Chinese variety is best, as it is milder and sweeter in flavour than the European kind. If it is not available, however, the inner leaves of a Savoy are almost as good.

Rinse the cabbage leaves and cut away the thick part of the stems. Blanch, one at a time, in a shallow pan of boiling water, for no more than a few seconds, just long enough for them to become limp. Drain and dry on kitchen paper.

With a pair of chicken shears or kitchen scissors cut along each side of the tough membrane on the underside of the bug tails. Lift away the membrane and ease out the flesh from the shells with the fingers. Bring the wine and brandy to the boil, lower the heat and poach the bugs for 1–2 minutes, until the flesh turns white. Take out immediately and drain. Put the shells in the wine, raise the heat and simmer for 20 minutes. Strain off the stock and discard the shells.

Butter a small, deep fireproof dish (a soufflé dish is good) and line it with the cabbage leaves, leaving enough overhanging the edges for them to be folded over the top when the filling is put in. Cut the bugs into thick slices and pile all the slices except two into the centre of the cabbage. Put these two bug pieces with the crème fraîche and some ground black pepper into a blender and puree to a smooth sauce. Pour this over the bugs, reserving about 2 tablespoons. Fold over the cabbage leaves so that the filling is completely enclosed, pour on the rest of the sauce, and cook for 10 minutes in a medium oven, until the sauce is bubbling and the cabbage tender. *Serves 2.*

CHILLI BUGS

4–6 green bugs
2 dried chillies
2 tablespoons hot water
¼ teaspoon each cumin and
  coriander seeds

pinch saffron
pinch pepper
1 tablespoon lemon juice
2 tablespoons sesame oil
mint for garnish

Cut away and discard the membrane, legs and centre part of the head from the underside of the bugs. Loosen the flesh in the shell, but don't take it out.

Discard the seeds from the chillies and chop the pods into small pieces. Soak in 2 tablespoons of hot water for 5 minutes. Add the cumin, coriander, saffron, pepper, lemon juice and sesame oil. Mix together, and pour into the bug shells, rubbing the marinade into the flesh. Set them aside to marinate for at least 1 hour before cooking.

To cook the bugs, drain the marinade into a dish and grill them over charcoal or under a hot grill, shell sides to the heat for the first minute. Baste the flesh with the marinade, turn and continue to cook for another 2–3 minutes, until the flesh is white and firm. Sprinkle with chopped mint and serve at once. *Serves 2.*

BUGS AND CORAL SAUCE

4–6 green bugs
1 tablespoon crème fraîche

1 egg yolk
pepper, freshly ground

Shell the bugs, making sure all the coral comes away, and set the flesh and coral aside. Place the shells in a saucepan, cover with water, bring to the boil, and simmer for 20–30 minutes. Strain the liquid into a shallow pan and discard the shells.

Carefully detach the coral from the bug tails. Heat the stock until just below boiling point, and poach the flesh until just white and firm. Arrange on a pre-heated serving dish and keep warm while the sauce is being finished.

Boil the stock until reduced to about 2 tablespoonfuls, then grind in a little pepper, withdraw from the heat and cool slightly. Blend together the crème fraîche and egg yolk with the coral. Add to the stock, stirring all the time over a very low heat (or in a bain marie) until the sauce becomes thick and smooth. Don't allow it to get near boiling point or the egg will separate. Pour over the bug tails and serve at once. *Serves 2.*

BUGS AND SNOW PEAS

4–6 green bugs　　　　　　*1 piece fresh ginger*
10–12 snow peas　　　　　*3 tablespoons water*
1 spring onion　　　　　　*1 tablespoons light soy sauce*
1 clove garlic

Take the flesh from the shells and cut in half lengthways. Arrange the pieces in a shallow heatproof dish with the snow peas. Cut the spring onion into short lengths and lay on top. Crush the garlic, grate the ginger, mix them both together with the water and soy sauce, and pour over the bugs and snow peas. Cover the dish and set aside to marinate for an hour or so, turning the bugs occasionally to make sure all the sides are impregnated with the mixture.

Bring a pan of water to the boil, place the dish in a steamer over the pan, and steam for 3–5 minutes.

If the bugs are very thick, they could take longer than 5 minutes to cook, but check them after 3 minutes to make sure. If the dish is overcooked, they will become tough and the snow peas limp. *Serves 2.*

BUGS WITH SPICY ORANGE SAUCE

4–6 green bugs　　　　　　　*1 tablespoon Japanese rice*
juice and grated rind of 1　　　*vinegar or 1 teaspoon white*
*　orange*　　　　　　　　　　*wine vinegar and ½*
1 teaspoon sugar　　　　　　*teaspoon sugar*
　　　　　　　　　　　　　　1 clove garlic
　　　　　　　　　　　　　　1 dried chilli

Shell the bugs, sprinkle the flesh with a little orange juice and set aside. Melt the sugar with the vinegar in a shallow saucepan and bring to the boil. Add the garlic and dried chilli (shake out the seeds first), lower the heat, put on the lid and simmer for 5 minutes. Pour in the orange juice with half of the grated peel, bring to just below boiling point, and poach the bugs until the flesh loses its translucency and the little tails curl and become striped with pink.

Transfer the bugs to a pre-heated serving dish and keep warm. Raise the heat once more, reduce the sauce a little and pour it over the bugs. Scatter the rest of the grated orange peel over the top and serve immediately.

Rice is good to soak up the spicy, orangey juices. Broccoli is also a good balance to the warmth of the sauce and the smoothness of the bugs. *Serves 2.*

BUGS WITH PORT SAUCE

4–6 green bugs	*pepper*
butter	*1 egg yolk*
50 ml (2 tablespoons) port	*vol-au-vent cases*
100 ml (½ cup) cream	*10 tiny mushrooms*

Shell the bugs and chop the flesh into thick slices. Heat some butter in a saucepan. As soon as it foams put in the bug pieces. Stir until the flesh becomes opaque, pour in the port and bring to the boil, turning the pieces all the time. As soon as the port starts to bubble, transfer them to a pre-heated dish to keep warm.

Reduce the port a little and pour in the cream and some pepper. Bubble fiercely for a minute or so, then remove from the heat and let cool slightly.

Beat the egg yolk, use a little of it to glaze the vol-au-vent cases and spoon a little cream into the rest. Add some of the sauce, mix thoroughly and pour back into the pan, whisking all the time over a very low heat until it thickens. Put the bugs back in the sauce to heat through.

Toss the mushrooms in butter for a few minutes, then stir them into the sauce with the bugs. Pile the mixture into the vol-au-vents and serve at once.

Sugar snap peas, cooked for no more than 30 seconds so that they are hot but not softened—they must remain crunchy—are a good accompaniment. Their clear and brilliant green is a foil to the golden cases of pastry and the faintly blush-tinted sauce. *Serves 2.*

BUGS IN ZUCCHINI WRAPPERS

6 green bugs	*1 tablespoon dry vermouth*
1 large zucchini	*150 ml (¾ cup) cream*
black pepper, freshly ground	*1 tablespoon crème fraîche*

Cut 6 thin parallel slices lengthways from the zucchini, and drop these into simmering water to blanch for 30 seconds. Drain the slices on kitchen paper.

Shell the bugs, season with pepper, and wind a zucchini strip diagonally round each one, like the binding on a racquet handle, to completely enclose it. Bring a pan of water to the boil. Place the zucchini-wrapped bugs in a muslin-lined steamer, making sure the loose end of the wrapping is underneath so it can't unravel, put it over the boiling water, cover, and steam for 3–5 minutes.

In the meantime, put the rest of the zucchini, the vermouth, cream and crème fraîche into a blender and whizz to a smooth consistency. Pour into a saucepan, bring to the boil and season with a little salt and some freshly ground black pepper. Arrange the zucchini-wrapped bugs on plates, pour the sauce over them, and serve.

The same rolls can also be threaded onto skewers, wiped with melted butter, then grilled under a medium grill. Bugs are also very good wrapped in spinach and steamed in the same way as Prawns in Spinach Leaves. *Serves 2.*

SLIPPER LOBSTERS or FLAPJACKS

These crustaceans rank in size between bugs and rock lobsters. They are usually caught in the nets of prawn trawlers and are not always available, but are well worth purchasing if they can be found. They have heavy, bumpy carapaces, small legs and flattened heads, although the bodies are quite rounded. They are kept live in lobster tanks.

Slipper lobsters yield between 35 to 40 per cent flesh. As with all live crustaceans choose energetic specimens that feel solid and heavy for their size.

Like rock lobsters, slipper lobsters should be drowned in fresh water or chilled in the freezer before cooking so that they die painlessly. Also like rock lobsters, the flesh can cling tightly to the shell. The meat is delicious but soft and easy to tear, so while it can be taken raw from the shell with care and the help of a very sharp knife, it's often easier to cook flapjacks first and shell them afterwards, which makes them ideal for salads and cold dishes.

SLIPPER LOBSTER WITH MAYONNAISE

1 live slipper lobster
black pepper, freshly ground
1 tablespoon dry sherry

mayonnaise
1 bunch watercress

Chill the slipper lobster. Place in a large pan of cold water, put on the cover, and bring to the boil. Lower the flame and simmer for 7 minutes. Turn off the heat and let the lobster cool in the water for 30 minutes before taking it out.

Lay it shell side down on a board and cut in half lengthways (a Chinese meat cleaver is the best tool for this task. If you don't have one, cut along the centre line of the thick ribs of bone and the membrane with chicken shears or strong kitchen scissors. Using the same scissors, cut away the undershell of the head and the legs. Chop through the flesh along the same line with a very sharp, heavy knife).

Scrape out the guts and gritty sac from the head. Wipe the cavities with kitchen paper so they are completely clean, and remove as much as possible of the intestinal tract that runs along the back (bits of it will be found in both halves). Loosen the flesh from the shells so that it's easy for the eater to get out, and sprinkle with freshly ground black pepper and a little sherry. Pour some mayonnaise into the head cavities and along the centre of the meat, and serve on a bed of watercress. *Serves 2.*

SLIPPER LOBSTER TAIL AND BASIL TORTELLINI

1 small live slipper lobster
1 handful fresh basil leaves
pepper
2 tablespoons unsalted butter

400 g (14 oz) pasta in one
  sheet
semolina
1 tablespoon heavy cream

Chill the slipper lobster for an hour or so. Lay it shell side down on a board. Cut along each edge of the membrane, the undershell of the head and around the legs with sharp, strong scissors. Carefully peel away the undershell and membrane, and, with the fingers and a small, flexible and very sharp knife, scrape the flesh from the shell so that it comes away in one piece. Cut one-third of the meat into 4 neat medallions and set aside. Chop the rest finely, together with the basil, and season with a little pepper. Melt 1 tablespoon of the butter over a low heat, stir in the lobster and basil mixture and cook for a few seconds. Remove the pan from the heat and cool.

Roll out the pasta and place the mixture in tiny spoonfuls, 2 cm apart in straight lines, on one half. Damp the lines between the spoonfuls and fold over the other half, pressing along the dampened lines to seal the two sides together. Cut out the little mounds with a small circular cutter, sprinkle with semolina and set aside for 5 minutes. Bring a large saucepan ¾ full of lightly salted water to the boil and cook the pasta for 3 minutes.

Meanwhile, heat the second spoonful of butter and cook the medallions gently for about 1 minute, turning them carefully so they don't break up. As soon as the flesh firms and whitens, remove the pan from the heat.

Drain the tortellini thoroughly and serve in a pre-heated dish with the medallions, the melted butter from the pan, and a tablespoonful of thick cream. For total luxury, steam or poach 4–6 scallops and add them to the dish at the last minute.

Basil butter is another good idea for the sauce, or, even better, chervil butter. *Serves 4–6.*

POACHED SLIPPER LOBSTER

1 small live slipper lobster	*1 small carrot*
2 tablespoons brandy	*1 stick fennel*
1 onion	*peppercorns*
1 bay leaf	*1.5 l (48 fl oz) water*
1 handful parsley	*fennel fronds for garnish*

Kill the slipper lobster by putting it in the freezer for an hour. Bring the brandy, onion, bay leaf, parsley, carrot, fennel and peppercorns to the boil with the water in a large saucepan. Boil for 5 minutes. Lower the heat so that the water is barely simmering and put in the slipper lobster to cook for 10 minutes. Take it out of the pan and plunge into cold water to stop the cooking process.

Turn up the heat under the stock and boil rapidly until reduced by about half. Strain into a clean pan through a muslin-lined sieve so that the liquid is clear of any impurities, and bring back to the boil.

Meanwhile, shell the slipper lobster, slice the flesh into thick medallions, and divide between four hot soup plates. Carefully pour the simmering stock over them, drape a few fronds of fennel on the top of the lobster pieces, and serve at once. *Serves 4.*

SLIPPER LOBSTER FEUILLETES

1 live slipper lobster
100 ml (½ cup) dry white
* wine*
1 leek
4–6 peppercorns
1 bay leaf

1 tablespoon crème fraîche
250 g (8 oz) puff pastry
butter
150 g (5 oz) sugar snap peas
150 g (5 oz) button
* mushrooms*

Chill the lobster for an hour in the freezer until it dies painlessly. With a pair of heavy kitchen scissors or chicken shears break the bony ribs which hold in place the flexible membrane on the underside of the lobster. Cut along the inside edge of the carapace on each side, and lift away the skin like a flap. With the scissors, cut through the underside of the head where the legs join the body and lift away the centre part of the shell. With the fingers and a very sharp, flexible knife, carefully and gently ease away the shell, taking care not to tear the fragile flesh. Sprinkle the meat with a little white wine and set aside.

Rinse the shell, discarding the guts and gritty sac, and place it in a deep saucepan with the cleaned, chopped leek, white wine, peppercorns and bay leaf. Cover with water and bring to the boil with the lid on. Lower the heat and simmer for 30 minutes. Remove the shell, scrape out any remaining flesh into a blender, and blend it with the leek, peppercorns, a ladleful of the stock and the crème fraîche to a smooth, creamy-pink consistency.

Roll out the puff pastry into an oblong measuring 12 cm × 10 cm (5″ × 4″) and 1.5 cm (½″) thick. Cut it in half so that there are two pieces, each 6 cm × 10 cm (2½″ × 4″). Place them on a lightly buttered baking sheet, brush the tops with melted butter, and cook in a hot oven for 20 minutes, until well-risen and golden-brown. Split them open horizontally and scoop out any uncooked dough. Return them to the oven and keep warm.

Meanwhile, string the sugar snap peas and cook them in lightly salted water for 1 minute. Drain and toss in a little butter, and arrange around the edges of a pre-heated serving dish. In a frying pan, melt some more butter and cook the mushrooms until soft. Push them to one side and add the lobster pieces. Cook them carefully, turning in the butter, for 1 minute. Pour in the sauce, bring to the boil and remove the mushrooms and lobster.

Arrange the lower halves of the feuilletes on the centre of the serving dish. Pile the lobster and mushrooms on top, pour over the boiling sauce, place the lids on top, and serve at once. *Serves 2.*

SLIPPER LOBSTER SOUFFLÉ

1 small live slipper lobster　　*50 ml (¼ cup) cream*
2 tablespoons unsalted butter　*pepper*
1 heaped tablespoon plain　　*dry sherry*
　flour　　　　　　　　　　*3 eggs, separated*
100 ml (½ cup) milk　　　　*1 tablespoons butter*
100 g (3–4 oz) grated gruyère　*1 tablespoon brandy*
　cheese

Melt the butter over low heat in a heavy saucepan, sift in the flour, and stir for a minute or so to cook the flour. Add the milk little by little so there are no lumps. Stir until the mixture boils. Add the grated cheese, cream and some pepper and remove from the heat to cool.

Meanwhile, chill or drown the slipper lobster. Shell it and cut the meat into thick rounds, sprinkle with sherry and set aside.

Separate the eggs and beat the whites until they stand in peaks. Mix the yolks into the soufflé base and then gently cut and fold in the whites. Pour into a well-buttered soufflé dish and place in a hot oven to cook for 30 minutes, until risen and puffy.

While the soufflé is cooking, melt some butter in a small pan over a low heat and turn the lobster medallions in it until just cooked. Pour over 1 tablespoon of brandy, set alight, and shake the pan so that all the pieces are coated with the burning alcohol.

Take the soufflé out of the oven. Cut a couple of deep slashes into the puffy, heaving top, and into them press the lobster pieces. Pour over the rest of the brandy in the pan and serve at once. *Serves 4.*

SLIPPER LOBSTER WITH TOMATO AND CAPSICUM SAUCE

1 live slipper lobster　　　*2 tomatoes*
1 onion　　　　　　　　　*½ teaspoon paprika, basil*
1 clove garlic　　　　　　　*and thyme*
1 tablespoon olive oil　　　*½ teaspoon cumin*
½ each red and green　　　*pinch saffron*
　capsicums　　　　　　　*1 tablespoon red wine vinegar*

Peel the onion and garlic. Seed the capsicums and strip out the white pith, and peel and seed the tomatoes. Chop them all finely. Cook the onion and garlic in the oil until soft. Add the capsicum and tomato, cover the pan, and cook for 5 minutes. Mince the herbs, grind the cumin, crumble the saffron, mix them all together with the red wine vinegar and pour the mixture into the capsicum and tomatoes. Put the lid back on, lower the heat as far as possible, and cook for 2 hours.

Meanwhile, chill the slipper lobster. Place it in a large pan, cover with water, and bring to the boil to cook for 7 minutes. Drop the lobster into cold water to stop the cooking process. As soon as it's cool enough to handle take off the shell, cut the flesh into thick slices and add them to the sauce to cook for 1 minute longer.

This can be served hot or cold. Rice is a good accompaniment if hot. It's best cold (it tastes like an incredibly luxurious ratatouille) and needs nothing except perhaps some pitta bread to scoop up the sauce. *Serves 2.*

SLIPPER LOBSTER AND WALNUTS

1 small live slipper lobster   *1 tablespoon light vegetable oil*
½ green capsicum   *2 tablespoons light soy sauce*
30 g (2 tablespoons) walnuts   *1 tablespoon rice wine*

Chill the slipper lobster, then carefully remove the flesh and chop into thick pieces. Discard the seeds and any white pith from the capsicum and cut into slender slices. Chop the walnuts roughly.

In a frying pan heat the oil and stir-fry the slipper lobster pieces for 30 seconds. Add the capsicum slices and the walnuts and stir for a few seconds more. Then add the soy sauce and the rice wine, and bring to the boil. As soon as the liquid starts to bubble, transfer the lobster, capsicum and walnuts to a pre-heated serving dish and keep warm. Let the sauce bubble fiercely for a few seconds longer, pour over the lobster and serve at once, with plenty of rice. *Serves 2.*

Scallops

The curved, ridged, scroll-edged scallop shell is one of the most famous of all Western decorative designs. It has graced ceilings and columns, mosaic pavements, classical friezes and niches. Carved in marble, scallop shells held water as basins or fountains. Scallop shells bordered Greek vases and framed Roman busts. Raphael's nymph Galatea rides in one, pulled by two dolphins, as she turns her head to the song of a love-sick giant: Botticelli's Venus rises from the waves in one; and Holbein's Virgin Mary stands in a shell-topped niche looking down at the adoring couple in his painting *Virgin with the Family of the Burgomaster Jakob Meyer*. The scallop shell, worn in the hat and at the belt, became the universal badge of pilgrims, first those who travelled to Santiago de Compostella, and then by extension to pilgrims everywhere. The scallop shell was the symbol or emblem of Saint James, who according to legend crawled out of the sea after a shipwreck in the far north-west of Spain, covered with scallops. One species is actually called the pilgrim scallop, and the French name for the creature is Coquille Saint Jacques.

However, while the shell may be of great artistic, historic and symbolic value, it's what's inside that makes this one of the most delicious of all shellfish. The scallop is a creature with a thick white muscle and a soft orange and cream coral, set in a mantle of pink and transparent paleness. The muscle and coral are the edible bits, although the mantle can be used for soups and flavouring.

Scallops belong to the family Pectinidae, and there are various species throughout the world. They live in coastal waters and along the continental shelf in colonies, moving about by jetting water as their shells open and close. They are harvested by trawling, and are available all year round, although sometimes in variable quantities. They can be purchased in various ways, from live in the shell to processed packs (sometimes even covered in crumbs) from the shelves of the deep-freeze cabinets. But by far the greatest bulk of the catch is sold already shelled and cleaned, packed into deep trays, then covered with water and frozen for transport, later to slowly defrost on the ice in the fish markets (something to be remembered if you want to freeze them yourself), absorbing some of the water as they do so. This added water changes the balance of the tissue, making the muscle soft and smooth and round (and very white) instead of firm, cream-coloured and with defined, squared-off edges, as they are when shelled without soaking. Dry-shucked scallops can usually be purchased in good fishmongers, although they may cost a little more. So, if possible, buy them either dry-shucked or live in the shell.

To shuck live scallops, slide the knife between the two shells, flexing the blade against the flat side. As the blade touches the mantle, the scallop will open. Carefully scrape the white muscle from its anchorage on the flat shell (which is usually on the right-hand side towards the hinge), sliding the knife under the mantle so that the muscle isn't cut in half. Turn the shells over so that the deep side is cupped in your hand, and cut around the black sac that sits in the deep curve beneath the hinge, then gently slide the knife between the shell and the muscle, easing them apart. Lift out the creamy muscle, the coloured coral, and the gritty, pink and white transparent frill or mantle, and gently pull this away from the rest. Pinch out the long, hard black line that once attached to the black sac, rinse the scallop quickly under cold water to get rid of any grit or sand, and drain.

If the only scallops available are the already shelled, block-frozen ones, don't despair. Check to see if the black trail needs to be removed and place them in a colander or sieve set over a bowl to drain for an hour or more before cooking. Use the collected liquid to add to the water or wine for poaching, or adding to a sauce. One of the best ways of treating scallops that have been transported in this fashion is to marinate them in a tablespoon of whisky and their juices for two or three hours before straining them.

If you are buying them live in the shell, 1 kg usually yields 250–300 g (8–10 oz) of meat (or from 12 to 15 scallops). This amount is enough for two people, as the flesh is dense and very high in protein. One other consideration, of course, is time. Shelling scallops is relatively easy, but until one gets the knack it's also slow. Already shelled ones that have been dry-shucked need no attention other than removing the black line, and block-frozen ones need draining as well, but that's all. I have never bought deep-frozen scallops so can't comment on them, but the 'ready-to-cook' processed and crumbed packs are no use at all so far as I can see, and should be avoided like the plague.

Scallops vary greatly in size according to species. The very large European pilgrim scallop measure up to 14 cm, while the commercial scallop of southern Australian waters usually measures about 8 centimetres. Larger ones obviously take longer to cook, but regardless of size scallops are ready when the flesh turns opaque, and the texture tightens a little. They should still feel soft and slightly squishy, and be no more than warm inside, for the longer they cook the smaller, drier and tougher they become.

SCALLOPS AND ALMONDS

12–14 scallops
1 egg
pepper
dried breadcrumbs
60 g (3 tablespoons) unsalted
* butter*

30 g (2 tablespoons or 1 oz)
* blanched almonds*
juice ½ lemon
parsley

Beat the egg, season with pepper, and dip the scallops first in the egg and then in the breadcrumbs. Place them on a plate and chill for at least 30 minutes, turning them halfway through.

Heat the butter in a frying pan and toss the almonds until they start to turn golden. Remove from the pan and drain. Put in the scallops and fry quickly, stirring them so that all sides become crisp and golden brown. Just before they have finished cooking return the almonds to the pan to reheat (almonds burn with astounding speed, so this will take no more than a few seconds). Transfer the scallops and almonds to a heated serving dish and keep warm.

Pour the lemon juice into the pan, add some finely chopped parsley, stir to amalgamate and spoon into a warmed bowl.

Serve with sugar snap peas, or broccoli sprinkled with black pepper and lemon juice, and cooked for only a few minutes so that the stems are still crisp and crunchy. *Serves 2.*

SCALLOPS WITH APRICOTS

8 scallops
4 ripe fresh apricots
30 g (1½ tablespoons) unsalted
  butter

1 slice fresh ginger
1 tablespoon cognac
20 g (1½ tablespoons) ground
  almonds

This is a very pretty dish, with the hot-gold flesh of the apricots counterpointing the coral and white of the scallops. For this reason the scallops are steamed to retain their pearly purity.

Make sure there is none of the mantle or the trail left on the scallops to mar their whiteness. Steam them over boiling water for 30–50 seconds until the translucency is gone. Arrange on a heated serving dish and keep warm. If you like, detach the corals and place them in the centre, surrounded by the white muscles.

Blanch the apricots in boiling water for 1 minute. Drain, skin and halve. Melt the butter in a shallow pan, grate in the ginger and add the apricots, turning them to ensure all sides are exposed to the heat. Pour in the cognac and set it alight, shaking the pan so that the apricot halves are impregnated with the flavours. As soon as the flames die down, arrange the apricots around the scallops and return the dish to the oven. Add the ground almonds to the juices in the pan, stir until thickened, and pour over the apricots so that it coats them like a glaze.

Serve on its own, or with Basmati rice, or, better still, with just a few snow peas. *Serves 2.*

SCALLOPS AND ARTICHOKES

6 scallops
6 mussels
1 onion
2 cloves garlic
1 slice fresh ginger
2 tablespoons sesame oil
2 artichokes

1 tablespoon soy sauce
1 tablespoon water
2 small hot chillies
1 stick lemon grass
coriander leaves, freshly
  chopped, for garnish

Scrub, beard and steam open the mussels and discard the shells, reserving the liquid. Set them aside with the scallops.

Peel the onion, garlic and ginger, chop them all finely and cook in the hot sesame oil in a frying pan until the onion is soft. Remove the outer leaves from the artichokes, cut off the tops and trim the stems. Slice into quarters or eighths if they are very large, remove the chokes and add the slices to the pan, stirring them gently in the oil until the surfaces are lightly browned. Pour in the mussel juices, soy sauce and water, add the chillies and lemon grass, lower the heat and simmer for 10 minutes, or until the artichoke slices are cooked.

Add the scallops and stir for 1 minute. Put in the mussels and allow them to heat through. Arrange on a pre-heated serving dish, discarding the lemon grass stick, and scatter liberally with freshly chopped coriander leaves. Serve at once, with plenty of white rice. *Serves 2.*

SCALLOP AND CUCUMBER SALAD

8 scallops	*4–6 pink peppercorns*
½ cucumber	*2 tablespoons mayonnaise*
salt	*1 soft-leaved lettuce*
2 tablespoons dry white wine	*dill for garnish*

Peel the cucumber, cut in half lengthways, scoop out the seeds and sprinkle the flesh with salt. Leave it in a colander to drain off the bitter juices for 30 minutes. Rinse thoroughly, drain, and dry on kitchen paper.

Bring the white wine to the boil with the pink peppercorns. Simmer for 5 minutes, then lower the heat so that the liquid is just below boiling and poach the scallops for 1 minute until the muscle loses its translucency. Drain them on kitchen paper and set aside.

Bring the liquid back to the boil to reduce by half, then withdraw from the heat. As soon as it's cool, strain it into the mayonnaise, pressing down on the peppercorns to release all the flavour, and stir well. Fold in the scallops carefully, making sure they are all coated with the sauce.

Cover two salad plates with lettuce leaves. Cut each cucumber half into 4 lengths and arrange the pieces, scooped-out side upwards, on top. Spoon the scallop mayonnaise into and over the cucumbers, scatter some dill fronds over the top, and serve. *Serves 2.*

SCALLOPS FLAMED IN BRANDY

12–14 scallops	*6–8 green peppercorns*
1 tablespoon brandy	

Put the brandy and the peppercorns in a saucepan and crush the corns slightly to release their aroma. Warm the pan, set the brandy alight, and add the scallops, shaking the pan constantly so that all of them are in contact with the flaming liquid.

Cook for no more than 1 minute, so that the scallops have just lost their translucency, and are warmed through rather than hot. They should retain their shape and slight squishiness. Transfer them to a pre-heated dish, pour the juices from the pan through a sieve over them and serve at once, on their own. *Serves 2.*

SCALLOPS GLAZED WITH SHERRY

8 scallops
2 tablespoons dry sherry

1 leek
unsalted butter

Marinate the scallops in half the sherry for 1 hour. Drain and dry, reserving the marinade.

Clean the leek, remove the tough tops and outer leaves, and chop the white part into thin rounds. Melt some butter in a shallow pan and cook the leek rounds until soft, then transfer them to two salad plates and keep warm in the oven.

Stir the scallops for 1 minute in the same butter, then take them out of the pan and keep warm. Turn up the heat, add the marinade and the second tablespoon of brandy and boil until the liquid is reduced to little more than a glaze. Put the scallops back in the pan, turning them in the glaze so that they are coated on all sides. Arrange them on the bed of leeks and serve. *Serves 2.*

SCALLOPS WITH GINGER BERNAISE

12–14 scallops
1 slice fresh ginger
1 shallot
2 tablespoons dry white wine
1 egg yolk

65 g (2 oz tablespoons)
*   unsalted butter, chilled*
salt
pepper

Peel and finely grate the ginger, peel and mince or chop the shallot, and put them both in a saucepan with the white wine. Cook over a medium heat until the shallot is cooked and the wine reduced to about ½ a tablespoon. Remove the pan from the heat, let it cool a little, then break in the egg yolk, stirring over a low heat until the mixture thickens slightly. Beat in the butter, cut into small, chilled cubes, a few at a time, until the mixture is thick and smooth and glossy golden. Season with salt and a small amount of pepper, and pour into a sauce boat, sprinkling the top with some shavings of ginger.

Steam the scallops over boiling water for 1 minute, or until the flesh loses its translucency, and serve with the ginger bearnaise. *Serves 2.*

SCALLOPS AND SWEET POTATO

12 scallops, preferably in their shells
1 medium, orange-fleshed sweet potato
2 tablespoons melted unsalted butter

2 tablespoons cream
4–6 pink peppercorns
16 sugar snap peas
black pepper, freshly ground

Choose a straight, slender sweet potato, as these cook more evenly. Bake it in a medium oven for about 45 minutes until ¾ cooked. Cut into 12 rounds. Butter a fireproof dish large enough to take the sweet potato slices in one layer. Put them in, grind over a little pepper, and brush the tops with melted butter. Cover with tinfoil and return to the oven to cook for another 15 minutes.

Meanwhile, shell the scallops. Detach the mantles and rinse them thoroughly under running water to get rid of any grit and sand trapped in the frilly edges. Drain on kitchen paper for a minute or so before blending with the cream and pink peppercorns. Pour into a saucepan, bring to the boil, lower the heat and simmer for 5 minutes, then withdraw from the heat and cool. As soon as the sauce is cold, put in the scallops and marinate for at least 1 hour.

Cook the sugar snap peas in boiling water for 1 minute. Drain, and return to the heat in the dry saucepan for a few seconds to get rid of any moisture. Arrange them between the rounds of sweet potato on the dish in the oven and keep warm.

Bring the sauce back to just below boiling and poach the scallops for 1 minute, until the muscle turns white and the flesh firms slightly. Place a scallop on each sweet potato round, spoon a little of the sauce over, and serve at once.

The mantle gives body and texture to the sauce as well as flavour. If you cannot find scallops in the shell get at least two extra to blend with the cream for the sauce. Alternatively, substitute Gin and Juniper Cream which gives a smoky, subtle flavour to the dish. *Serves 2.*

SCALLOP AND SWEET POTATO SOUP

6 scallops
1 orange-fleshed sweet potato
unsalted butter
200 ml (1 cup) chicken stock

1 tablespoon dry vermouth
pinch chilli powder
black pepper, freshly ground
chopped parsley for garnish

Peel the sweet potato. Cut it into cubes, and cook in a shallow pan with a little butter for a minute or so, stirring so that all the sides are coated. Pour in the chicken stock and the vermouth and bring to the boil.

Simmer for 10 minutes, or until the sweet potato is soft. Remove from the heat and cool. Add a pinch of chilli and a good grinding of black pepper, pour into a blender or food processor and blend until smooth. Return to the pan, and bring to the boil once more. Lower the heat, put in the scallops (and any liquid that has been strained off them, if they are defrosted ones) and cook very gently for 1 minute, remembering that they will go on cooking in the hot soup. Pour into warmed soup plates, and serve at once, sprinkled with finely chopped parsley. *Serves 2.*

SCALLOP AND SWEET POTATO SALAD

8 scallops
½ small, orange-fleshed sweet
   potato
2 tablespoons olive oil

½ tablespoon lemon juice
salt
black pepper, freshly ground
3 spinach leaves

Bake the sweet potato in its skin until soft. Cool. Remove the skin and cut the flesh into small cubes. Mix together the oil and lemon juice, salt and freshly ground pepper and pour some over the sweet potato. Grind over some extra pepper.

Heat some water in a shallow pan and poach the scallops for about 1 minute, until they lose their translucency. Drain, and add to the sweet potato. Drop the spinach leaves into the simmering water and remove them instantly with a slotted spoon. Drain on a piece of kitchen paper, slice the leaves into thin ribbons and drape them over the scallops.

Shake the remaining vinaigrette and pour over the salad. Served still warm, this is one of the best and simplest of seafood salads. *Serves 2.*

MARINATED, SKEWERED SCALLOPS

12–14 scallops	*squeeze lemon juice*
1 teaspoon curry paste	*salt*
1 tablespoon water	*pepper*

Mix together the curry paste, water, lemon juice, some salt and pepper in a bowl and marinate the scallops in this for at least 1 hour. Drain and thread onto skewers.

Preheat a grill to very hot and cook the scallops quickly for about 90 seconds, turning them once. They should be heated through, but still large, fat and juicy. Serve on their own, or with some boiled, buttered rice and a salad. *Serves 2.*

SCALLOPS AND BUGS IN PASTRY SHELLS

4–6 scallops, with 4 shells	*2 tablespoons ginger wine*
4–6 green Bugs	*1 piece fresh ginger, grated*
200 g (7 oz) puff pastry	*1 teaspoon lemon juice*
1 tablespoon dry white wine	*100 ml (½ cup) cream*

Roll out the pastry and cut into 4 pieces. Butter both sides of 4 deep scallop shells and press the pastry into one of them, then lay the second shell on top, pressing down to imprint the pattern on it. Trim the dough to fit the shells and put into a hot oven, placing them so that the convex side is uppermost.

Bake for 10 minutes. Remove the top shells and continue to bake for another 5 minutes, or until the pastry is risen and golden. Take them out of the oven. Cool on a rack for a few minutes, then remove the bottom shells (if you try to remove them while the pastry is still hot, the fragile shapes could break). Return the pastry shells to a low oven to keep warm.

Bring the wine, ginger wine, grated ginger and lemon juice to the boil and reduce the liquid by half. Add the cream, return to the boil, and cook to a smooth, rich, creamy-gold sauce. Lower the heat, add the scallops and bugs, and cook gently until the flesh turns opaque.

Place a shell on each plate, pile in the scallops, bugs and sauce, and top with the second shell. Serve immediately. *Serves 2.*

SCALLOP AND MUSSEL TERRINE

6–8 scallops
12–16 mussels
1 slice white bread without
  crusts
1 tablespoon milk
400 g (14 oz) snapper fillets
1 large egg, separated

pepper
nutmeg
60 g (3 tablespoons) unsalted
  butter
1 tablespoon gin
1 tablespoon crème fraîche

Beard, scrub and steam open the mussels. Shell them and set aside with the scallops. Soak the bread in the milk for 1 minute, then squeeze it dry and mince into breadcrumbs. Discard the skin and bones from the snapper fillets, and separate the egg.

Grind the fillets in a food processor or blender, add the egg yolk and process until smooth. Put in the breadcrumbs, some pepper and nutmeg, half the butter (softened) and half the gin. Pour the mixture into a bowl, cover with plastic wrap and chill for an hour. Take the bowl out of the fridge, whip the egg white stiffly and work into the mixture with the crème fraîche. Cover and return to the fridge to chill for a further 30 minutes or so.

Meanwhile, melt the rest of the butter in a saucepan and cook the scallops for 30 seconds. Add the mussels and the rest of the gin and flame, shaking the pan so that all the shellfish are impregnated with burning alcohol.

Line a terrine with buttered tinfoil and spread the bottom with some of the fish mixture. Arrange a layer of shellfish on top and continue to build up alternate layers, ending with the forcemeat. Cover with the ends of the tinfoil, put on the lid, place in a bain-marie of simmering water and cook in a pre-heated medium oven (100°C or 200°F) for 1½ to 2 hours. Cool at room temperature then refrigerate overnight for 24 hours before serving. *Serves 6.*

SCALLOP AND GRAPEFRUIT SALAD

6 scallops
100 ml (½ cup) dry white
  wine
1 grapefruit

1 teaspoon sugar
1 tablespoon crème fraîche
black pepper, freshly ground
mint for garnish

Poach the scallops in the white wine and set aside. Peel the grapefruit, discard the membranes from the segments, and sprinkle the flesh with the sugar, turning them over and over so that they are all impregnated.

Bring the wine back to the boil and reduce to about 1 tablespoonful. Stir in the crème fraîche, season with black pepper (or, better, mix some pepper with the sugar and macerate the grapefruit segments in it). Arrange the grapefruit with the scallops on salad plates. Pour over the dressing, scatter some finely chopped mint over the top, and serve. *Serves 2.*

SCALLOP CEVICHE

8 scallops
1–2 small red or green fresh
  chillies
juice 1 lime

2 tablespoons coconut milk
handful fresh coriander leaves
  for garnish

Discard the seeds from the chillies and put the pods into the lime juice. Add the scallops, turning them gently so that all sides are coated with the marinade.

Cover the dish and place in the refrigerator for at least 4 hours, or preferably overnight. The longer the chillies stay in the dish, the hotter the marinade will become. Taste it after an hour or so, and discard the chillies when the lime is spicy enough for your taste.

To serve, pour over the coconut milk and sprinkle with chopped coriander leaves. *Serves 2.*

SCALLOPS IN BASIL

14 scallops
100 ml (½ cup) dry white
  wine

2 tablespoons heavy cream
6–8 basil leaves
black pepper, freshly ground

In a shallow pan bring the white wine to the boil. Lower the heat and poach the scallops until the flesh turns white. Take them out and set aside.

Add the cream to the wine, bring to the boil and reduce by half to a rich, thick, smooth sauce. Mince or chop the basil very finely, add to the sauce with some freshly ground black pepper, and return the scallops to the pan to reheat.

Serve the scallops in their glossy, pale-green sauce on a bed of buttery, peppery spinach, contrasting the two greens. *Serves 2.*

SCALLOP SOUFFLÉ

8–10 scallops
100 ml (½ cup) dry white
  wine
4–6 pink peppercorns

1 large egg, separated
100 ml (½ cup) cream
1 tablespoon crème fraîche

Boil the white wine with the pink peppercorns until reduced to 1 tablespoonful, then set aside to cool. Detach the coral from 4 of the scallops and set aside.

Put the scallops, egg yolk, wine, peppercorns, cream and crème fraîche into a food processor or blender and process to a smooth puree. Beat the egg white until it stands in peaks, fold in the scallop mixture, and pour into two small, well-buttered, fireproof ramekins, adding the reserved corals halfway through so that they are well covered by the soufflé mixture.

Cook in a hot oven for 7–10 minutes. Serve them the instant they are ready, for there's nothing to hold up the fragile, airy puffs once they are removed from the heat and they collapse very quickly. However, they are so delicious—like scallop-flavoured air—that it's worth the effort to get them to the table immediately. *Serves 2.*

SCALLOPS AND HEART OF PALM SALAD

8 scallops
2 tablespoons dry white wine
2 tablespoons mayonnaise

black pepper, freshly ground
1 small tin heart of palm

Poach the scallops in 2 tablespoons of white wine and a little water for 30–60 seconds, just until the flesh loses its translucency. Remove from the pan and drain.

Reduce the poaching liquid to no more than 1 tablespoonful. Cool and mix with the mayonnaise and some freshly ground black pepper.

Drain the heart of palm and arrange on salad plates. Top with the scallops, and put some mayonnaise on the side. *Serves 2.*

Scampi

Scampo is the Italian name for a crustacean that belongs to the same family—Nephropsidae—as the northern hemisphere lobster. Scampi is the plural term. It's a much better name for the creatures than the English one which is, or was, Dublin Bay prawns (a title both cumbersome and incorrect: they aren't prawns) as it has the advantage of being short, simple and easy to remember. Unlike lobsters, scampi are found in both hemispheres. They are caught in waters as far north as the western coast of Britain, throughout the Mediterranean, especially in the Adriatic (the Italian connection); in the rich fishing grounds of the Gulf of Thailand; and along the eastern fringes of the Indian Ocean to the northern edges of Western Australia.

Like northern hemisphere lobsters, scampi have two large claws, but they are much smaller—usually about the same size as freshwater crayfish (yabbies), or large tiger prawns, but with thicker, meatier bodies. They have fragile shells like prawns, are pale pink in colour, and because of their size have very little meat in the claws. Wherever they are caught, the large part of the catch goes for export, and they are frozen for transport, packed side by side in shallow trays, sitting with their tails curved under them, all facing the same way and looking rather like frosty, pink-sugar-icing mice. Like all shellfish, they taste much nicer fresh than frozen, but for most people frozen is the only way they can buy them. They are usually displayed in their trays on the ice in fish markets and shops where they slowly defrost, so they should be cooked as soon as possible after purchasing, and never refrozen.

Even after freezing, however they have a sweet, delicate flavour, and are well worth buying, although the nicest way to eat them (poached and cooled, with lots of lemony mayonnaise) is best kept for when you can find fresh ones. They go very well with such vegetables as asparagus and artichokes.

To poach scampi, bring a wide, shallow pan of water to the boil. Lower the heat until the water is barely moving and put in the scampi. Poach for 2–3 minutes until pink and firm, then take them from the pan and cool.

Remove the undershell and loosen the flesh from the carapace. Arrange them sitting right way up with their tails curved underneath and the claws crossed in front. Serve with mayonnaise that has been sharped with lemon juice rather than vinegar.

SCAMPI WITH ARTICHOKE HEARTS

4 scampi
4 artichokes
6 tablespoons olive oil
2 tablespoons lemon juice

black pepper, freshly ground
parsley
fresh mint
1 soft-leaved lettuce

Cut off the tough tops of the artichokes, peel away the outer leaves, trim the stems, and cook them in plenty of lightly salted boiling water, uncovered, for 15–20 minutes.

While the artichokes are cooking, blend the olive oil and lemon juice with some black pepper and a generous quantity of parsley and mint to a smooth green sauce. Arrange the lettuce on four salad plates and set aside. As soon as the artichokes are cooked drain them, cut in half and remove the chokes, and pour a little of the vinaigrette over them. Steam the scampi for 3 minutes and remove the shells while they are still warm. Arrange the artichoke hearts and the scampi on top of the lettuce, pour over the sauce, and serve at once.

This very simple salad relies on everything being prepared just before serving. The artichokes and scampi must be warm, and the different flavours in the vinaigrette still fresh and distinct. *Serves 4.*

SCAMPI AND ASPARAGUS

6 scampi
150 g (6 spears) fresh
  asparagus
2 tablespoons dry white wine
black pepper, freshly ground

1 stick celery
unsalted butter
fresh parsley
fresh mint

Peel the asparagus, snap off the tough lower parts of the stems, and put these with its peel and the white wine in a saucepan with some freshly ground pepper and enough water to cover. Bring to the boil, lower the heat and simmer for 10 minutes. Strain the liquid and discard the peel and stems.

Cut the asparagus into short lengths. Bring the stock back to the boil and put in the asparagus and the scampi. Lower the heat and poach for 3 minutes. Check to see the scampi are cooked and remove them, with the asparagus tips, to a pre-heated serving dish. Cut along the shell edges of the membrane on the undersides of the shellfish, loosen the flesh with the fingers so that it will be easy for the eater to remove, and arrange on the centre of the dish, surrounded by the asparagus tips.

Strip the strings from the celery and cook it quickly in a little butter until slightly softened. Arrange a few of the slices on the dish, and add the rest to the asparagus stock and stems. Pour into a blender with the mint and parsley and whizz to a smooth sauce. Return to the heat, check the seasoning, and pour around the scampi. Sprinkle a little fresh parsley over the asparagus tips, and serve at once. *Serves 2.*

SCAMPI IN HERBS AND LEMON JUICE

6 scampi	*1 sprig each parsley, oregano,*
1 tablespoon unsalted butter	*basil and tarragon*
	juice ½ lemon

Shell the scampi. Melt the butter in a shallow pan, and stir them in it until the flesh turns white and firm, then add the chopped fresh herbs. Shake the pan for a few seconds more, add the lemon juice, swirl into the butter, and serve at once. *Serves 2.*

SCAMPI IN TOMATO CREAM

6 scampi	*unsalted butter*
1 large, ripe, red tomato	*black pepper, freshly ground*
150 ml (¾ cup) cream	*chopped chives for garnish*

Peel the tomato, remove the seeds, and puree in a blender with the cream until smooth and thick.

Melt some butter in a shallow pan. Shell the scampi, stir them in the butter until the flesh firms and whitens, then pour in the sauce.

Grate in some black pepper, bring to the boil and immediately remove from the heat. Arrange the scampi on a pre-heated serving dish, pour over the sauce, sprinkle with chopped chives and serve at once. *Serves 2.*

SCAMPI AND SPINACH IN VERMOUTH CREAM

6 scampi
1 bunch spinach
1 tablespoon butter

black pepper, freshly ground
150 ml (¾ cup) cream
2 tablespoons dry vermouth

Shell the scampi. Clean the spinach in many changes of water, strip out the central stems, and cook for no more than 1–2 minutes in the water still clinging to the leaves. Drain thoroughly and squeeze dry. Stir in 1 tablespoon of melted butter and plenty of ground black pepper, and divide into 2 lots. Place one half of the spinach into a blender with the cream and the vermouth, and blend to a smooth puree, then pour into a saucepan. Bring to the boil, simmer for 1 minute, add the rest of the spinach and simmer for 1 minute longer, and finally put in the scampi. Turn in the sauce until the flesh becomes firm and white, then arrange with the sauce and spinach on a pre-heated serving dish and serve at once. *Serves 2.*

SCAMPI IN WALNUT CRUMBS

6 scampi
1 tablespoon unsalted butter

60 g (2 oz) walnuts
2 tablespoons ghee

Shell the scampi and poach them for 1 minute in a shallow pan of water. Drain them on kitchen paper and coat with the melted butter.

Grind the walnuts finely and press the crumbs onto the scampi, covering all the surfaces thickly. Put them on a plate and place in the fridge to chill for 30 minutes.

Heat the ghee in a shallow pan until very hot and put in the scampi. Stir-fry over a high heat (the cold scampi will lower the temperature of the ghee considerably) until the walnut coating is brown and crisp. Drain for a few seconds on kitchen paper and serve at once, with a walnut tarator or baba ganoush and plenty of tabbouli. *Serves 2.*

SCAMPI AND PEACHES

6 scampi   pepper
2 ripe peaches   mint for garnish
1 tablespoon Pernod

Choose ripe, luscious peaches that are sweet and full of sugar, otherwise they taste disconcertingly sour when cooked. Poach the scampi and remove the membranes from the undersides, then loosen the flesh in the shells and set them aside.

Peel the peaches and cut into thin slices. Heat the Pernod and poach the slices (very gently so they don't break up) for 5 minutes or so. Remove them to the dish with the scampi, arrange the slices round the shellfish, and pour the juices from the pan over them (turn the scampi on their backs and drizzle some of the juices into the shells so that they can marinate in the liquid). Cover with plastic and set aside for at least 1 hour before serving, or preferably put in the refrigerator overnight, and take out at least 2 hours before it is needed. Sprinkle mint over the dish just before serving. *Serves 2.*

Sea-urchins

Some people never take to sea-urchins, usually for some reason totally unconnected with eating them—like having stepped on one at the age of four, and still remembering the agony it caused. However, this is not a logical attitude (indeed, one would think that eating them would be a sensible sort of revenge), as sea-urchins are a great delicacy.

They are fascinating creatures to watch, looking like spiky balls as they roll around the rock pools and shallows of the sea shore. There are several species, with spines varying in thickness from hair-thin to pencil-thick. But beware. They may look charming rolling about the rock pool, but the spines mean business, and they should be handled with very thick gloves and a lot of care.

Sea-urchins can occasionally be bought live at the fish markets, but they are most often sold already processed, with the roe presented and packed in little wooden boxes, ready to be eaten raw as sashimi. If live ones are available, or if you come across easily-handled ones in an unpolluted pool, they are quite easy to open with a pair of strong scissors. Cut around the equator of the sphere and open up the two halves. Inside, the five roe, separated each in its own compartment, are very easy to scoop out, either with a thin 'soldier' of bread and butter, or with a knife blade. Sprinkle the roe with pepper and a little lemon juice and eat them as they are, with the bread and butter. They have a smooth, rich flavour and texture, as though they have been blended with thick cream.

To eat as sashimi, arrange them on a plate with a mound of grated white radish, another of grated carrot, some shredded ginger and little bowls of soy sauce. A good contrast to their smooth richness is thinly sliced whiting, with its tight, firm texture, translucent flesh and sea-water flavour.

ARTICHOKES WITH SEA-URCHINS SAUCE

roe from 2 sea-urchins   *pepper to taste*
2 artichokes   *1 tablespoon sherry*
1 slice lemon   *1 tablespoon crème fraîche*
unsalted butter

Cut away all the outside leaves, trim the stems, and chop off the tops
of the artichokes. Rub the cut surfaces with a lemon, and cook in
plenty of boiling water, uncovered, for 20 minutes, or until a fork
pierces the stems easily. Drain, cut in halves, scoop out the chokes,
and brush with melted butter. Arrange on two small, pre-heated plates.
Sprinkle with pepper and keep warm.

   Put the urchin roe in a blender with the sherry, crème fraîche and
a little more pepper. Blend to a smooth consistency and pour into
a saucepan. Heat it carefully but don't let it boil or the urchin roe
will have a regrettable tendency to become lumpy and coagulate. When
hot enough pour over the artichoke halves and serve at once. *Serves 2.*

SEA-URCHINS WITH SCRAMBLED EGGS

roe from 1 sea-urchin   *black pepper, freshly ground*
2 eggs   *pinch chilli powder*
20 g (1 tablespoon) unsalted   *chives, finely chopped*
   butter

Beat the eggs, melt the butter in a saucepan and pour them in. Season
with freshly ground black pepper, a pinch of chilli, and lots of chopped
chives, and cook, stirring all the time, very slowly until the mixture
starts to thicken. Add the urchin roe. Stir until the correct consistency
(creamy-smooth and still slightly runny) and spoon onto buttered, hot
toast. Eat at once. *Serves 1.*

Snails

Snails have been eaten by humans for thousands of years. Excavations in Turkey have uncovered middens that included snail shells amongst those of crabs and mussels and small turtles. Ancient Romans considered them a delicacy: snails were bred in special enclosures and fed on milk, or bran and wine, before being cooked and served in the inevitable garum sauce. The Chinese roasted them; the Italians considered taking them from someone else's property to be stealing, punishable by a stiff fine; in England glassblowers thought that eating them would enhance their breathing capacities; and throughout medieval Europe snails were classified as 'abstinence fare', suitable to be eaten on the many fast days.

For eating, specially bred snails aren't necessary—common or garden ones will do just as well—but preparing live snails is a long, slow process, and one can't just leap into the garden after rain, crying 'Let's have snails for dinner tonight'. For a start, garden snails eat all sorts of things (including snail bait) that are toxic to humans, so they should be starved or fed for a week on non-toxic food such as lettuce leaves, fennel, milk or, like the Romans, oatmeal and wine—but I suggest you boil off the alcohol first, or they could all die of alcohol poisoning.

After a week of fattening, the snails should be cleansed of their slime by placing them in a bowl with plenty of coarse salt and some vinegar to just cover. Leave them, stirring occasionally, until they start to foam (about 10 minutes), then rinse them thoroughly under cold water. Boil a large pan of water, tip in the snails, boil them for five minutes and drain, plunging them into cold water to cool. As soon as they are cool enough to handle, take the flesh out of the shells by poking it out with a pin or wide-pronged fork, and remove the black intestinal tip at the very end of the snail. Rinse the shells, scrub them if necessary, boil them for ten minutes or so in a large quantity of water with a spoonful of vinegar or a pinch of bicarbonate of soda, and drain. Poke the snails back into their shells and cook them in a stock of water and wine, with a bay leaf, herbs (such as parsley, thyme and oregano), cloves, peppercorns and a small onion for two hours. And then, at last, after a week and three hours the snails are ready to be eaten.

There are, of course, some major difficulties inherent in this process. The quantity of snails to be found on the way home from the office, or on the balcony of a seventh-floor apartment, for instance, can be counted on the fingers of no hands. Perhaps while feeding the creatures for a week, one could become too fond of them to eat them—though it's probably more likely one would just forget them completely. But there is another avenue open to high-rise-dwelling snail lovers, and that is going into the nearest delicatessen and buying a can of French snails, already prepared, their shells attached in a cellophane bag. Then all you have to do is rinse away the brine they are packed in and choose your recipe.

SNAILS WITH GARLIC BUTTER

12 prepared snails
1 large clove garlic
1 small shallot
parsley

60 g (3 tablespoons) unsalted
butter
lemon juice

Crush the garlic, mince the shallot and some parsley, and mix with the softened butter until smooth. Season with a little lemon juice, and pack into the shells on top of the snails. Place the shells, opening upwards, on metal snail plates, or on fireproof plates well carpeted with rock salt into which the shells can settle without overturning. Cook in a hot oven for 5 minutes, until the butter is bubbling. Serve at once.

This is probably the most famous way of serving snails, and one of the most delicious. *Serves 2.*

SPANISH STUFFED SNAILS

12 prepared snails
1 small onion
1 clove garlic
olive oil
¼ red capsicum

1 ripe, red tomato
1 fresh red chilli
lemon juice
1 tablespoon fresh white
*   breadcrumbs*

Peel the onion and garlic, chop them both finely and cook in some olive oil until soft. Skin and seed the capsicum and the tomato, seed the chilli, chop them like the onion and garlic and add to the pan to cook for 5 minutes longer. Put in some lemon juice and the breadcrumbs and withdraw from the heat.

Mince or finely chop the snails and stir them into the mixture. When everything is well stirred press spoonfuls of it into each shell. Put the stuffed shells on snail plates on heatproof dishes carpeted with rock salt, and cook in a hot oven for 5 minutes. Serve at once.

For both the above dishes, snail holders and forks are really necessary, as it's difficult to get snails out of their shells. Partly for this reason, but also because it tastes good, the Spanish-stuffed snail recipe can be adapted to stuff vegetables such as zucchini. Choose medium-sized zucchini, cut them into short lengths, and remove the centres with an apple corer. Stuff the cavities with the snail mixture, place the zucchini in a well-buttered fireproof dish, pour in 2 tablespoons of wine and dot the vegetables with butter. Cover the dish and cook in a medium oven for 20 minutes. *Serves 2.*

SNAILS IN RED WINE

24 prepared snails
500 ml (2½ cups) water
150 g (5 oz) polenta
1 tablespoon olive oil

1 clove garlic
100 ml (½ cup) red wine
unsalted butter

Bring the water to the boil, pour in the polenta, and stir until the water returns to the boil. Lower the heat and continue to cook for 30 minutes, stirring frequently, especially towards the end as it starts to get very thick. When it has become very stiff, turn it out onto a board, shaping it quickly into an oblong, and leave it to cool completely before cutting it into small squares.

Heat the olive oil and chop the garlic. Cook it in the oil for a few minutes, then add the wine and bring to the boil. Lower the heat and simmer for 5 minutes.

If you have collected fresh snails, they should go into the sauce after they have been cleaned and shelled, to cook gently for 2 hours. If you can only get canned ones, let the sauce cook for an hour or so, and only add them to the pan for the last 5 minutes.

Place the squares of polenta on a grill rack, brush them with melted butter on all sides, and grill under a high heat until the outside is crisp and golden. Arrange the squares on a heated serving dish, pour over the snails in their sauce, and serve. *Serves 2.*

SNAILS WITH BEANS

24 prepared snails
200 g (1 cup) dried white
  beans
1 bay leaf
1 onion
40 g (2 tablespoons) unsalted
  butter

salt to taste
black pepper, freshly ground
1 clove garlic
1 tablespoon lemon juice
parsley for garnish

Cook the beans until soft with the bay leaf and the onion. Drain, discard the bay leaf, chop the onion, and mix in half the butter with a little salt and plenty of freshly ground black pepper. Place in a preheated bowl and keep warm.

Heat the rest of the butter in a saucepan and cook the minced garlic for a few seconds, then add the lemon juice and the snails. Stir them around so they become coated with the garlic-lemon butter and are heated through. Mix carefully with the beans, sprinkle with plenty of finely chopped parsley, and serve. *Serves 2.*

SNAILS IN MUSHROOMS

24 prepared snails
8 medium-size mushrooms
unsalted butter
salt and pepper to taste
1 clove garlic

1 tablespoon brandy
2 tablespoons thick cream
lemon juice (optional)
parsley

Remove the stems from the mushrooms and chop them finely. Wipe the caps inside and out with melted butter and set them aside, inside up, on a rack in a baking dish. Sprinkle with salt and pepper and cook in a medium oven (170°C or 350°F) for 10 minutes, or until they start to soften and release their liquid.

Melt some butter in a saucepan, mince the garlic and cook in the butter with the chopped mushroom stems, turning up the heat to evaporate the liquid. Pour in the brandy and the cream and boil to reduce by about half. Add the snails, stir in the sauce to heat them, check the seasoning and squeeze in a little lemon juice if the taste seems too bland. Spoon the snails and their sauce into the mushroom caps and bake for 5 minutes more. Sprinkle with finely chopped parsley before serving.

This is a very rich little first course, and doesn't need to be served with anything else, but a variation on the same theme is to use smaller mushrooms, cook them in the butter with the garlic, brandy and cream, and pile them, with the sauce and the snails, into pre-heated pastry cases such as vol-au-vents or feuilletes. Or make bread cases from firm bread and deep-fry them, and use these as holders instead. With this sort of treatment, and a green vegetable like broccoli to balance the flavours, the dish can become a smart main course instead. *Serves 4.*

SNAILS IN ROLLS

16 prepared snails
150 ml (¾ cup) milk and
  water mixed together
15 g (½ oz) fresh yeast
250 g (8 oz) plain flour
1 teaspoon salt

milk for glazing
unsalted butter
2 cloves garlic
1 handful chopped parsley
extra pinch salt

Warm the milk and water until just tepid and dissolve the yeast in it, stirring to ensure it dissolves evenly. Sift together the salt and flour into a bowl and mix in the yeast solution. Cover the bowl and leave to rise for 1–2 hours, or until it has risen to twice its original volume.

Punch the dough down, knead a little and divide into 16 pieces. Roll each into a ball, put on a floured surface, and press them out flat with the heel of the hand or a rolling pin. Place a snail in the centre of each and bring up the sides of the dough, folding them over the top like an envelope. Press the edges together to seal them, brush the tops with milk and cover them again to rest until they have regained their bulk and size (about 30 minutes should be long enough).

Pre-heat the oven to hot (200°C or 400°F), put the little rolls on a lightly floured baking sheet and bake for 20–30 minutes. Brush the tops with milk once more and return them to the oven for a few minutes longer, so that the tops are shiny and golden.

Melt some butter in a saucepan. Crush the garlic with a little salt and mix with the chopped parsley. Stir into the just-melted butter and serve with the little buns. Ideally, they should be broken open and a little of the sauce poured onto the snail inside before eating. *Serves 4.*

WALNUT-CRUSTED SNAILS

24 prepared snails
2 tablespoons ground walnuts
2 tablespoons fresh white
  breadcrumbs
1 clove garlic

fresh parsley, finely chopped
pepper to taste
2 tablespoons butter
oil or ghee for frying

Mix together the ground walnuts, breadcrumbs, crushed garlic and some finely chopped parsley and pepper. Brush the snails with melted butter and coat them with the walnut mixture, pressing it on each one firmly. Chill the snails for at least 30 minutes before cooking so that the coating dries, and then fry them in oil or ghee until crisp and golden on the outside. *Serves 2.*

TOMATO AND SNAIL CASSEROLE

24 prepared snails
1 onion
1 clove garlic
olive oil
2 large, ripe, red tomatoes

1 sprig each basil, rosemary
  and oregano
black pepper, freshly ground
1 tablespoon pesto

As with Snails in Red Wine, the snails for this recipe should be cleaned and shelled, but not fully cooked. If you can only get hold of the canned ones, add them 5 minutes before serving.

Peel the onion and garlic, chop them both finely, and cook in some olive oil until soft. Skin and seed the tomatoes, reserving all the juice, and chop the flesh roughly. Add the tomatoes and their juice to the pan, put in the herbs and a good grinding of black pepper, cover and simmer for 5 minutes. Add the snails and cook over a very low heat for 2 hours, or until the snails are tender.

To serve, remove the herbs from the sauce, and stir in the pesto just before the casserole goes to the table. *Serves 2.*

Squid

'The squid', writes Buchbaum in *Animals Without Backbones*, 'is one of the most highly developed of all invertebrates'. Squid are cephalopods, relatives of octopus and cuttlefish and, more distantly, of clams; for cephalopods are, or were, molluscs, but have outgrown their molluscness so to speak. The shell is no longer required for protection and has adapted and atrophied into a quill-shaped, transparent stiffening that is completely enclosed by the mantle. At this stage of their evolution, squid rely on intelligence and speed to get them out of trouble.

With the other cephalopods, squid are some of the most fascinating creatures in the sea, or indeed anywhere else. Like cuttlefish they have ten arms, two of which are longer than the rest and end in flat, suckered paddles, presumably for scooping up the food. These arms are attached to the head just below the eyes (which are very close in structure to human eyes), and surround the curved, parrot-like beak of a mouth. Squid can change colour and pattern with astonishing rapidity, and some deep-sea species are luminescent as well. They have large brains, well-developed nervous systems and complex sensory organs, and there are more than 100 different species spread throughout the world's oceans, living in habitats as varied as the lower depths of the Atlantic and the inshore shallows of Pacific islands.

They range in size from tiny, transparent creatures difficult to see without a microscope to real Monsters-of-the-Deep straight out of horror stories or sci-fi movies. There aren't all that many recorded sightings of these monsters, probably because of the depths at which they normally live. But one recorded as having been washed up, dead and decaying, on an Irish beach in the 1600s measured 6 m without its head. In 1860 the French warship *Alecton* met one in the Atlantic. It was nearly 18 m long, excluding tentacles, and 6 m in circumference. Another, washed up on an Australian beach, measured more than 7 metres.

Luckily however, these monsters (the largest of all invertebrates) keep to the deep ocean where the only predator they have is the sperm whale, which is specially adapted for squid eating. But even a creature as massive as a sperm whale might baulk at tackling something 18 m long—if the giant squid put up a battle as good as it got, it could be a moot point as to who was predating who. Squid that live close to shore are much smaller and easier to deal with and, although they can measure more than 90 cm and weigh over 1 kg, they are usually caught when they are between 7 cm and 30 cm long.

Squid of one sort or another are always available at the fish markets, although the species may vary. Most of the inshore ones are members of the family Loliginidae and the main commercial catch includes arrow or flying squid, which have long, slender mantles and short fins set to the rear, and (southern) calamari, which have rounder bodies and fins that stretch the full distance of the mantle. There are others available at various times, and they are all very good to eat.

Squid are tenderer than cuttlefish, with a sweeter, more subtle flavour, and are much easier to clean. Humans have eaten them for centuries: the Romans, according to Apicius, served them with rue and honey and boiled sweet wine (and, inevitably, garum); in Japan slender, milk-white squares are eaten raw as sashimi; the Chinese dry them, to add to such dishes as red-cooked pork; the Thais enliven the subtle flavour by adding tiny, fiery chillies; the Spanish use the ink as a dark, rich sauce to cook them in; the Italians serve minute specimens in exquisite salads of rice or fresh vegetables; and in France, as all round the Mediterranean, they are cooked in garlic, olive oil, tomatoes and red wine. Squid can be poached, grilled, or baked. They can be stuffed with pine nuts and ginger, rice and garlic, raisins and walnuts. They can be braised in soy sauce or coconut milk, red wine or rice vinegar. They can be marinated, steamed, stewed and deep-fried. Indeed, they can be cooked almost any way you like, but they must *never* be overcooked. The longer squid are exposed to heat, the tougher they become, and their smooth, silky sweetness rapidly turns into unpalatable rubber. So, cook them whatever way appeals, but for a few seconds only.

To clean squid, pull the head away from the mantle and all the inner organs will come away with it. Pull out the flexible transparent quill or shell from its envelope, rub off the mucus-like skin (unlike cuttlefish skin, this will peel off easily under running water), turn the hood inside out to rinse thoroughly, discard any inner organs still attached and peel away the transparent film-like inner skin (very small squid don't need to be skinned, just cleaned and rinsed). Cut the tentacles from the head just below the eyes so that all ten are still joined together by a thin rim of flesh, but unless the creatures are very large there is no need to skin these as they are slender and fragile and could easily break.

If the ink sacs are needed, set them aside as soon as the head is pulled out. There are two, attached to the organs behind the head. They are small, black and iridescent, and their size seems totally inadequate to hold the enormous amount of jet-black liquid which can shoot all over cook and kitchen as the result of one misguided movement.

Squid can be purchased fresh and whole; ready cleaned and skinned, either whole (mantle only) or sliced into rings; or cleaned and frozen—again, mantles only—in packs. The dense, tight, white flesh freezes well, so if that's the only way they are available there's no problem. They can also be bought crumbed and ready for frying, frozen in large packs, but I have a feeling that these are the ones that are so disappointing in some restaurants—vast, thick rings of chewy, stale-tasting rubbery substance coated with brown concrete. Fried calamari can be delicious, and are well worth cooking at home with care and attention.

DEEP-FRIED SQUID

2 squid mantles	*dried breadcrumbs*
1 egg	*oil for deep-frying*
pepper	

The tentacles aren't used for this dish, so buying ready cleaned and skinned hoods, whether fresh or frozen, means it can be prepared very quickly.

Beat the egg and season with pepper. Cut the hoods into thin rings and dip them first into the egg and then into the breadcrumbs, making sure all the surfaces are coated. Lay the rings on a dish and refrigerate for 30 minutes, or until ready to cook.

Heat enough oil for deep-frying in a heavy saucepan until a piece of bread turns brown in 1 minute. Drop in the squid rings, a few at a time, taking them out as soon as they turn crisp and golden—no more than 30–50 seconds. Drain them on kitchen paper and serve with wedges of lemon and sauces such as tartare or pine nut tarator.

Squid rings can also be cooked in the same batter as deep-fried cuttlefish. Again, cook them in the hot oil for no more than 30–50 seconds. *Serves 2.*

DEEP-FRIED SQUID WITH TOMATO SAUCE

2 medium-sized squid
100 ml (½ cup) water
2 ripe, red tomatoes
pepper
1 sprig fresh tarragon
1 bay leaf

100 ml (½ cup) red wine
light, tasteless cooking oil
60 g (3 tablespoons) plain flour
1 tablespoon crème fraîche
freshly chopped tarragon for
    garnish

Skin and clean the squid. Discard the guts, ink sacs and heads but retain the tentacles.

Cut the hood into small squares, lightly scoring the inside in a diamond pattern with a knife. Bring the water to the boil, toss in the squid squares and the tentacles, lower the heat at once, and poach for 30–50 seconds. Strain the squid from the stock, retaining the liquid, and drain the pieces thoroughly on kitchen paper.

Skin and seed the tomatoes and chop them roughly. Add to the stock with some pepper, the tarragon, bay leaf and wine. Simmer for 20 minutes. Rub through a fine sieve and return to the stove to reduce if necessary (this depends on the amount of liquid in the tomatoes. The sauce should have a rich, smooth consistency).

Heat some light, tasteless cooking oil to the point where a piece of bread will brown in 1 minute. Toss the well-dried squid pieces in flour, and cook them, a few at a time, until golden brown. Drain them on kitchen paper and keep warm in the oven until all the pieces are cooked.

Add the creme fraîche to the tomato sauce. Sprinkle on a small amount of freshly chopped tarragon, and serve with the squid. *Serves 2.*

SQUID WITH PEANUT SAUCE

2 medium-sized squid	*1 small fresh or dried red*
plain flour	*chilli*
1 small potato	*juice 1 lemon*
50 g (2 tablespoons or 1½ oz)	*olive oil*
unsalted peanuts	

Clean the squid, discard the ink sacs, heads and guts and remove the skin. Rinse thoroughly to remove any grit or sand and set aside.

Just before cooking, toss the hoods and tentacles in flour. Boil the potato until cooked, and skin and mash it as soon as it's cool enough to handle. Grind the peanuts, seed and mince the chilli, and mix them both with the potato and 1 tablespoon of lemon juice. Put the mixture into a bowl and chill for at least 1 hour.

Heat 2 tablespoons of olive oil in a frying pan. Add the lightly-floured squid and stir-fry for 30 seconds. Add the potato, peanut sauce and another tablespoon of lemon juice and continue to cook very gently for 1 minute until the squid is done, adding more olive oil or lemon juice if the sauce is too heavy.

The best way to serve this is on its own, with a tomato salad to follow. *Serves 2.*

CALAMARI AL NERO

400 g (14 oz) small squid	*2 cloves garlic*
1 tablespoon olive oil	*juice ½ lemon*

Clean the little squid and discard the guts, heads and quills but retain the tentacles and the ink sacs. Skin the hoods, dry them inside and out and set aside with the tentacles.

Heat the olive oil in a shallow pan. Put in the squid and cook for 1 minute, stirring constantly. Take out and keep warm on a pre-heated dish in the oven. Prick the ink sacs and carefully press out the ink into the pan. Add the crushed garlic and the lemon juice and simmer gently for 5 minutes. Return the squid to the pan to heat through gently, but don't let it boil.

Serve at once, with rice. *Serves 2.*

GRILLED STUFFED SQUID

400 g (14 oz) small squid   *50 g (2 tablespoons) fresh*
1 small onion   *white breadcrumbs*
1 clove garlic

Skin the squid and discard the guts and quill but retain the tentacles. Rinse the hoods inside and out, dry them thoroughly, then cut off the flaps and mince them with the tentacles.

Peel and finely chop the onion, crush the garlic, and cook them gently in a little olive oil until soft. Add the minced squid and continue to cook for 30 seconds. Stir in the breadcrumbs and withdraw from the heat. Spoon the mixture into the hoods, leaving them no more than ¾ full to allow for expansion, and close the mouths with toothpicks. Brush with olive oil and place on a grid under a hot grill to cook for 2–3 minutes, turning them once.

Serve with rice and any of the leftover stuffing. *Serves 2.*

CALAMARI SALAD

300 g (10 oz) small squid   *vinaigrette*
pepper   *1 carrot*
lemon juice   *4–6 leaves soft-leaved lettuce*
½ cucumber   *mayonnaise*
1 zucchini   *parsley*

Skin the calamari and remove the ink sacs and guts. Rinse in plenty of cold running water and dry thoroughly. Cut the hood into rings, leaving the tentacles whole. Bring a saucepan of water to the boil and poach the calamari for no longer than 30–40 seconds. Drain and sprinkle with pepper and a little lemon juice.

Peel and seed the cucumber, slice it with the zucchini into matchsticks, and salt them both in a colander for 30 minutes. Rinse them under running water, dry on kitchen paper and toss in vinaigrette. Peel the carrot, discard the inner core if it's an old one, and slice into the same size batons as the other vegetables. Blanch for 1 minute in boiling water. Drain, dry, and mix with the zucchini and cucumber.

Arrange the lettuce on salad plates. Heap the calamari in the centres, and surround with the vegetables. Spoon some mayonnaise over the calamari, scatter with finely chopped parsley and serve. *Serves 2.*

GINGER-STUFFED SQUID

400 g (14 oz) squid
2 slices fresh ginger
1 generous handful fresh
  coriander leaves
60 g (3 tablespoons) pine nuts

6–8 peppercorns
dried breadcrumbs
tasteless vegetable oil for
  frying

Clean the squid, discard the ink sacs and guts, and place the flaps and tentacles in a blender or food processor with the ginger, coriander, pine nuts and peppercorns. Process until all the ingredients are well minced and mixed, then stuff the hoods about ¾ full with the mixture. Seal the openings by sewing or with toothpicks. Dip each stuffed squid in beaten egg before rolling in the breadcrumbs. Chill for at least 30 minutes to dry the coating.

Heat some tasteless vegetable oil in a deep saucepan until a piece of bread will turn brown in 1 minute. Fry the squid, a few at a time, until the breadcrumbs are crisp and golden (no more than 1–2 minutes, or they will become tough). Serve with fresh tomato sauce plentifully flavoured with ground cumin. *Serves 2.*

SQUID AND RICE SALAD

100 g (3½ oz) tiny squid
100 g (3½ oz) long-grain rice,
  preferably Basmati
vinaigrette
black pepper, freshly ground

salt
1 tablespoon mint leaves
1 tablespoon basil leaves
½ red capsicum

The best rice for salads of this sort is Basmati, which adds its own subtle perfume to the dish, and remains separate and unbroken when mixed with other ingredients. Cook it in boiling water for 10 minutes, then drain and toss to get rid of any moisture, and mix in some vinaigrette and plenty of freshly ground pepper with a little salt to taste.

Clean the squid (but don't skin it) and discard the guts, ink sacs and heads. Poach the tentacles and hoods for no more than a few seconds. The tentacles will curl back on themselves so that they look like tiny purple flowers, and the hoods will swell into shell-like shapes of different colours. Dry them all on kitchen paper and fold into the rice.

Chop the herbs very finely, skin and seed the capsicum and cut into small dice, and mix them all into the rice, adding more salt and pepper and vinaigrette if necessary. Set the salad aside for at least 1 hour so that all the flavours come together, and serve as a first course, or part of a smorgasboard. *Serves 2.*

SQUID AND MUSHROOM SALAD

100 g (3½ oz) tiny squid
100 g (3½ oz) small white
  mushrooms
1 tablespoon lemon juice
1 tablespoon olive oil

pinch mustard
pinch pepper
salt to taste
1 large handful chives,
  chopped

Clean the squid, discard the guts, ink sacs and heads. Poach the hoods and tentacles for a few seconds. Drain on kitchen paper.

Dice the mushrooms into small cubes. Mix together the lemon juice, oil, mustard, salt and pepper and pour over the mushrooms and the squid. Chop lots of chives, mix into the salad, and leave aside for at least 1 hour before serving. *Serves 2.*

SQUID SOUP

300 g (10 oz) medium-sized
  squid
½ red capsicum
1 tomato
1 carrot
1 small potato
1 clove garlic
1 stick celery

1 tablespoon olive oil
200 ml (1 cup) water
2 tablespoons fresh tomato
  puree
1 sprig each tarragon, oregano
  and rosemary
black pepper, freshly ground

Clean and skin the squid, discard the guts and ink sacs, and chop the hoods and tentacles roughly. Skin and seed the red capsicum and tomato. Peel the carrot, potato and garlic, string the celery and dice them all finely. Heat the olive oil and fry the carrot, celery and potato for 5 minutes, then lower the heat, cover the pan, and continue to cook for another 5–10 minutes, or until the potato and carrot are almost cooked.

Push the vegetables to one side and add the squid to the pan. Raise the heat and fry in the oil for a few seconds. Pour in the water and bring to the boil with the red capsicum and the tomato puree. Simmer for 5 minutes. Stir in the chopped tomato and the finely chopped herbs with plenty of black pepper, check the seasoning, and serve. *Serves 4.*

STUFFED SQUID FETTUCINE

2 medium-sized squid	1 sprig each parsley, oregano,
1 onion	rosemary
2 cloves garlic	2 tablespoons olive oil
1 tomato	black pepper, freshly ground
1 slice white bread without	2 tablespoons tomato puree
crusts	250 g (8 oz) thin fettucine
	salt

Clean the skin the squid, discard the guts and ink sacs, dry thoroughly, then mince or chop the wings and tentacles very finely.

Peel the onion and garlic. Skin and seed the tomato. Grate the bread to fine crumbs, and chop the herbs very finely.

Dice the onion, crush the garlic, mix them together and set half the mixture aside. Cook the rest in olive oil until soft, add the chopped squid and some of the herbs, stir-fry for 30 seconds, then combine the mixture with the breadcrumbs, black pepper and 2 teaspoons of the tomato puree. Spoon the stuffing into the squid hoods, leaving enough room to allow for expansion during cooking, and seal the opening with toothpicks or by sewing them up (it doesn't matter if all the stuffing isn't used, as it can just be added to the sauce). Pour the rest of the oil into the pan, turn up the heat and fry the squid for 1 minute turning so that all sides are exposed to the heat. Remove and drain.

Put the rest of the garlic and onion into the oil and cook until soft. Add the tomato, tomato puree, and the rest of the herbs and simmer for 10 minutes. Return the squid to the pan and cook gently for another 3–5 minutes, or until the flesh can be easily pierced with a fork (but remember that squid get tougher the longer they cook and 3 minutes should be the most they require).

Bring a large pan of water to the boil and cook the pasta with a little salt and a spoonful of oil to stop it from sticking. Drain thoroughly and arrange around the edges of a pre-heated dish.

Cut the squid (with a very sharp knife, otherwise all the filling will squish out) into slices and place in the centre of the dish. Pour the sauce over the top and serve at once. *Serves 2.*

SQUID WITH PEAS

4–6 medium-sized squid
200 g (7 oz) fresh green peas
1 small onion
1 clove garlic
½ small green capsicum

2 tablespoons olive oil
1 slice white bread
1 sprig parsley
black pepper, freshly ground

Clean and skin the squid, discard the guts and ink sacs and chop the wings and tentacles finely. Drain on kitchen paper and set aside. Shell the peas, cook them for 2–3 minutes in boiling water, and strain.

Peel the onion, garlic and capsicum and chop them all finely. Heat the oil in a frying pan and cook the onion until soft. Add the capsicum, garlic and chopped squid and cook for 1 minute more.

Blend the bread to fine crumbs and stir into the mixture with the chopped herbs and plenty of black pepper. Spoon the stuffing into the squid hoods, filling them no more than ¾ full. Close the openings with toothpicks or by sewing them up, and stir-fry in the oil until lightly browned on all sides. Lower the heat, put back into the pan any left-over stuffing and the peas, put on the cover and continue to cook gently for 3–5 minutes, or until the squid is tender.

A spoonful of water can be added if the squid seem to be drying out too much, but the dish should be dry rather than sloppy, and the squid themselves will give off some liquid. The peas and the shellfish absorb each other's tastes while retaining their own specific textures, and they taste delicious. This is best served on its own, with a salad to follow. *Serves 2.*

SQUID ON SKEWERS

4 large squid
1 clove garlic
1 sprig each rosemary, thyme
  and oregano

1 tablespoon lemon juice
3 tablespoons olive oil
pinch chilli powder
dried breadcrumbs

Clean the squid, discarding everything except the hoods. Score the inside of the flesh lightly, then cut into small squares. Crush the garlic, mince the herbs, and blend them together with the lemon juice, olive oil, and chilli powder. Pour over the squid and marinate for at least 2 hours, turning occasionally so that all the surfaces are covered.

Drain the squid pieces and toss in the breadcrumbs. Thread onto the skewers and grill (preferably over charcoal) for no more than 2 minutes.

Serve with the marinade as a sauce. *Serves 2.*

BARBECUED SQUID

400 g (14 oz) small squid
black pepper, freshly ground
1 clove garlic
1 sprig rosemary
lemon juice
olive oil

Clean the squid and discard the guts, pen and ink sacs. Just below the eyes cut off the tentacles so that they are joined together by a thin rim of flesh. Skin the hoods if you wish, but it's not necessary. Sprinkle the squid with black pepper. Crush the garlic, chop the rosemary, combine with some lemon juice and olive oil and pour over the squid. Cover and leave to marinate for at least 1 hour, or until they are to be cooked.

To cook, heat a hotplate until very hot and wipe it with some olive oil. Drain the squid and grill them, constantly turning and brushing with the marinade, for about 2 minutes. They will swell up, and quickly brown on the outside, leaving the inside white and tender and the tentacles will crisp slightly. Make sure they don't cook any longer, or they will become tough.

This is one of the easiest and nicest ways of cooking and eating squid. They can also be cooked on a grid over hot coals.

JAPANESE GRILLED SQUID

200 g (7 oz) cleaned, skinned
*   squid hoods*
3 tablespoons mirin
½ tablespoon dark soy sauce
1 teaspoon lemon juice
1 slice fresh ginger, grated

Only the hoods are used for this, so ready skinned and cleaned ones are fine.

Slit the hoods so that they open flat and score the inner side in a diamond pattern. Mix the mirin, soy sauce, lemon juice and ginger together and pour over the squid. Leave to marinate for an hour or so, turning occasionally to make sure all sides are well impregnated.

Drain the hoods from the marinade. Thread them flat on small skewers. Arrange them along the sides from the pointed tail end to the top of the triangular piece of flesh (or thread the skewers diagonally, crossing them in the centre like a brace). Place them on a grid over very hot coals and cook for 30–50 seconds on each side, turning once and basting with the marinade. Serve at once.

These marinated squid should taste slightly burnt on the outside and soft and tender inside. They cook very quickly because of the action of the marinade, so unless they are very large 30 seconds each side should be ample. *Serves 2.*

CALAMARI RIBBONS

200 g (7 oz) cleaned, skinned
 squid hoods
black pepper, freshly ground
1 tablespoon dry vermouth

4 tablespoons water
1 tablespoon crème fraîche
1 handful chervil

Cut the squid into narrow ribbons and sprinkle with pepper. Bring the dry vermouth (the French Noilly Prat has a subtle flavour which goes perfectly with shellfish) to the boil with 4 tablespoons of water in a shallow pan. Simmer for 2 minutes. Lower the heat so that the liquid is no longer bubbling and put in the squid ribbons. Poach them for no more than 30 seconds, then drain on kitchen paper and place on a pre-heated dish to keep warm.

Raise the heat under the pan, add the crème fraîche, and boil until reduced to a rich, smooth consistency. Meanwhile, chop the chervil finely and add it to the sauce. Check for seasoning, adding some more pepper if necessary, and return the squid ribbons to the pan to reheat (but make sure the sauce doesn't boil, or they will toughen) for a minute or so.

Serve the ribbons with thin pasta, or on a bed of spinach, or with a warm salad of zucchini matchsticks, snow peas and tiny tomatoes. *Serves 2.*

Casseroles &
Other Combinations

Combinations of shellfish range from austerely elegant arrangements of one scallop, one mussel, one oyster and a spray of fennel to hearty, heavy slices of polenta packed with mussels and clams. In between range regional celebrities such as Spanish paella, American jambalaya and gumbo, and French bouillabaisse. And of course, Italian fritto misto, and North African couscous. The following recipes are really a cross-section of methods that can be used rather than faithful reproductions of regional dishes—an attempt to get to the spirit of the food, so to speak. If one of the shellfish specified isn't available, either buy more of those that are, or something different—cockles instead of clams, for instance.

For most of these dishes there is a fair amount of preparation involved as the shells have to be cleaned and scrubbed, or soaked in many changes of salted water, or both. Because of this and because the amounts that need to be purchased make more sense (it's hard to buy two oysters, or one scallop), most of the following recipes are for four or more people. Specific instructions as to how to shell and clean any shellfish will be found in its own section.

JAMBALAYA

1 jar oysters
12 scallops
500 g (16 oz) cockles
400 g (14 oz) green medium-
    sized prawns
2 fresh hot chillies
2 onions
2 cloves garlic

1 slice fresh ginger
oil
1 red and 1 green capsicum
2 ripe, red tomatoes
2 drops Tabasco
pinch each black and green
    pepper

'Jambalaya' (like 'gumbo', 'chowder', 'bouillabaisse', 'paella' or 'suppa de pesce') is a word whose meaning is as elastic and all-embracing as the ingredients which go into the pot. While each one has some ingredient or cooking method which differentiates it from the others (okra for a gumbo, for instance, or the use of milk as the cooking liquid in a chowder), they all make use of their local varieties of seafood.

First of all, strain the liquid from the jar of oysters into a saucepan. Seed the chillies, cut into thin strips, add to the oyster liquid and bring to the boil. Lower the heat, cover and simmer for 30 minutes.

Soak and scrub the cockles, remove the black trail from the scallops, peel the prawns and add the shells to the oyster stock. Set the shellfish aside.

Peel and thinly slice the onions and garlic, shred the ginger, and cook in a little oil until the onion is soft. Cut the capsicums into thin strips, discarding the seeds and white pith, and add them to the pan. Peel the tomatoes and squeeze out the seeds over a sieve, rubbing the juice through into a basin. When the capsicum has cooked for 5 minutes, add the roughly chopped tomatoes and their juice, the oyster liquid, a little black and green pepper and Tabasco to the pan. Put on the lid, and simmer gently for 30 minutes, or until the sauce is rich, dark and aromatic.

Add the cockles to the pan first and stir for 30 seconds. Add the scallops and prawns, cook for 1 minute longer, and last of all add the oysters. Check the seasoning—it should be spicy and hot but not fiery—and serve at once with polenta or rice. *Serves 6.*

SHELLFISH POLENTA

250 g (8 oz) assorted shellfish:	*200 g (7 oz) polenta*
small squid, mussels,	*2 tablespoons olive oil*
cockles, prawns	*2 tablespoons butter*
500 ml (2½ cups) fish stock	*black pepper, freshly ground*

Clean and skin the squid, cut the hood into small squares and chop the tentacles roughly. Scrub the mussels and the cockles, removing beards and barnacles. Bring the fish stock to the boil, lower the heat, and drop in the shellfish a few at a time to cook. First the prawns, fishing them back out as soon as they turn pink; next the mussels and the cockles, lifting them out as soon as the shells open; and last the squid pieces, poaching them for no more than 1 minute, until the flesh turns pearly white. Peel the prawns, shell the cockles and mussels, and tip any liquid from the shells back into the stock.

Pour the liquid through a fine, muslin-lined sieve into a heavy-based saucepan. Return to the boil, grind in some black pepper, and pour in the polenta slowly, stirring all the time to make sure it doesn't go lumpy. Cook over a low heat for 15–20 minutes, stirring occasionally, until the mixture becomes very thick and leaves the sides of the pan cleanly. Remove from the heat. Mix the shellfish into the polenta, and pour into a straight-sided, shallow, well-buttered dish. Cool to room temperature, then cover and refrigerate for at least 4 hours, and preferably overnight.

Turn the polenta out onto a board and cut into small squares. Heat the oil and butter together in a frying pan and cook the squares until crusty and golden on all sides.

Serve them hot, with a sauce to dip them in—fresh tomato sauce, say, or capsicum sauce, or even a hot chilli and tomato sauce. But don't make it too fiery or it could destroy the taste of the shellfish.

This is extremely heavy and solid food, and is probably better served in very small pieces with drinks at a party, rather than as a meal in itself. In small doses, however, these crisply-golden, shellfish-packed pies are delicious.

CIOPPINO

1 green spanner crab	*1 fresh hot chilli*
12 cockles or clams	*1 sprig each rosemary, thyme,*
12 scallops	*parsley*
12 green medium-sized prawns	*1 bay leaf*
2 tablespoons olive oil	*200 ml (1 cup) red wine*
1 leek	*2 ripe, red tomatoes*
1 onion	*1 spring onion, finely chopped*
1 clove garlic	

Scrub the cockles or clams and leave them to soak in salted water and oatmeal for at least 6 hours, changing the water 2 or 3 times. Peel the prawns and the scallops and set aside.

In a large saucepan, heat the olive oil. Peel the leek and onion and slice them thinly. Crush the garlic, seed the chilli and chop them finely with the herbs. Cook them all in the oil until the onion is soft. Pour in the wine and ½ cup of water, bring to the boil and simmer for 5 minutes. Put in the crab and continue to cook for 7 minutes, then take it out and plunge into cold water to stop the cooking process.

As soon as it's cool enough to handle, remove the flesh from the body, crack the claws, and set them aside with the scallops and prawns.

Tie the crab shells up in a piece of muslin and return them to the pan. Peel and seed the tomatoes, chop them roughly, add them as well, and simmer for 20 minutes before taking out and discarding the muslin bag full of crab shells.

Turn up the heat, take off the lid and boil the soup vigorously for 5 minutes. Lower the heat once more and put in the cockles to cook for 30 seconds before adding the scallops and prawns. Cook for 30 seconds longer, then add the crab meat and claws and stir gently into the soup so that they are warmed through. Ladle into four pre-heated soup plates, sprinkle the finely chopped spring onion on top, and serve at once, with plenty of fresh bread. *Serves 4.*

SHELLFISH FRITTO MISTO

2 medium-sized squid
8 green medium-sized prawns
8 scallops
8 clams
1 small egg
30 g (2 tablespoons) dried breadcrumbs

tasteless vegetable oil for frying
80 ml (⅓ cup) beer
30 g (2 tablespoons) self-raising flour
30 g (2 tablespoons) plain flour

Clean the squid and discard everything except the hoods. Skin them, cut into narrow rings, and dry thoroughly on kitchen paper. Beat the egg and dip the rings first into the egg and then into the breadcrumbs. Put them on a plate and into the refrigerator for at least 30 minutes to allow the coating to dry.

Peel the shells, leaving on the tail shells, and remove the trails. Shell the scallops and the clams. Clean and rinse them under cold running water, then drain on kitchen paper. Heat some tasteless vegetable oil in a deep pan until a piece of bread turns brown in 1 minute. Just before cooking, blend together the beer and the self-raising flour, and dip in the scallops and clams. Dust the prawns with the plain flour. Cook them all with the squid rings, a few at a time in the hot oil, taking each piece out as soon as it turns golden and crisp. Drain on kitchen paper and serve at once, with plenty of lemon quarters. *Serves 4.*

SHELLFISH SALAD

4 blue swimmer crabs
8 green bugs
16 green medium-sized prawns
8 New Zealand green mussels
   or
16 black mussels
8 scallops in the shell
8 oysters

6 tablespoons olive oil
2 tablespoons lemon juice
2 tablespoons crème fraîche
pepper
1 handful mint leaves
lemon slices, parsley, mint,
   sorrel, and tiny tomatoes to
   garnish

Clean and steam all the shellfish except the oysters. Crabs take 8–10 minutes to steam; bugs 5–8 minutes; prawns 2–4 minutes; mussels and scallops 1–2 minutes.

Twist off and crack the crab claws, take the meat from the bodies and pile into the top shells (break off the brittle undersides). Cut away the tough membrane from the bugs and loosen the flesh in the shell. Peel the centre section of the prawns, leaving on the heads and tails. Check the mussels for any beard or grit, discard the tough outer rings and separate the flesh from the ligaments. Discard the flat scallop shells, leaving the meat in the deep half. Cover a large, flat serving dish with a bed of lettuce and arrange all the shellfish (not forgetting the oysters) on top.

Blend together the oil, lemon juice, crème fraîche, some pepper and finely minced mint to a smooth green sauce. Drizzle a little into each shell and pour the rest into a bowl to be served separately. Decorate the plate with lemon slices, sprigs of parsley and mint and strips of sorrel. Scatter some tiny Tom Thumb tomatoes between the shells and serve. *Serves 8.*

SHELLFISH AND BROCCOLI

24 cockles
6 small squid
24 green medium-sized prawns
24 mussels
500 g (1 lb) kingfish cutlets
200 ml (1 cup) dry white wine
1 onion
2 cloves garlic
1 red capsicum

2 ripe, red tomatoes
1 fresh red chilli
1 sprig each sage, parsley,
   basil and mint
2 tablespoons olive oil
1 large head broccoli
few threads saffron
salt and pepper to taste

Scrub the cockles and soak them in many changes of salted water for at least 6 hours. Skin the squid, discarding the ink sacs and guts. Rinse and dry the hoods and cut into rings but leave the tentacles whole. Peel the prawns, clean and beard the mussels, remove the skin and bones from the kingfish cutlets and chop the flesh into large cubes.

Place the fish bones and skin and the prawn shells in a saucepan with the wine and add enough water to cover. Bring to the boil and simmer for 20 minutes. Strain the stock through a fine sieve, pressing down on the shells to extract all the flavour.

Peel and slice the onion and garlic. Skin and seed the capsicum and tomatoes, remove the seeds from the chilli and slice them all roughly. Chop the herbs finely.

Heat the oil in a large saucepan and put in the chilli. Stir for a few seconds, then add the fish cubes and the prawns and stir-fry for 1 minute, making sure all sides are sealed. Remove the fish and prawns from the pan and set aside. Cook the onion until soft in the same oil, add the garlic, capsicum, herbs and tomatoes, pour in the stock and bring to the boil. Lower the heat, cover the pan and simmer for 30 minutes.

Place a steamer over the pan and steam open the mussels and cockles, tipping their juice into the sauce below as they open. Arrange them on the half shell and set aside with the prawns and fish. Cut the thick base from the broccoli, peel off the outer layer of the stems, separate into small heads and steam for no more than 5 minutes. Place in a deep bowl and keep warm in the oven with the fish and shellfish.

Bring the soup to the boil and reduce by around one-third. Check the seasoning, crumble a few threads of saffron into it and pour over the broccoli, fish and shellfish. Serve at once, with plenty of bread. *Serves 8.*

SEAFOOD CASSEROLE

200 g (7 oz) clams or cockles
200 g (7 oz) small green
*   prawns*
8 scallops
1 small cooked spanner crab
1 shallot

200 ml (1 cup) dry white wine
1 tablespoon brandy
150 ml (¾ cup) cream
pinch cayenne pepper
chopped chives for garnish

Scrub the clams or cockles and soak them for at least 6 hours in salted water (and oatmeal, if using clams).

Skin the shallot, chop or mince finely, and put into a saucepan with the wine and brandy to simmer for 5 minutes. Peel the prawns and add the shells, preferably tied up in muslin so that they are easy to lift out. Continue to simmer for another 20 minutes. Discard the prawn shells, pressing out as much liquid from the bag as possible.

Place a muslin-lined steamer over the pan and steam open the clams, removing them as soon as the shells open and tipping the liquid into the pan below. Shell them and set aside. Poach the prawns and the scallops in the liquid for 30 seconds. Take them out and set aside with the clams.

Turn up the heat under the pan so that the stock comes to a rapid boil, and reduce to about ¾ cup. Pour in the cream and bring back to the boil. Add the shellfish, stir in a pinch of cayenne pepper, and heat everything through. Serve at once, liberally sprinkled with chopped chives. *Serves 4.*

SCALLOP AND BUG TAIL MOUSSE

14 scallops   *1 egg, separated*
6 small green bugs   *black pepper, freshly ground*
* or 6 frozen bug tails*   *150 ml (¾ cup) heavy cream*

Rinse the scallops quickly under cold running water and drain them thoroughly on absorbent paper. Shell the bugs, and set 4 aside. Put the other 2 with the scallops and the egg yolk into a blender or food processor and process to a smooth puree, then add the egg white and blend again. Finally, grind in a little black pepper, pour in the cream, and blend once more. Pour the mixture into a buttered terrine or other deep, fireproof dish. Smooth the top and cover with a lid or tinfoil, then place it in a shallow pan of simmering water and put into a moderate oven (170°C or 350°F) for 25–30 minutes. Take it out of the oven and let it cool for a few minutes.

Meanwhile, poach the remaining bug tails in a little water and keep them warm. Unmould the terrine, arrange the bug tails on top, and serve with a saffron and cream sauce. *Serves 4.*

PASTA WITH SEAFOOD AND PRAWN SAUCE

4 green mussels
1 small cutlet fresh eel
4 scallops
6 prawn killers (mantis
* shrimp)*
2 tablespoons dry white wine
1 leek

butter
1 tablespoon cream
1 tablespoon sour cream
black pepper, freshly ground
500 g (1 lb) mixed green and
* white fettucine*

Scrub and beard the mussels, then steam them open over a pan of boiling water. Strain the liquid into the pan, take out the meat, discard the shells, and cut each mussel in half. Skin the eel and separate the flesh from the bones so that there are 4 tiny fillets. Clean the scallops and cut in halves.

Pour the white wine into the mussel liquid and continue to simmer, uncovered, for 5 minutes, then remove from the heat. Put in the prawn killers and poach them for about 1 minute (prawn killers go from soft to collapsed without ever reaching firm), shell the creatures and discard the carapaces, placing the flesh in a blender or food processor. Peel and clean the leek. Cook in some butter until soft, then add to the blender with the stock, the cream, sour cream and some black pepper, and blend until smooth. Pour back into the pan, bring to the boil, and simmer, uncovered, until it reaches the consistency of cream.

Cook the pasta in plenty of boiling water to which a little salt and oil have been added and strain. Stir the scallops into the sauce, add the eel, mussels and lastly the fettucine. Continue to stir for only a few seconds more, then transfer to a pre-heated serving bowl and serve at once. This is a fairly runny sauce, and although salty from the prawn killers it's very good indeed with pasta. *Serves 4.*

LEEKS AND SHELLFISH

250 g (8 oz) cockles or clams
500 g (1 lb) mussels
200 g (7 oz) green prawns
6 scallops
2 leeks

50 g (2 tablespoons) unsalted
* butter*
1 clove garlic
200 ml (1 cup) dry white wine
black pepper, freshly ground
parsley for garnish

Scrub the cockles and soak in salted water for at least 6 hours. Scrub and beard the mussels and shell the prawns.

Peel the leeks, slice them thinly and cook in the butter with the garlic until the leek slices are soft but not brown. Pour in the wine, grind in a little black pepper and simmer for 5 minutes, then put in the cockles and mussels. Put the lid on and cook for 1 minute. Add the scallops and prawns and continue to cook for 1 minute more.

Serve, sprinkled with parsley and accompanied by fresh bread, in pre-heated soup bowls. *Serves 6.*

MERMAID'S HAIR

12 mussels
12 green prawns
400 g (14 oz) Chinese rice
  noodles

100 ml (½ cup) cream
1 tablespoon brandy
black pepper, freshly ground

Soak the rice noodles in cold water for at least 1 hour before cooking, then drain them in a colander. Scrub and beard the mussels and shell the prawns. Bring a shallow pan of water to the boil, place a muslin-lined steamer over the top and steam open the mussels, taking them out as soon as they open and tipping the liquid from the shells into the water below. Shell the mussels and set aside. Poach the prawns and the scallops in the same water, and keep them warm with the mussels.

Turn up the heat under the pan and reduce the liquid to about half. Add the cream and the brandy and continue to boil until the sauce is rich and smooth. Lower the heat, put in the noodles, and stir them in the sauce for 2–3 minutes, until they are cooked. Return the mussels, prawns and scallops to the pan and stir them into the sauce, tangling them with the noodles. Grind in some pepper, pile onto a pre-heated serving dish, and serve at once. *Serves 4.*

PAELLA

250 g (8 oz) mussels
250 g (8 oz) squid
3 blue swimmer crabs
250 g (8 oz) green prawns
200 g (7 oz) fresh green peas
1 large onion
2 cloves garlic
250 g (8 oz) chorizo sausage
1 large red capsicum
3 ripe, red tomatoes

1 handful parsley
200 ml (1 cup) chicken stock
olive oil
6 chicken thighs
500 g (1 lb) long-grain rice
black pepper, freshly ground
pinch saffron
pinch cayenne pepper
chopped parsley for garnish

Paella is one of those dishes that's hardly worth making for less than 6 people. Chock-full of rice and chicken, peas and squid, tomatoes and prawns, garlic and capsicums and saffron, it seems to hold the very essence of hospitality. Like so many other famous regional (in this case, almost national) dishes, paella takes its name from the shallow iron pan, usually two-handled, in which it's cooked. It isn't a polite dish—there are chicken bones, prawn and mussel shells, perhaps even lobster tails or crab claws to deal with—so finger bowls are necessary. It's an expanding, expensive affair, to be placed in the centre of a table surrounded by expectant people, and accompanied by chilled red wine—or Spanish rosé—and argument about politics and art and what should or shouldn't be found in a paella.

Paella is a dish of rice-and-additions, with chicken, prawns, mussels, tomatoes, capsicums and peas as the usual basics, and other ingredients put in depending on the availability and the season. The ingredients list is a guide, but vegetables such as artichokes, or shellfish like rock lobster or freshwater crayfish can be added if the season and the pocket allow.

Shell the peas; peel and slice the onion and garlic; scrub and beard the mussels. Clean the squid, discarding the guts and ink sacs, and skin the hoods. Cut the tentacles from the head so that they are tied together by a thin band of flesh. Slice the hoods into narrow strips.

Take the flesh out of the crab bodies and crack the claws; shell the centre sections of the prawns, leaving on the heads and tails; slice the chorizo into thick rounds. Peel and seed the capsicum and tomatoes, reserving the juice from the latter, and chop them both roughly. Chop the parsley. Bring the chicken stock to simmering point in a small saucepan.

To cook the paella, use a wide, shallow pan that will hold all the ingredients comfortably and go direct from stove to table. Into it pour some olive oil. As soon as it's hot add the chicken pieces, turning them so that all sides are sealed. Lower the heat and cook for 5 minutes, then put in the onion and garlic and continue to cook, stirring occasionally, for another 5–10 minutes, until the onion is softened and transparent (but not browned).

Push the chicken pieces to one side and add the rice, stirring it into the oil so that each grain is coated and translucent. Add the capsicum, tomatoes and their juices and 2 ladles of the simmering chicken stock. Grind in some black pepper, add a good pinch of saffron and another of cayenne, stir and leave to simmer, uncovered, for 10 minutes, or until the rice has absorbed all the liquid.

Pour in another ladleful of the stock, and put in the crab claws, chorizo, and prawns. Stir very carefully to make sure that the rice hasn't stuck to the pan, cook for another 5 minutes, add the squid, mussels and crab meat and continue to cook for a further 5 minutes, until the mussels open. Unless the rice is very dry and seems in danger of burning, don't add any more chicken stock after the mussels go into the pan as the shells will release their liquid as they open.

Try a grain of rice to make sure it's cooked through (it should be just soft, but never soggy or mushy). Check the seasoning, adding more cayenne if necessary, sprinkle the dish liberally with chopped parsley, and serve. *Serves 6.*

SEAFOOD COUSCOUS

200 g (7 oz) cockles or clams	*1 potato*
500 g (1 lb) small octopus	*1 ripe, red tomato*
200 g (7 oz) green prawns	*1 large onion*
75 g (2½ oz) chick peas	*1 zucchini*
2 tablespoons olive oil	*pinch cayenne pepper*
1 carrot	*pinch saffron*
1 capsicum	*300 g (10 oz) couscous*

Soak the chick peas overnight, and the cockles or clams for at least 6 hours in salted water (adding some oatmeal if clams are used) to degrit them. Shell the cockles and prawns and clean the octopus.

In a couscoussier (if you're lucky enough to have one) or in a deep saucepan which will take a colander or steamer with a perforated base (the Chinese bamboo-slatted sort won't do for this) heat the olive oil.

Put in the drained chick peas and cook them over a low heat for 30 minutes. Meanwhile, peel the vegetables (not the zucchini) and cut them into chunks. Discard the seeds from the tomato and the capsicum, but retain the tomato juice. Put the onion into the pan with the chick peas and continue to cook for another 30 minutes, then pour in 500 ml (2 ½ cups) of water, add the cayenne and saffron and bring to the boil.

Place the couscous in the steamer, sprinkle with cold water and sieve through the fingers so that no lumps form, and put the steamer on top of the saucepan. Make sure the liquid can't touch the steamer and that the steam isn't escaping round the sides and cook, uncovered, for 15 minutes.

Take the steamer off the saucepan, immediately put in the vegetables and the little octopus. Transfer the couscous to a deep bowl and stir it thoroughly with a wooden spoon, or even better a wooden fork, to break up any lumps that may have formed. Sprinkle with a little cold water once more, return to the steamer, put it back on the pan and cook for a further 15 minutes.

Turn the couscous into a pre-heated bowl, and put the prawns and cockles into the broth to cook for a minute or so. Lift out the vegetables, octopus, cockles and prawns and arrange them on top of the couscous. Pour a ladleful of the liquid over it, and serve the rest in a separate bowl.

This is just the barest outline of a couscous. All sorts of things could be added. Quinces, for instance, or raisins; squid or cuttlefish; mullet, crabs, bug tails, or sardines; green capsicums, chillies, and perhaps dates or almonds. The sauce can be enlivened with harissa, or left as it is (it shouldn't be too hot for a fish or shellfish couscous, as otherwise it completely overpowers all the other tastes), or divided into two separate bowls: one hot, the other au naturel, so to speak. *Serves 6.*

Sauces

A sauce can be either a complementary or a contrasting element, but it should always enhance—display, if you like—the essential flavour and texture of the food it's served with. While many sauces are integral to one particular dish, others are used so widely that it seems sensible to give their recipes in a separate section, especially as so many use two or three basic methods to which flavours and textures can be added as required. Of course, even if a sauce is given for, say, octopus or squid, there's no reason why it shouldn't be used for something else. Sauce Americaine/Amoricaine, originally created for lobster, has been teamed with octopus, which may be unclassifical but is undoubtedly delicious.

Sauces can be as simple as mixing lemon juice and olive oil together, or as complex as combining egg yolk and butter into a thick emulsion, but the function of all of them is to add to the tastes and textures of the food they accompany. Their success relies also on the goodness and freshness of their own ingredients. Fresh eggs, good unsalted butter, olive oil, herbs picked just before using, tomatoes chosen for taste and not long shelf life. . .with these and some attention to detail it's hard for things to go wrong. Not, of course, impossible: don't try and make mayonnaise, even in a blender or food processor, while a thunderstorm rumbles and grumbles in the atmosphere, because it could curdle. And if you make a large enough batch to store in the refrigerator (always a good idea, as it will keep for at least a week) make sure it doesn't freeze, as freezing will break down the consistency to such a degree that it can't be reconstituted.

Blenders and food processors come into their own where sauces are concerned. With them, it's possible to create a fresh-tasting, brilliantly-coloured puree in seconds, and the possibilties are endless. These are the simplest kinds of sauces, and the following recipes are only an indication of what can be done.

RED CAPSICUM SAUCE

1 large red capsicum
olive oil

salt and pepper to taste

Seed the capsicum and grill it over a gas flame until the skin blackens and lifts away from the flesh. If you don't have a gas stove, cut the capsicum into strips and put them under an electric grill until the skin bubbles and chars. As soon as they are cool enough to handle, while the skin is still puffed away from the flesh, peel it off, scraping away any charred bits of flesh. Put the capsicum into a food processor or blender. Whizz for a few seconds to chop it finely, then slowly pour olive oil through the funnel or top until the oil and the capsicum amalgamate into a brilliant scarlet sauce. Taste to see if it needs salt and pepper, and serve with cold mussels, deep-fried squid or grilled prawns.

Additions and variations
• Add a little lemon juice to the blender before pouring the oil in.
• Seed a fresh hot chilli and add it at the same time as the capsicum so that it blends smoothly.
• Add herbs like mint, basil or a little rosemary.
• Pour in 1 tablespoon of sour cream or crème fraîche and a little water.

MAYONNAISE

1 large egg yolk or 1 egg
2 teaspoons white wine
*   vinegar or lemon juice*

olive oil
1 teaspoon mustard
salt and pepper to taste

If you're making mayonnaise in a food processor or blender, it's better to use a whole egg. If you're beating it by hand, use the yolk only.

Mix together the egg, vinegar or lemon juice, salt, pepper and mustard. When thoroughly blended start adding the oil, little by little, until the mixture starts to thicken. Slowly increase the oil flow until it's running in a thin stream and continue to whisk or blend until the mayonnaise is thick and heavy, and won't accept any more oil.

Additions and variations
• *Aioli* Add 3 cloves of garlic to the lemon juice, crushing them with a little salt, and continue with the egg yolk and olive oil.
• *Aioli-in-a-hurry* Crush 2 cloves garlic and add them to the finished mayonnaise.
• *Basil* Mince or finely chop a handful of basil leaves and stir into the mayonnaise.
• *Mustard* Stir in extra mustard to taste. Try some of the grainy varieties, which add texture as well as taste to the sauce.
• *Rouille* Crush 3 cloves of garlic. Seed a small hot red chilli, and mince or chop it finely. Mix the garlic and chilli with a pinch of saffron and some salt, and stir into the mayonnaise.
• *Saffron* Stir in a few strands of saffron, or add a pinch of powdered saffron.
• *Sherry* Use sherry instead of vinegar or lemon juice. Better than any of them, use sherry vinegar.
• *Tartare (or Remoulade)* Mix together 1 finely minced shallot, 1 teaspoon capers, ½ a teaspoon French mustard, and a sprig each of parsley, tarragon, chervil and chives and ½ a small gherkin, all very finely chopped. Stir into the mayonnaise.

TOMATO SAUCE

400 g (14 oz) ripe, red   *salt and pepper to taste*
*   tomatoes, preferably*
*   home-grown*

Skin the tomatoes by first dipping them for a few seconds into boiling water. Remove the seeds. Push them into a strainer set over a bowl and rub them to strain through the juice. Put the flesh and juice into a blender and whizz until the tomatoes are pureed. Season with salt and pepper to taste, and serve with grilled or fried shellfish, or with octopus tapas. If this is made with good tomatoes it has a beautifully clean, refreshing flavour. Don't blend it too smoothly: it should still be slightly lumpy with pieces of tomato.

Additions and variations
• Add plenty of basil leaves or mint.

• Grind a teaspoon of cumin and a teaspoon of coriander seeds, heat them over a low flame to release their aromatics, and mix with the tomatoes.

• Add the juice of ½ a lime and a seeded, finely chopped chilli.

• Blend in 1 tablespoon heavy cream and heat the sauce, but don't let it cook or all the freshness will evaporate.

• Try blending other vegetables with cream to make a fresh sauce: zucchini (bring it to the boil before serving), broad beans, asparagus, peas, sorrel, avocadoes and cucumbers.

BUTTER-BASED SAUCES

The following sauces are all based on using butter as the amalgamating agent. They should be served warm rather than hot, as butter will separate into oils and solids if it is heated beyond 30°C. The best method of controlling the heat is to have the butter very cold and cut into small cubes which should be added to the sauce a few at a time. Stir in the next batch as soon as the first lot melt. A double boiler, so long as the water beneath it isn't allowed to boil, is a good method of controlling the butter temperature. Always use unsalted butter so that the flavour of the sauce is not drowned.

SPICED BUTTER

65 g (3 tablespoons) unsalted   *1 tablespoon dry sherry*
   butter   *few drops Tabasco*

Bring the sherry and the Tabasco to the boil and simmer for 1 minute. Lower the heat and beat in the chilled, cubed butter, a few pieces at a time, until the sauce is thick and smooth. Serve with crab cakes or bug tails.

MUSTARD BUTTER

65 g (3 tablespoons) unsalted   *1 tablespoon vermouth*
   butter   *1 teaspoon French mustard*

Mix together the vermouth and the mustard and bring to the boil. Simmer for 1 minute. Remove from the heat and beat in the butter over a low heat, adding the cubes a few at a time, whisking until the sauce is thick and smooth. Serve with abalone or prawns, or poached yabbies.

Additions and variations
• *Chervil butter* Put a large handful of fresh chervil into a food processor with 1 tablespoon of dry vermouth and process to a puree. Spoon into a saucepan, bring to the boil, and add the chilled butter cubes away from the heat, whisking until thick. This sauce is a sharp, vivid green, looks wonderful with scallops and octopus, and tastes wonderful with almost anything. If you can't get hold of chervil, which seems to be one of those herbs that has to be grown at home, use the flat-leaved kind of parsley. The colour will be almost as good, but the flavour will be more delicate. Other herbs that can be used in the same way are *mint* and *basil* and *sorrel*.

HOLLANDAISE

75 g (4 tablespoons) unsalted
   butter
1 tablespoon water

1 tablespoon lemon juice
1 egg yolk

Put the water and the lemon juice into a saucepan, bring to the boil and reduce by half. Take the pan off the heat and cool a little. Beat in the egg yolk and return the pan to the stove on a very low heat. Whisk continuously until the yolk thickens and the mixture is the consistency of cream.

Cut the chilled butter into small cubes and add them, a few at a time, to the egg yolk, putting in more cubes as soon as the first batch melts, until all the butter is incorporated and the sauce is thick and smooth.

Additions and variations
• *Curry* Add a teaspoon of garam masala and a pinch of chilli powder.
• *Ginger hollandaise* Grate a slice of fresh ginger and add to the pan with the lemon juice and water.
• *Herbs* Add tarragon, oregano or juniper berries to the lemon juice, infusing the flavour. Remove them before beating in the egg yolk and butter.
• *Saffron* Crumble a few strands of saffron into the sauce just before serving.

• *Sherry* Use 2 tablespoonfuls of dry sherry instead of lemon juice and water.

BROWN BUTTER SAUCE

65 g (3 tablespoons) unsalted   *1 slice fresh ginger*
   butter   *1 large egg yolk*

Grate the ginger and put in a shallow pan with the butter. Heat until the butter just starts to turn brown, then withdraw from the heat and cool for a moment. Beat in the egg yolk, whisking it with the browned butter until thick and smooth.

CAPSICUM AND ALMOND SAUCE

1 green capsicum   *1 tablespoon olive oil*
1 small hot green chilli   *100 ml (½ cup) water*
30 g (2 tablespoons) blanched
   almonds

Seed the capsicum and chilli and chop them roughly. Put into a blender with the almonds, olive oil and water and blend to a smooth sauce. (More water might be needed, as it depends very much on the water content of the green capsicums. Generally, the fresher, shinier and tighter skinned capsicums are, the more moisture they have and the less water needs to be added to the sauce.)

COCONUT AND TOMATO SAUCE

1 clove garlic   *butter*
1 green capsicum   *100 ml (½ cup) coconut milk*
1 ripe, red tomato

Peel the garlic, remove the seeds and white pith from the capsicum, peel and seed the tomato, and chop them all into small chunks. Cook for a minute or so in some butter. Pour in the coconut milk, bring to the boil and serve.

    The tastes, textures and colours of this sauce should be kept as separate as possible, so try not to stir it once the coconut milk goes in.

CORIANDER AND ALMOND SAUCE

1 dried chilli
50 ml (¼ cup) water
30 g (2 tablespoons) blanched
  almonds
1 handful fresh coriander
  leaves

1 spring onion
2 cloves
1 sprig oregano
pinch ground cinnamon

Split the dried chilli and shake out the seeds, then soak in the water for 1 hour. Toast the almonds in a hot oven for 5 minutes. Put all the ingredients in a blender and whizz to make a smooth sauce.

HAZELNUT TARATOR

1 slice white bread without
  crusts
100 g (½ cup) blanched
  hazelnuts

1 clove garlic
1 tablespoon lemon juice
salt and pepper to taste
50 ml (2 tablespoons) olive oil

Put the bread into the blender and whizz to fine crumbs, take them out and in turn put in the hazelnuts and grate them finely. Crush the garlic, put it into the blender, and add the crumbs, lemon juice, salt and pepper and half the oil. Blend over a high speed, adding more oil in a thin stream until the sauce thickens to a mayonnaise consistency.

Additions and variations
• *Almonds* Use blanched almonds instead of the hazelnuts, use ½ water and ½ lemon juice instead of all lemon juice, and leave out the garlic.
• *Pine nuts* Substitute pine nuts for the hazelnuts.
• *Walnuts* Use walnuts instead of the hazelnuts, and put in 4 tablespoons tahina paste instead of breadcrumbs.

PESTO

40 g (1 ½ oz) parmesan cheese
40 g (1 ½ oz) basil leaves

40 g (2 tablespoons) pine nuts
1 clove garlic
olive oil

Grate the parmesan, chop the basil leaves, grind the pine nuts, and blend them together with the garlic in a blender or food processor, pouring in the oil slowly until the sauce amalgamates into a thick, green sauce which is still not entirely smooth. Pour into a jar, cover with olive oil, and leave for at least 24 hours in the refrigerator before using to allow the flavours to meld.

Additions and variations
- *Chervil* Use chervil and walnuts.
- *Mint* Use mint leaves (or ½ *mint and* ½ parsley) instead of basil.
- *Walnuts* Use ½ walnuts and ½ pinenuts, or just walnuts.

TOMATO AND CAPSICUM SAUCE

1 onion
1 clove garlic
½ each red and green
  capsicums
2 ripe, red tomatoes
1 tablespoon olive oil

½ teaspoon ground cumin
  seeds
½ teaspoon paprika
sprig each basil and thyme
1 tablespoon red wine vinegar

Peel the onion and garlic, seed the capsicums and strip out the white pith. Peel and seed the tomatoes. Chop them all finely.

Heat the oil and cook the onion until soft. Add the garlic, capsicums, and last of all the tomatoes. Finely chop the herbs and mix with the spices and the red wine vinegar, and pour into the tomato and capsicum mixture. Lower the heat and cook over a very low heat for 2 hours, or until the vegetables have all melded together into a thick, dark sauce.

This is particularly good with Shellfish Polenta, and cockles and mussels.

BABA GHANOUSH SAUCE

1 aubergine
juice 1 lemon

2 tablespoons tahina paste
1 clove garlic

While baba ghanoush is usually served as a dip with pitta bread, it is delicious as a sauce for prawns and mussels. It is very good used instead of mayonnaise, piled on top of prawns which are themselves piled on wholegrain bread and butter.

Grill the aubergine until the skin chars, then peel as soon as it's cool enough to handle and squeeze out as much juice as possible. Put the flesh in a blender or food processor and puree with the lemon juice, tahina and garlic until thick and smooth. Let the baba ghanoush sit for at least 1 hour before using so that all the tastes have time to come together.

CAPSICUM AND CREAM SAUCE

1 red capsicum   *2 tablespoons cream*

This would have to be amongst the easiest, as well as the nicest, of all sauces.

Grill the capsicum until the skin is charred and blackened, peel off the skin and discard the seeds and white pith. Cut into pieces, place in a blender with the cream and blend until smooth. Serve cold with mussels and crab or lobster.

GREEN CAPSICUM AND GINGER SAUCE

1 onion   *1 slice fresh ginger*
olive oil   *1 small green chilli*
1 green capsicum   *salt to taste*

Peel the onion, chop finely and soften in a little olive oil. Grill the capsicum, take off the skin, remove the seeds and chop roughly. Put it into a blender or food processor with the ginger, onion, chilli and some salt and blend until smooth with olive oil, adding it as you would when making mayonnaise.

This is very glossy, very green, and very hot. It's a great sauce for lobster or crab, or very large tiger prawns which are strong enough to hold their own against such heat. If you really don't like very hot tastes, leave out the chilli, and the sauce will have a sweet, almost nutty flavour. But either way it does need the salt, to add a sourer, sharper note.

ORANGE SAUCE

1 tablespoon butter
1 tablespoon plain flour
juice and grated rind of 1
    orange
1 tablespoon white wine

100 ml (½ cup) cream
pepper
salt (optional)
1 egg yolk

Melt the butter and sift in the flour. Mix them together to a smooth paste, then stir over a very low heat for 2–3 minutes so that the flour is cooked.

Pour in the orange juice and white wine, stirring all the time. Add the cream and bring to the boil. Lower the heat and cook very gently for 10 minutes, uncovered, every so often skimming off the skin which forms on the top. Check the seasoning, adding pepper quite lavishly (white pepper doesn't show, but then again neither does black pepper all that much) and salt if necessary. Remove from the heat and cool slightly.

Break the egg yolk into a basin, beat lightly, and add a spoonful of the sauce, mixing them together thoroughly. Return the mixture to the sauce and put back on the heat, stirring all the time until it becomes thick and glossy. On no account allow it to boil or it will curdle. Pour into a sauce boat, sprinkle with the grated orange rind, and serve.

PUMPKIN SEED SAUCE

50 g (2 tablespoons) pumpkin
    seeds
juice 1 lemon
1 handful fresh coriander

leaves
pinch cayenne pepper
1 tablespoon vegetable oil

Blend all the ingredients together to a smooth puree, adding more oil or lemon juice if necessary until the sauce has the consistency of mayonnaise.

PEANUT AND POTATO SAUCE

1 small potato
50 g (1 tablespoon) peanuts
juice 1 lime

1 tablespoon peanut oil
salt and pepper to taste

Bake the potato in its jacket until soft. Crush the peanuts finely, then blend until smooth with the lime juice and the peanut oil. Mash the potato and mix with the peanuts, tasting to see if it needs salt and pepper—a little cayenne goes rather better than black pepper. More lime juice or oil may be needed, depending on the juiciness of the lime.

Don't try to put the potato in the blender as well as the peanuts, lime and oil. The instant result is glue—potatoes and blenders or food processors don't seem to mix.

GIN AND JUNIPER SAUCE

4 juniper berries
2 tablespoons gin

1 tablespoon cream
1 tablespoon crème fraîche

Crush the juniper berries and place in a saucepan with the gin. Bring to the boil and simmer until reduced by half. Add the cream and crème fraîche and continue cooking until thick.

Marinades for Shellfish

ORANGE MARINADE (1)

1 spring onion
1 clove garlic
black pepper, freshly ground

juice ½ orange
juice ½ lemon
1 tablespoon olive oil

Grate the spring onion and garlic finely. Mix with the pepper, orange and lemon juices and olive oil.

This marinade is good for prawns, scallops or crabs. They should be marinated for at least 1 hour before being steamed.

ORANGE MARINADE (2)

1 tomato
1 spring onion
1 small fresh green chilli

juice ½ lime
juice ½ orange
pinch salt

Peel the seed the tomato, reserving the juice. Mix together with the finely chopped spring onion, the little green chilli (take the seeds out first or it will be too hot), the lime and orange juices and a pinch of salt. This is especially good with prawns, which should be marinated for at least 1 hour before cooking in the same sauce.

LIME AND CAPSICUM MARINADE
WITH AVOCADO

1 ripe, red tomato
½ small red capsicum
1 small fresh green chilli
2–3 green olives
juice of 1 lime

1 handful fresh coriander
  leaves
1 spring onion
1 tablespoon olive oil

Peel the seed the tomato, reserving the liquid. Scrape the seeds from the capsicum and the chilli, pit the olives, put everything in a blender and blend until smooth. Suitable for crab or scallops. Put them in a bowl and cover with the mixture and refrigerate for at least 12 hours so the shellfish has time to 'cook' in the marinade. Serve with cubes of avocado mixed with the marinade and shellfish.

LIME AND MINT MARINADE

1 spring onion
1 handful fresh mint leaves

juice 1 lime
pinch chilli powder

Mince the spring onion and mint leaves finely and mix with the lime juice and chilli powder. This one is very good with oysters, which should soak in the mixture for at least 2 hours.

GREEN ALMOND MARINADE

1 small fresh hot green chilli
1 clove garlic
1 spring onion
1 handful coriander leaves

1 handful parsley
2–3 leaves butter lettuce
20 g (1 tablespoon) blanched
  almonds

Remove the seeds from the chilli, peel the garlic, and blend everything together in a blender or food processor. Marinate steamed mussels or cockles for at least 2 hours before serving.

HOT ALMOND MARINADE

*20 g (1 tablespoon) blanched
  almonds
unsalted butter
1 spring onion
1 small hot fresh green chilli*

*1 hard boiled egg
2 tablespoons fresh white
  breadcrumbs
100 ml (½ cup) fish stock*

Heat some butter and toss the almonds in it until they turn pale gold. Drain on kitchen paper.

Peel the spring onion, seed the chilli and cook them both in the same butter until soft. Place in a blender or food processor with all the rest of the ingredients and puree to a thick, smooth consistency. Use for steamed mussels or poached prawns. Mix with the marinade and refrigerate for 2 hours before serving.

Index